DATE DUE

Demco, Inc. 38-293

Women of Color on the Rise

Women of Color on the Rise

Leadership and Administration in Social Work Education and the Academy

HALAEVALU F. OFAHENGAUE VAKALAHI
AND WILMA PEEBLES-WILKINS,
EDITORS

Columbia University Press   *New York*

Columbia University Press
Publishers Since 1893
New York   Chichester, West Sussex
Copyright © 2010 Columbia University Press
All rights reserved
Library of Congress Cataloging-in-Publication Data
Women of color on the rise : leadership and administration in social work education and
the academy / Halaevalu F. Ofahengaue Vakalahi and Wilma Peebles-Wilkins, editors.
p. cm.
Includes bibliographical references and index.
ISBN 978-0-231-14476-6 (cloth : alk. paper)
1. Women in social work education—United States.   2. Minorities in social work
education—United States.   3. Social work education—United States.   I. Vakalahi,
Halaevalu F. Ofahengaue.   II. Peebles-Wilkins, Wilma Cecelia.   III. Title.

HV11.7.W665 2009
361.3071'173—dc22
2009024190

Columbia University Press books are printed on permanent and durable acid-free paper.
This book is printed on paper with recycled content.
Printed in the United States of America
c 10 9 8 7 6 5 4 3 2 1
References to Internet Web sites (URLs) were accurate at the time of writing. Neither
the author nor Columbia University Press is responsible for URLs that may have expired or
changed since the manuscript was prepared.

Contents

Contents

Foreword

LORRIE GREENHOUSE GARDELLA

Women of color have been leaders from the time that the world began. They have guided and sustained families, nurtured and encouraged communities, created and cultivated social movements and institutions, instilled faith, and, whatever the circumstances, inspired hope in the possibilities of social change. In social work agencies and in higher education, women of color were once denied credentials for their knowledge, skills, and expertise. They often led from behind the scenes, even though their contributions were there for all to see. In contrast, the authors of this book belong to the first generations of women of color in the United States who gained access to higher education and to leadership positions with professional titles that name their work. Many dedicate their narratives as they have dedicated their accomplishments, to the mothers, grandmothers, teachers, and mentors who came before them.

Perhaps the most distinctive commonality in the women's stories is the confidence and competence that they have applied at every phase of their careers. Aware of their abilities at an early age, they were motivated less by altruism or personal ambition than by a sense of purpose that obliged them to fulfill their potential. In contrast to self-help books that present the professional aspirations of women in conflict with their family responsibilities, the authors of this book suggest that the capacity for caring expands with use. Whether at home, at church, in the community, or in the academy, devotion to a purpose has energized and integrated the women's lives.

The authors of this book followed various professional paths, and their stories reveal complex facets of leadership rather than simplistic prescriptions for success. Somewhere along the way, however, each of the women discovered a personal mission that allies with the values and goals of social work: "To enhance human wellbeing and help meet the basic human needs of all people, with particular attention to the needs and empowerment of people who are vulnerable, oppressed, and living in poverty" (NASW 1999: Preamble). They are "keeping the movement alive" from their positions as leaders in higher education.

Women of Color on the Rise is a book for every social worker who has imagined an academic career. If you have considered entering graduate school or earning a doctoral degree or teaching a college class or leading a university, then these stories will enrich your sense of what is possible. Whether you are a student, practitioner, educator, or administrator, you too have the potential to keep the movement alive by engaging the academy in building a more equitable and humane society.

Introduction

This work is part of a lifelong commitment to critically examining and utilizing the unique experiences of women of color in the academy to build and rebuild culturally respectful academic systems and institutions as a means of promoting social change and social justice. We recognize that we are not in this effort alone, as many mainstream women, men, systems, and institutions have begun the journey of rebuilding and reinventing (Vakalahi, Starks, and Hendricks 2007). During the final stage of this writing, on November 4, 2008, a piece of history for which many have died, but perhaps have never thought possible, came into fruition. Barack Obama was elected as the forty-fourth president of the United States of America, the first African American to occupy this leadership position. On January 29, 2009, President Obama signed his first bill into law: the Lilly Ledbetter Fair Pay Act, which reinforces the ability of women to challenge unequal pay for equal work. These events epitomize social change and social justice in the twenty-first century and solidify our hope in and commitment to women of color as leaders and administrators in the academy.

The narratives in this book are a contribution to this movement commenced by the struggles, ambitions, strengths, and successes of pioneering women and men leaders in academia who have risen and paved the way for all who follow. Keeping this movement alive is grounded in the mission and standards of the profession of social work in relation to respect and appreciation for human diversity, inclusiveness, and social and economic justice (CSWE 2001; NASW 1999). It is the hope of the editors that this work will advocate for opportunities in self-assessment, innovations, and building culturally competent academic institutions that specifically support diversity in leadership and administration and include women of color.

The title *Women of Color on the Rise* purports to emphasize the themes of social change and social justice shown through the personal stories of selected women of color who have risen and have become leaders and administrators in social work education and the academy. The stories of these women represent the collective hope and courage for present and future women of color aspiring to leadership and administrative positions in academia. Each author was asked to address three basic elements: strategies for pursuing one's aspiration to a leadership position; strategies for successful leadership and administration upon securing a position; and methods for keeping the movement alive. In describing their journey to leadership and administration, authors were asked specific questions:

- Was the journey planned or unplanned?
- What self-assessment tools did you use to determine your leadership aspirations?
- What are the do's and don'ts of pursuing leadership and administration positions?
- Describe the personal characteristics that have contributed to your success in leadership and administration.
- In what ways have culture, ethnicity, and race impacted your leadership style?
- Describe the role of mentorship, collegiality, and networking in your successful leadership and administration.
- What is the role of formal education and training in your successful leadership and administration?
- Describe any institutional strategies, policies, and supports for advancement in your career.
- What is the role of leadership programs?
- What is the role of professional social work organizations?
- Describe what life or nonacademic experiences and extracurricular activities that have influenced your drive to pursue leadership and administration positions.

Introduction

- Describe your role and responsibility in keeping alive the movement of promoting women of color in leadership and administration.
- What are relevant policies, programs and services for which you are advocating to keep the movement alive?

The women in this book are representative of the five federally defined historically disadvantaged ethnic/racial groups of color in the United States: African American or Black, Asian American, Latina or Hispanic American, Native American or American Indian or First Nations, and Pacific Islander. To provide specific lessons learned and strategies for success in pursuing leadership and administrative positions in academia, the stories are organized into four clusters: administration on the university level, deanship in multidisciplinary schools and colleges, deanship in schools of social work, and chair/directorship in social work departments and programs. Of importance is the fact that some of the women have crossed clusters from occupying university-level administration positions to social work department or program director positions. However, authors are placed in specific clusters to provide examples specific to those positions. Additionally, it is a goal of this work to continue cultivating the idea of inclusion and the need for partnership with all women and men in academia regardless of race/ethnicity or gender, in order to experience true social change and social justice. To this end, Dr. Rebecca Turner, author of chapter 1, gracefully accepted the invitation to address the issue of leadership development of all women in the academy, thus providing a larger framework for the personal stories in this book.

Significance of This Work

In the words of Spelman College's president, Dr. Beverly Daniel Tatum, "Our mission calls us to be intentional about the cultivation of the leadership potential of women of color as we prepare for their wise stewardship of their world" (Spelman College, *College News*, May 7, 2004). Grounded on this idea, the overarching purposes of this work are to (1) honor leaders and administrators who are women of color in social work education and the academy; (2) pay homage to pioneers who have successfully led and administered in a system that has historically been oppressive and discriminatory; (3) advocate for inclusion and partnership with all women and men in academia as a means for producing future generations of women of color as leaders and administrators; (4) explore leadership styles and issues that are relevant to leadership development of women; (5) provide lessons learned for future women of color that may inform their leadership and administrative practices; (6) contribute to the literature on diversity in leadership and administration by ethnicity/race and gender; and (7) promote respect and acceptance toward race/ethnic and gender-related leadership paradigms that have been historically devalued and suppressed in the academy. Overall, the authors hope that the voices of these women of color who are leaders and administrators will inspire positive changes in individuals and in the institutions in which they exist.

In keeping the movement alive, this book will bring women of color as leaders and administrators in social work education and in the academy to the forefront of discussion, resolution, and visibility. In addition to filling gaps in the existing literature and emphasizing culturally based leadership paradigms of women of color, the authors hope to assist in dispelling myths, misunderstandings, misconceptions, and misrepresentation of the phenomenon of women of color as leaders and administrators in social work education and in the academy.

References

Council on Social Work Education (2001). *Handbook of Accreditation Standards and Procedures*. Alexandria, Va.: Council on Social Work Education.

National Association of Social Workers (1999). *Code of Ethics*. Washington, D.C.: National Association of Social Workers.

Peebles-Wilkins, W. (1999). "Women in Leadership Roles," National Association of Deans and Directors of Schools of Social Work, Savannah, Ga., October.

Spelman College Center for Leadership and Civic Engagement (2004). *Conference on Women of Color Leadership in the 21st Century: It's Our turn.* Spelman LEADS, May 12–13. Available at http://www.collegenews.org/x3295.xml (accessed November 22, 2006). Atlanta, May 7 (AScribe Newswire).

Vakalahi, H.F.O., S. Starks, and C. Ortiz Hendricks, eds. (2007). *Women of Color as Social Work Educators: Strengths and Survival*. Alexandria, Va.: Council on Social Work Education Press.

Women of Color on the Rise

[PART ONE]

Administration on the University Level

The Leadership Development of Women

REBECCA TURNER

From my vantage point as a woman and the first woman vice president at Jacksonville University, I see that women have not done an exemplary job of developing women of color and other women to be leaders. There has been the token mentoring effort here and the modest tutoring there, but overall our contributions to the development of women leaders are embarrassingly meager. My criticism includes criticism of my own efforts at developing women leaders because, as I reflect on those attempts at leadership development of other women, they fall short of my expectations. Yes, I have observed those who have followed along behind me, learned from me, and who now are themselves leaders, but those numbers could be so much higher. It is my hope that by writing this chapter for your consideration you will find information to assist you in developing women of color and other women to be leaders and, at the same time, find tools to help you become a successful leader in your own right. After all, within each of us women is a leader waiting to blossom.

Building Blocks to Leadership

According to Zichy (2001), there are six building blocks to leadership, the first of which is *self-knowledge*. In my own leadership development, self-knowledge in relation to leadership development began this way. My leadership opportunities began early in life, as the eldest of five children, born to young parents, who often relied on me to maintain order in the household. I was given responsibilities at much too young an age, and I grew up much too fast. My past, in relation to social work education, began when I was a college sophomore, searching for the right major for me at a time when women in higher education were mostly studying to be schoolteachers. In fact, my father advised me to "be a teacher" because in his opinion it was a suitable field of study and work for women. At this point, it is important to mention that I am a first-generation college student. I was the first in my immediate family to earn a college diploma. I attended a college preparatory high school on an academic scholarship, so there was never any doubt on my part nor on the part of my parents that I would go to college. But there was considerable doubt about what I would study and what work I would eventually do. So, in 1967, when I began my college experience, my search for a field to study began along with the continued search for self-knowledge.

Zichy states that self-knowledge is followed by *self-management*, which for me began soon after I discovered college courses that interested me. I fell in love with the subjects of psychology, philosophy, and sociology and, like a dork, sat through some lectures twice. I began to ask questions of my teachers, questions like "what can you do with majors like these?" And "what kind of work does one do with information or knowledge like that which is found in psychology and sociology?" Unfortunately, my faculty was of no help to me. Remember, this was 1967–68, before undergraduate social work education was well on its way. So I turned to my mother's good friend, an educated woman, who was first a schoolteacher and then an elementary school principal. Her name is Estelle Robertson. Sometime toward the end of my freshman year, I asked Estelle about careers that were suitable for someone with an interest in psychology or sociology. She knew me well (through my mother and in church). Almost without hesitation she said that social work was a field I should consider. Looking back now, Estelle was a mentor—a leader who pointed me in the right direction and encouraged me to reach an appropriate career goal in social work that led me into social work education.

Because I was unfamiliar with the profession of social work at the time, she made a quick referral to a woman named Margaret Copeland, who was the director of our local public child welfare office. I met with Ms. Copeland, spent a summer doing volunteer work in child welfare, fell in love with child welfare, and immediately knew what I should study. But where? There was no social work major at my university. I began to research the major in social work in Alabama schools and found one at the University of Montevallo (formerly Alabama College), a small liberal arts school about a hundred miles from my home and university. So I transferred to Montevallo in 1969, studied social work, and graduated proudly in 1971, knowing I had found the right field for me.

Self-confidence is Zichy's third building block in leadership development. My self-confidence developed slowly, or so it seems, and in the following manner. The degree in social work led to a job in public child welfare, then three years later led me to a master's of social work program at the University of Alabama. Two significant career-influencing events resulted from the MSW. The first was an elective I persuaded my major professor, Dr. Phillip Crunk, to allow me to take. It was a course for doctoral students, and the subject was social work education. This was 1975 and 1976, just after baccalaureate social work programs became accredited by the Council on Social Work Education (CSWE) in 1974. And I was an MSW student, not a doctoral student at that time. It was in this course on social work education that I learned about accreditation and CSWE. I learned about curricula and the foundation content areas (the original five), and I formed a keen interest in social work education. I took that interest in social work education back with me to the agency, where within months I was promoted to supervisor, which was the second significant event resulting from my MSW.

In that supervisory role my self-confidence further grew as I oriented new employees to the agency, provided supervision to social workers, and offered field instruction supervision to baccalaureate social work students at three Alabama universities: Montevallo, Auburn, and Troy, all moving into initial accreditation with CSWE. As I oriented new employees to the agency, I quickly realized the distinct and profound differences between employees hired to do social work tasks without the bachelor's of social work degree and those with the BSW degree. The differences were significant and amazing. I can say without a doubt that new social workers with the BSW degree only needed orienting to the agency. They possessed knowledge, skills, and values to practice social work with minimum supervision from me. Such was not the case for those employees hired to do social work but without a social work education foundation. Those employees were hardly ready to make field visits alone at the end of a year. They required more direct supervision and lacked the professional judgment required for entry-level social work practice. Their professional code of behavior was missing. This supervisory experience (my first leadership opportunity in social work) and the corresponding realization that baccalaureate social work education is necessary for good entry-level social work practice led me to my next role—that of social work educator.

I suppose Zichy's fourth building block to leadership, *accomplishment*, was underway during the confidence-building phase, but the greatest accomplishments for me occurred after my field of practice changed from public child welfare to baccalaureate social work education. In the spring of 1981 I read an ad in the *NASW News* that advertised a social work faculty position at my first university, Jacksonville State University, in my home county. The ad announced a need for faculty to lead in the development of a BSW program that could be accredited by CSWE. At the time there was a minor in place in a multidisciplinary department with sociology, gerontology, anthropology, and archeology. I found the job announcement to be interesting indeed, so I applied, interviewed for the position in July, and began teaching that fall.

The transition from practice to education was a whirlwind, and I had many doubts and second thoughts about it in the beginning, but after awhile and upon further evaluation, it was pretty clear that the change of primary focus from practice to education was the right step for me. And now, looking back, the timing was perfect. After all, how many of us get to return to our roots and improve the opportunities for those who follow us in social work? I did. I returned to the university that did not offer me a BSW in the late 1960s to develop a BSW program for those interested in that career path in the mid-1980s and beyond. That work is one of my proudest accomplishments. It is work that offered me many leadership opportunities and exposed me to many leaders who in turn influenced me.

I was named the first program director for the newly approved social work program. I was the program director when the program achieved candidacy (1988), initial accreditation (1992), and its first reaffirmation of accreditation (1996). During my years as director we brought social work education leaders to our campus—people like, Drs. Brad Shaeffor, Grafton Hull, Charles Zastrow, Kay Hoffman, Barbara White, and others—thus providing our students and faculty with opportunities to learn from the leaders in social work education. Somehow along the way, I earned a doctorate in social work in 1990, by studying part time and working full time, just like many women in higher education have done and continue to do, day in and day out. In my doctoral studies, Dr. Beulah Roberts Compton was my major professor and mentor. She was such a leader in social work education for so long and I know from speaking with others over the years that she was a mentor to many in social work education.

Following accomplishments, Zichy says the next building block to leadership is *self-esteem*. While it is unlikely that self-confidence and accomplishments can occur without some measure of self-esteem, I do agree with Zichy that self-esteem is enhanced through accomplishments and that believing in oneself, self-confidence, contributes positively to successful accomplishments. And I also believe that the more we attempt to accomplish something of value, the more successes we will experience, and with those successes, the more confident we become and the more enhanced our self-esteem will be.

As other leadership opportunities opened up to me, Zichy's last building block in leadership development, *leadership*, emerged more apparently. I was encouraged and motivated by others who led before me to seek those opportunities for leadership and service. I was mentored by some great leaders in social work education. Harry Macy, my first mentor in social work program administration, who later became my friend and coauthor, had a profound influence on me. He believed I had something to contribute, and he allowed me to make some of those contributions with him. Other mentors, like Drs. Kay Hoffman, Dean Pierce, Steve Holloway, and Barbara White, come to mind when I think about individuals who inspired, encouraged, and appointed me to leadership roles. For example, I served on the board of directors of the Association of Baccalaureate Social Work Program Directors (BPD) and chaired the membership committee of that organization for many years. I was appointed to the Commission on Educational Policy (now the Commission on Curriculum and Educational Innovations), followed by two consecutive appointments to the Commission on Accreditation of the Council on Social Work Education. For nine years I served on those commissions where I was inspired, motivated, encouraged, and stimulated by others to continue making contributions to social work education: to lead.

On my campus I was appointed to the program review committee in the early 1990s where I first served as secretary, then chairperson. During that same period of time, I was appointed head of the multidisciplinary department that hosted social work, then in 1998 I was asked to serve as interim associate vice president for academic affairs, at which time I stepped down from the social work program director role I had held since 1988. In 1999 I was named associate vice president for academic affairs and left the department head position. Then, in January 2002, I was named the first woman vice president at my university when I became vice president for academic and student affairs, a position I continue to hold today. I am the only woman vice president and the only vice president with an earned doctorate on my campus. When offered the vice presidency, I asked my president if he thought our community was ready for a woman vice president. His reply was, "Ready or not, here we come." And we are still going strong more than six years later.

In Zichy's six building blocks of leadership, there is much development of self, much emphasis on self, and much focus on self. Why are introspection, self-control, understanding, risk taking, achievement, and sense of self so important to a true leader? How can you lead without a direction, a purpose, a passion, or a calling? How can you lead if no one deems you worthy of following? Leaders must inspire, motivate, encourage, and stimulate others to follow them, but leaders also inspire, motivate, encourage, and stimulate others to develop into leaders themselves.

Leadership is influential. It can not exist in a vacuum. To lead is to "conduct along a way," according to Webster. To lead requires action on the leader's part and someone who will follow. Unfortunately, it is entirely possible to sit in an administrative role day in and day out, year after year, without leading. And unfortunately some administrators do just that: they may be great at getting things done, but they do not lead. Leading requires proactive behaviors that encourage others over and over, again and again, day after day, and year after year.

In our roles as administrators, we perform many tasks on any given day. We have systems in place to organize the workload. We have deadlines to meet, executive summaries to prepare, phone calls to make, and meetings to attend, coordinate, or address. We *get things done* in our administrative roles. However, occupying an administrative role does not automatically make us leaders. To be an administrator who leads, we will also need to mentor others, teach, inspire, encourage, motivate, and stimulate others to perform tasks unknown to them, to learn what they do not know, to serve in new ways, to develop confidence, to enhance self-esteem, to accomplish goals, and to *lead* in the future. For women administrators, this challenge to lead other women and women of color is even more important. Finding ways to develop other women leaders should be at the top of our list of priority activities, constantly.

Institutional Supports for Leadership Development

Currently, higher education offers opportunities and challenges for leadership development of women and women of color. Similar opportunities are found across institutions of higher education, such as equal employment opportunity and affirmative action policies and procedures. Some of us have benefited from those policies, at least in the employment stage. Recruitment and hiring are certainly influenced by equal employment opportunity and affirmative action policies and procedures found on most campuses. Hiring women and women of color is important and necessary to developing women leaders in higher education, but also important is the ongoing effort to provide professional development or enhancement opportunities for those women who are hired and employed. Leadership development opportunities offered or supported by universities are necessary to the growth and development of women leaders. Programs that support educational pursuits for terminal degrees and programs that support research, publication, travel, and service are examples of ways that universities can endorse and fund professional development that nurtures leaders. These programs are found on my campus, through educational leave (with funding support), professional development leave (with funding support), research grants, travel grants, and other funded projects supported on a case-by-case basis. In particular is a *Grow Your Own* program on my campus that supports African American faculty, graduate students, and administrators in earning a terminal degree. So far two women faculty members of color have benefited from the three-year-old program and one more young woman of color has interviewed to express her desire to participate in the program on my campus.

As an administrator with oversight responsibility for promotion and tenure decisions, my practice is to provide needed support for faculty in tenure-track positions that will result in evidence in the areas of research and service in portfolios presented for promotion and tenure. It is also my responsibility to be constantly looking for opportunities for professional development of faculty and administrators—conferences, workshops, institutes, consultants, speakers, and other examples of avenues for leadership development that will encourage and support women and women of color who participate. Assigning women to leadership roles such as chairing university committees, chairing academic departments, or managing a research or service project offers ways for women to gain experience and develop leadership skills. Partnering with other women in research projects, writing projects, or making presentations at professional meetings are also examples of ways that women leaders can assist other women to develop leadership skills.

At the University of Michigan, Ann Arbor, the Women of Color Task Force, which has operated for more than twenty-five years, was organizationally located in the Center for the Education of Women in 2002 (http:// www.umich.edu). The task force holds an annual conference, workshops for career and personal development, award programs for woman of the year, and staff mentoring opportunities for members. According to the website, goals of the program include promoting leadership development and increasing professional skills and competencies, providing information and direction to identify and achieve career goals, and establishing a network of support services for staff, especially minority women employed by the university. These goals could be appropriately implemented in any university wishing to support leadership development of women of color and other women. Organizations like this center and its task force are empowered to move women ahead and support them in accomplishing their leadership goals.

In *Gender Equity or Bust!* (2001), Wenniger and Conroy write about the road to campus leadership for women in higher education. They point out the importance of women in higher education gathering together in support of one another and a common goal of gender equity (p. 67). Their advice is on point, if one is to accept the premise of Patricia Valdata in her 2006 article for *Diverse*, "Lonely at the Top?" Valdata interviewed six minority women university presidents and found that minority women college presidents have a lonely job in addition to a demanding one. Her research also showed that women are aware of their leadership styles, which are usually different from leadership styles of their male counterparts. In addition, women presidents are more likely to take risks, a trait not surprising to those of us women who have experienced many firsts. Dr. Juliet Garcia, president of the University of Texas at Brownsville, is the first Mexican American woman to become president of an American college or university (Valdata 2006:30). Dr. Karen Gayton Swisher, retired president of Haskell Indian Nations University, was the first woman president of Haskell and attributes her accomplishments to "strong female role models she observed growing up in the Standing Rock Sioux Tribe" (Valdata 2006:31). Like Zerrie Campbell, president of Malcolm X College, a community college in the Chicago City College system since 1992 (Valdata 2006:31), Dr. Swisher was a master team builder. Both women used their positions to broaden representation from across campus to create inclusion on the administrative team and build consensus for accomplishing goals. They were firsts. I am also a first: the first woman vice president on my campus, the first child in my family to earn a college degree, and the only one in my family to earn a doctorate. We are just three examples of first women, but our experiences are found everywhere there are women who are pushing forward, becoming leaders, ahead of their peers. These women did not become leaders overnight. Instead, their leadership development occurred over a series of years, through personal and professional development, with mentoring and support from others, and by one accomplishment at a time.

Strategies for Leadership Development

Many organizations offer training programs, affiliations, workshops, and websites to assist with the development of leaders in higher education. Just this week I received an email from a staff member at Inside Higher Education, a resource in Washington, D.C., offering an audio conference on the topic of mentoring minority faculty. The conference proposes to discuss how to provide minority professors with mentors and an inclusive environment. While the term leadership was not used in the advertisement, this workshop is a place for minority faculty to experience professional development in higher education, which is one building block to leadership development.

Another organization that provides opportunities for leadership development of women is the American Council on Education (ACE). Since its founding in 1918, ACE has served as a unifying voice for higher education. Leadership development opportunities are found in conferences, workshops for administrators, institutes for administrators, publications found on the website www.accnet.edu, and, for women, the Office of Women in Higher

Education. There is also a unique fellows program that purports to be "the nation's premier higher education leadership development program" (ACE Leadership Opportunities, 3). The ACE website is a great resource for executives or administrators in higher education needing opportunities to participate, network, and learn. According to the website, "the Office of Women in Higher Education offers regional leadership forums for emerging and mid-level women leaders ready to move into deanships and vice presidencies." In addition to the regional forums, "the ACE National Network for the Advancement of Women Leaders, supported by the Office of Women in Higher Education and the ACE Network Executive Board of presidents, is a state-based national network committed to strengthening women's leadership in higher education." Through this network, thousands of women are reached annually.

For women of color, ACE offers specific summits. Jointly sponsored by ACE's Center for Advancement of Racial and Ethnic Equity and the Office of Women in Higher Education (OWHE), the summits address the challenges faced by women of color in the academy (ACE website, Leadership Programs, 4). A review of the homepage for OWHE provides much useful information for women in leadership roles and those aspiring to be leaders. The OWHE states that it provides national direction for women's leadership development and career advancement in the following ways:

- Identifying women leaders in higher education
- Developing leadership skills of women in higher education
- Encouraging women leaders to make full use of their abilities
- Advancing women leaders into senior-level positions
- Linking women leaders at all levels to one another
- Supporting the retention of women in higher education

Another interesting organization is the International Women's Democracy Center, whose motto is "strengthening women's global leadership through training, education networking and research" (www.iwdc.org). While not focusing on leadership development for women in higher education per se, the organization still offers to train women leaders to effectively lobby legislators, to advocate for issues central to their organization's mission, and to manage issue-based campaigns, all important skills for women leaders in higher education.

At the University of Maryland, the James MacGregor Burns Academy of Leadership exists to deliver core offerings, leadership training, team building, organizational transformation, coaching, women's leadership, African American leadership, federal leadership, and customized programs (www .academy.umd.edu). According to the website, the academy can customize training sessions in a number of areas specifically targeted toward women, including mentors and advisers, with an emphasis on embracing risk, change, and power.

Still another organization in higher education, the National Association of Student Affairs Professional Administrators (NASPA), has an impressive bibliography on leadership development, women's leadership, and gender differences (www.naspa.org). One of the classics that meant a lot to me as a developing woman leader and is listed in the NASPA bibliography is Carol Gilligan's *In a Different Voice: Psychological Theory and Women's Development* (1982). Her discussion of the different perspective women bring to the leadership role is important to understand as we approach positions of leadership previously held by men, and as we relate to male leaders in higher education.

At the University of Delaware, the Institute for Public Administration includes a Women's Leadership Development Program (www.ipa.udel .edu). Although this program focuses on women in public service, skills acquired here would benefit women in higher education, where many women involved in social work move into during the course of their professional development and careers.

Another example of university-based leadership development programs is found at Simmons College in Boston, Massachusetts. Simmons College Center for Gender Organizations in the School of Management considers research in leadership, especially underrecognized aspects of leadership, and purports to give voice to the experiences and knowledge of women leaders, especially those from marginalized groups (www.simmons.edu).

Likewise, Rutgers University's Institute for Women's Leadership has a purpose "to examine and advance women's leadership in education, research, politics, the workplace, and the world" (www.rci.rutgers.edu). To its credit, Rutgers boasts on the top three programs in women's studies among the more than seven hundred such programs nationally. This women's studies program is one of five units at Rutgers that form the Institute for Women's Leadership Consortium, an impressive organization and combination of resources pertinent to leadership development of women.

Located in the Center for Public Policy at Virginia Commonwealth University, the Grace E. Harris Leadership Institute offers community and organizational training for women in higher education and faith organizations. According to the website, the objectives of the program are to teach women how to incorporate key leadership principles into their own professional and personal style and to foster leadership development and collaborative partnerships among women of color and women from diverse racial, ethnic, and religious backgrounds in higher education and faith communities (www.vcu.edu).

One website in particular, at the University of Illinois at Chicago (www .uic.edu/depts/owa/womens_centers.html), has a page on Women's Centers and Offices at American Colleges and Universities that is managed by the Office of Women's Affairs and provides eleven pages of alphabetically listed links to women's centers and offices around the United States. Surely many women will find this website to be a handy and useful resource. A similar master reference page is found at NASPA online, with a four-page list of references linked to leadership development organizations, publications, and opportunities for women. And finally, the American Association of University Women (AAUW) has a list of leadership development resources on their website at www.aauw.org.

Mentoring for Leadership Development

According to Stacy Blake-Beard (2005:6), "mentoring relationships offer phenomenal opportunity to support and be supported, to offer shelter and take risks." Similarly, Growe and Montgomery (1999:6) write that for "women to succeed in acquiring administrative positions in education, mentoring must occur." To summarize their points, consider the following benefits of mentoring:

- Mentoring can enhance income and promotion possibilities.
- Mentoring can meet the needs of women and institutions by attracting and retaining women in the academy.
- Mentoring reduces turnover and provides information about the organization that hastens adjustment to the work setting.

- Mentoring promotes a feeling of being supported in those being mentored.

Although women can and have been mentored by men (as is true in my own professional development), women mentoring other women is generally thought to be the best situation. For one thing, women share common perspectives and similar experiences. For another thing, women who travel through the professional development steps before other women can offer real-life accounts of examples from their own experiences of leadership development that will serve as powerful mentoring opportunities. Women mentors can also model successful survival skills to other women in the university—survival skills such as setting goals and working to reach them, persisting, recognizing deadlines and meeting them, learning to delegate effectively, demonstrating courage and determination, and developing and displaying confidence (Growe and Montgomery 1999).

Out of curiosity I did an Internet search on the terms "mentoring," "women," and "higher education" and asked for recent articles only. There were 39,200 displayed in 0.28 second. Remarkable, is it not? Yes, it is certainly remarkable that so much information is available at our fingertips. Useful? Yes, it is probably useful, but only if we review and use the information that is so readily available to us. It helps no one if no one is directed to the mentoring information or finds it without direction. In our social work discipline, through organizations like the Council on Social Work Education, the Association for Baccalaureate Social Work Program Directors, the National Association of Deans and Directors of Social Work Programs (NADD), the National Association of Social Workers (NASW), and others not listed here, we are provided with numerous opportunities for mentoring and being mentored. My own experiences with mentoring, through BPD and CSWE in particular, have played an important role in my own leadership development. Through those organizations I found role models, teachers, consultants, collaborators, and mentors. I learned from them, was reassured by them, found support among them, saw behaviors to emulate in them, and established collegial relationships with them. Through these organizations I learned how to be a leader in social work education by participating, observing, practicing, taking risks, and responding to opportunities that were presented to me. Through these organizations I also became a teacher, consultant, presenter, mentor, and leader. Mentoring new program directors, faculty, and commissioners is of significant importance to me and is one way I participate in developing leaders in social work education.

Mentoring can be formal, such as in training, workshops, classes, and institutes, or informal, such as between colleagues. According to Zichy (2001:200), "mentors excel at leading others to achieve their potential." For mentoring others to be successful, the mentor must check her ego at the door and enter into the mentoring relationship with generosity, affirmation, and compassion for the developing leader. The mentor must also have a desire to share, not withhold, knowledge, experiences, and resources. Even though we are stating the obvious, mentoring is a goal-oriented activity with an expected outcome for the person being mentored. Mentoring others is a giving activity, with no expectation of receiving anything in return except for the satisfaction one derives from helping others develop into leaders. Leadership development, especially in women of color and other women, is the true reward for mentors engaged in that process.

Conclusion

Institutions of higher education, organizations, and individuals all have roles to play in leadership development of women of color and other women in higher education. Some institutions have impressive programs, websites, and funding to support the development of women as leaders. Similarly, some organizations offer a variety of opportunities for women who want to develop leadership skills or have leadership experiences. Individuals also are great resources for leadership development. It is the individual mentor or role model whose influence is often cited by the developing leader as significant. That can be said of my own experience as a developing leader, and I hope it is being said by some who have been mentored by me over the years. For the profession to prosper and flourish, and for women to have opportunities for leadership, leadership development is everyone's responsibility.

References

Blake-Beard, S. D. (2005). "The Inextricable Link Between Mentoring and Leadership." In *Enlightened Power: How Women Are Transforming the Practice of Lead-*

ership, ed. L. Coughlin, E. Wingard, and K. Hollihan, pp. 101–10. San Francisco: Jossey-Bass.

Center for the Education of Women, University of Michigan, Ann Arbor (http://www.umich.edu).

Daresh, John C. (1995). "Research Base on Mentoring for Educational Leaders: What Do We Know?" *Journal of Educational Administration* 33 (5): 7–16.

Gilligan, C. (1982). *In A Different Voice: Psychological Theory and Women's Development*. Cambridge: Harvard University Press.

Growe, Rosilin, and Paula Montgomery (1999). "Women and the Leadership Paradigm: Bridging the Gender Gap." *National Forum of Educational Administration and Supervision Journal* 1E (4): 38–46.

Rhode, Deborah L., ed. (2003). *The Difference "Difference" Makes: Women and Leadership*. Stanford: Stanford University Press.

Valdata, Patricia (2006). "Lonely at the Top?" *Diverse* (November 16): 28–33.

Wenniger, Mary D., and Mary H. Conroy, eds. (2001). *Gender Equity or Bust! On the Road to Campus Leadership with Women in Higher Education*. San Francisco: Jossey-Bass.

Wisker, Gina (1996). *Empowering Women in Higher Education*. Sterling, Va.: Stylus.

Zichy, Shoya (2001). *Women and the Leadership Q, the Breakthrough System for Achieving Power and Influence*. New York: McGraw-Hill.

Resources

American Association of University Women (www.aauw.org)

American Council on Education (ACE), Office of Women in Higher Education, professional and leadership development opportunities (www.acenet.edu)

Association for Baccalaureate Social Work Education (BPD), professional and leadership development opportunities (www.bpdonline.org)

Council on Social Work Education (CSWE), professional and leadership development opportunities (www.CSWE.org)

Inside Higher Education (Inside_Higher_Ed@mail.vresp.com)

[2]

The Not-So-Accidental Leader

DARLENE GRANT

Pursuing Leadership and Administration

Appointed associate dean of graduate studies for the University of Texas at Austin in August 2003, I oversee the Graduate Recruitment and Outreach program as well as graduate admissions for over one hundred degree programs. I received a doctoral degree in social work from the University of Tennessee at Knoxville in 1993, after earning a bachelor's degree from Wittenberg University and a master's degree from Case Western Reserve University. My areas of teaching and research include social justice, culturally competent practice, human behavior and the social environment, clinical social work practice, research methods, and women with addiction and criminal justice involvement and their children. My research for the past ten years has focused on the evaluation of an in-prison visitation program involving wrap-around services for girl scouts with mothers who are incarcerated (Grant 2006).

My Journey to a Leadership Position

After receiving a failing grade on an assignment I was sure I had completed, turned in, and received back, I spent a half hour cleaning out my lift-top desk to find that piece of paper. Terrified, I walked to the desk of Mrs. Wright, a tall, regal Black woman, my fourth-grade teacher. I presented the graded "A" paper and tearfully asked her to change my grade while apologizing for contradicting her authority. In her booming voice she told me, in front of the entire class, that I had "perseverance." She had me look up the word, write it on a note card, and learn it as my own special word. Although I came from an all-Black neighborhood and school population in Cleveland, Mrs. Wright was the only African American teacher that I recall in the entire elementary school. I was simultaneously in awe and afraid of her. I was hungry for self-definition that legitimized my taking up space in a rough and threatening inner-city, family, and world, and Mrs. Wright gave me a word and a concept to positively define myself and my prospects for life. Perseverance in large part defines my path into higher education and subsequently into a leadership position. It is no coincidence that the concept of perseverance resonated with the teachings in the Black Baptist church, in which I was quite involved throughout my childhood and young adulthood.

Perseverance is defined as steady persistence in a course of action or purpose in spite of difficulties, obstacles, or disappointment. Coupled with commitment and passion for purpose and relevance, perseverance has long been the main reason I have landed in leadership positions. As a shy, bookish, clumsy introvert, in my senior year in high school I was elected runner-up to the homecoming queen. Homecoming queen was the third time that I campaigned for a pseudo- or real leadership position—I lost runs for minor positions on our junior and senior student councils. I ran for homecoming queen based on my visibility as an active member of our large and influential marching band in which I played a modest leadership role. While receiving recognition and a smaller tiara and winged award, I experienced the position of runner-up as a major embarrassment and loss, indicative of what happens to the bookish kid who quietly aspires to be more.

Graduating in the top 5 percent of my senior class, I went on to attend a predominantly White, private university in southern Ohio, applied to upon the recommendation of my high school guidance counselor. I spent my first semester wrestling with culture shock. It was the first time I ever perceived and experienced my race as a major deficit and barrier to success. I bore this debilitating experience without ever sharing these feelings with anyone—not even my fellow African American students. Ending my first semester in college with a 1.5 grade point average, I quickly learned that a straight-"A" student from a low-income inner-city public school is not the same as a straight-"A" student from a middle- or upper-class suburban public or private school system. Not only did I suspect, I had constant evidence in the form of failing grades that I was not as smart as my family and teachers believed. A pre-med schedule heavy in math and science and inexperience in knowing who or how to ask for help had also contributed to my failure.

Shortly after the beginning of spring semester I received a letter of dismissal. In tears, I collapsed in the hall outside of my dorm room. I could not return to Cleveland as a failure. What other options were there? A White student from down the hall, Ellen, stopped to find out why I was crying. For the first time ever, we shared more than a friendly hello as she read the letter from my outstretched hands. She sat down and sympathetically told me about the dean of women as a resource I could go to for a second chance. I did not know there was such a position or even an option to remain at the university after being dismissed. Ellen coached me in what to say and recommended the emotional and verbal stance I should take. I proceeded to the dean of women sure that my life was on the line and made a successful plea for a second chance.

Today, I realize that both Ellen and I bridged teachings and stereotypes about each other on that afternoon in the dormitory hallway. I risked trusting a white person, and she felt I was smart enough, just not savvy in terms of negotiating that complex system, which generations of her family had attended. My friendship with Ellen and her roommates grew as I continued to learn from them how to negotiate the world of college, how to study, how to approach and establish rapport with my instructors, how and when to ask for help, and, perhaps most important, that failing that first semester was not totally due to personal shortcomings. The system was set up to attract but not support an unknowingly underprepared minority student's success. Not until I received strategic informal peer mentoring did my grades reflect my intellectual abilities. Relieved of the burden of failure, I was presented with opportunities to expand my educational and social experience outside of books, study sessions, the library, and the three part-time jobs I had cobbled together in order to pay for school.

Two semesters later I participated in sorority rush (the screening process for new members) and was invited to join Sigma Kappa, Ellen's sorority. A year later I was elected the rush chair, one of the most coveted positions in a sorority. This position catapulted me into a campuswide leadership position with a seat on the Pan-Hellenic Council and expectations that I interact with the dean of students on several student committees. While my friendships with the handful of African American students continued, with subtle changes, the sorority became my home and my leadership grooming ground. By the end of my junior year I was elected the chapter president.

The most important leadership lessons learned during my time in college include the power of peer mentoring, the importance of cultural and organizational information, and that "access to higher education" is just a string of words unless you have assistance in learning how to concretely negotiate complex organizations and how to establish rapport with people in positions of power. I learned, for example, the importance of reading and constantly consulting the university's organizational handbooks for students and student leaders—cover to cover. I also learned the importance of nonjudgmental relationships and the benefit of sharing power and authority. The importance of working to purposefully bridge age, racial/ethnic, and class difference was affirmed many times.

Planned or Unplanned Leadership

I have frequently considered myself an accidental leader. Finding myself in leadership roles as a social work practitioner, university professor, and university administrator, I have often had to work hard to fight a self-perception of it all being "an accident." I never planned on being an administrator in higher education, for example, but I have always been purposeful in building my knowledge and credentials as a key team member in each position I have held. One might define the desire to play a role as a key team member as one among many definitions of leadership. Preparation for a role as a key team member has included attending conferences and workshops, collaborating with colleagues, subscribing to journals, reading broadly, consulting with supervisors, mentors, and colleagues, observing colleagues in similar roles, thinking about what I was doing, and always being genuine, ethical, and diplomatic.

Because these tendencies are what would be considered qualities that attract invitations to fill leadership positions, I am acutely aware of my lifelong prayer to be ready to help and even to lead, should I ever be called upon to do so. This conception has its foundation in church and family experiences and the complex experience of powerlessness mixed with feelings of hope for a better life and a fairer world. I have often wondered whether this is how someone like Rosa Parks felt as she attended workshops and participated in other leadership training via her church and her service as the secretary for her chapter of the NAACP, long before she took a stand for civil rights by refusing to give up her seat on that bus in Alabama on that cold December day in 1955.

When Professional Credibility Is Publicly Challenged

Thanks to mentoring and a research internship with a sociology professor, after college I went directly into the master's program in social work at Case Western Reserve University. After six years in direct social work practice, I had found my niche as a family therapist on an inpatient substance abuse treatment unit, with a small private practice and an adjunct faculty position at the University of Tennessee at Knoxville. I was respected across the hospital and frequently called upon by social workers on other units for case consultations. The only complication involved a staff psychologist who would frequently countermand my clinical judgment and case recommendations during our daily treatment team meetings. My initial reaction was to blame myself for not being clear—not speaking the language of psychology. So, determined to do better, I studied and meticulously prepared my presentations. Nothing changed. In hindsight I realize that my focus on the micro did not address the bigger social, professional, and organizational dynamics, including racism and the view of social work as a subordinate profession lacking clinical credibility.

The professional battle for credibility played out in the treatment team for over a year. Underlying issues of age, class, race, power, and privilege had irreparably damaged my professional credibility with the treatment team. I began doubting myself. One of the biggest threats to effective leadership is the daily alienation of confidence that grows until the only viable option seems to be to leave. Instead, I decided that a Ph.D. degree would place me on a more level playing field with this psychologist and would repair my credibility as a clinical practitioner. In 1990 I was accepted into the social work doctoral program at the University of Tennessee at Knoxville. My goal to return to clinical practice soon changed to that of teaching social workers pride of profession, culturally competent practice, and ways to better negotiate scenarios such as the one I had left. Graduating in December 1993, I accepted a faculty position at the University of Texas at Austin and began to pursue these very goals. The target of leadership changed from focus on the social worker, the psychologist, and the treatment team of one small psychiatric hospital to the hundreds of social workers that could be influenced by a university professor and mentor.

Self-assessment Tools Used to Determine My Leadership Aspirations

In February 2003, subsequent to a number of racially charged incidents at the university that resulted in a huge outcry for change, I was asked by Dr. Larry Faulkner, then president of the university, to chair a Task Force on Racial Respect and Fairness. This was an unplanned and quite daunting honor that immediately elevated me to university, state, and national notoriety. It was the big league of social change focused on race, one of the toughest dialogues in our nation. I was counting on my clinical social work skills to help me as the fifteen-member task force was convened, made up of students, faculty, and staff members. As part of the president's charge, we were asked to review procedures of the university's police department and examine the cross-cultural educational programs available to the university's police officers, look at the university's ability to exert greater influence over behavioral standards of student organizations, and analyze the effectiveness with which the university conveys the diversity (the "face") of the student population to the outside world. The executive summary of the report of the task force can be found at http://www.utexas.edu/news/2004/01/20/nr_respect/. The full report is available at http://www.utexas.edu/president/speeches/report_respect.pdf.

   Dr. King Davis, a colleague and mentor in the School of Social Work and executive director of the multimillion-dollar Hogg Foundation for Mental Health, gave me a bit of helpful advice early in my year as chair of the task force. He recommended that I keep a journal about my experience as chair, focusing on my strengths and weaknesses, highlighting the skills I brought to the position, the skills I needed to learn, the barriers I encountered, and the steps I took to overcome barriers and challenges. King reiterated this advice a year later, after I was appointed associate dean of graduate studies at the University of Texas at Austin. I took his advice and purchased a multiyear-format journal, which, with only four lines for the daily notes section, permits me to glance at eleven years in one page. Keeping my entries focused on my leadership and administrative experiences, I have been able to use this journal to organize my thoughts and goals. After three years as associate dean, I have been able to track themes and patterns, set goals for self-improvement in my leadership skills, and actually track changes in my skill set over time.

Robbins and Finley (2004:45) suggest that "self-assessment is a kind of assessment, and assessment—figuring out what's going on—is the leadership skill nobody talks about. Yet it is the foundation skill on which all other skills are built. Because if you don't know what you have, no change you achieve will matter because you won't be able to prove there was a change." Reading their book in preparation for writing this chapter affirmed much of my tendency toward self-assessment as my primary leadership tool. Another important leadership tool is mentoring. I am grateful for the mentoring that I have received from a number of colleagues across the years. So not only was I encouraged to purposefully self-assess, I was also encouraged to take care about how hard I was on myself. Perhaps it is the curse of being a woman leader, or being the oldest child, or my strict Baptist upbringing, or my fear of failure that drives me to fairly brutal self-assessment, but thank goodness for mentors who can step in to make sure we are judicious and fair in these processes that are designed to help, not hinder.

Blueprint for Pursuing a Leadership Position

My first five years as an assistant professor were spent learning and solidifying my credentials and legitimacy as a leader in the classroom and in the School of Social Work. I sought help from the university's Teaching Effectiveness Center. Learning that one does not automatically translate into the other, with the help of the center's staff I translated my nine years of clinical practitioner experience and skills into teaching skills. While student evaluations convinced me that my skills as a clinician did not readily translate into the skills of a teacher, changes in the focus of their critique have been indicative of my increasing experience and skill as a teacher. I read books on teaching and subscribed to the *Journal on Social Work Education*.

Another approach to credibility building included serving on the editorial board of several social work journals during these years. This service provided a way to increase my reputation nationally and to strengthen my own writing skills. I familiarized myself with *Robert's Rules of Order* for the numerous school and university-wide committees and community board of directors on which I served. The more I grew in my skills as a teacher and as a convener of committee meetings, the more I could effectively use my clinical experience to set the context and experience for student learning.

As an assistant professor, I worked to establish myself as a leader in the area of the recruitment and retention of students from historically underrepresented groups to the School of Social Work graduate program. This was an issue I could distinguish as my important civic contribution to the school as I worked for tenure. This work included chairing the school's recruitment and retention committee, recruitment travel, and collaboration with the university's Recruitment and Outreach Program in the Office of Graduate Studies. So that this leadership focus was not divorced from my research, writing, and publication activities, the stuff tenure is made of, the issue of recruitment and retention of minority students was incorporated into my research and resulted in two substantive publications (Grant 1994; Herrera, Murry, and Grant 1994). Later, this leadership focus led to an appointment to the university-wide minority recruitment and retention committee, which led to the appointment to chair the task force, which led to the invitation to join the Office of Graduate Studies with a focus on the recruitment of students from historically underrepresented groups to graduate programs at UT. The structure of these appointments emphasizes the nonaccidental aspect of my leadership experience.

Do's and Don'ts of Pursuing Leadership and Administration Positions

Of particular salience for me are three potential threats of undermining that woman leaders, in particular women of color as leaders, always face: insecurity, people management, and the lack of mentoring for leadership success. First, secret insecurities and doubt can undermine leadership. Second, colleagues and constituents might perceive the woman of color as undeservedly in the coveted position of power and authority because of being a double minority, a token, someone who is the go-to person for things related to diversity, not because of other sources of credibility. This suggests a second threat of undermining—one of the toughest challenges that women of color as leaders face, that of managing people, teams, and perceptions. Social work skills of listening, case management, advocacy, team building, interpretation, policy analysis, and problem solving are critical to managing people and administering a program, but not sufficient alone. For example, while I have shared with staff under my direct supervision my leadership style as working to their strengths and supporting efforts to strengthen areas in which they were challenged, that approach never guaranteed consistent cooperation or support for my vision or goals for the team. I have spent many sleepless nights trying to figure out how to get team members to do what needed to be done. There are times I would stay late at the office to double-check the work of others, or to simply do what needed to be done myself. The more often I resorted to solving our team-related problems in this way, the less effective I felt as a leader.

I am a big University of Texas (and, dare I admit publicly, University of Tennessee) women's basketball fan. Considering the skills needed to negotiate the dynamics illustrated in the example above, I am reminded of our women's basketball coach, who will often pull a player aside during a game for not playing to her full potential, causing a hole in team functioning on the court. As a guest coach seated directly behind the Texas player's bench, I have over heard our coach ask the player if she is willing to do what it takes to help the team win—"if not you can. . . ." I have rarely caught the words at the end of the coach's dialogue. And because of crowd noise, I have rarely heard the player's response. But I have had a view of their body language and the player's effort after the conversation, which is usually stepping up the pace and doing what needed to be done to help the team. As leaders with training in social work, women can demonstrate an ability to motivate but must also set clear boundaries—including how to clarify the consequences of not meeting performance expectations.

Mentoring from experienced leaders and consultation from trusted and professional human resources entities within the organization are invaluable ways to counter undermining that could negatively impact leadership success. In my confidential conversations with other leaders across the country who are women of color, the primary challenge is that of mentoring from experienced leaders, when we are expected to step into our positions as mentors to colleagues and students of color who aspire to leadership positions themselves. While we can offer important contributions to leadership mentoring, our resources are quickly used up and maximum effectiveness limited. We often discuss aspects of our role as administrators of color as "flying from the seat of our pants." I am clear, however, that we must always keep in mind that this sense of flying from the seat of our pants in leadership is in actuality based on experience, purpose, homework, consultation with colleagues and constituents, prayer, and a history of successes built upon successes in earlier leadership endeavors. Successful leadership from this perspective is formative, defined as susceptible to transformation by growth and development (*American Heritage Dictionary* 2006). There are, admittedly, weeks where we hold on to this definition for dear life.

Leading and Administering Successfully

Personal Factors Contributing to Success in Leadership

I like the stimulus of contrast—this seems to be a characteristic of most of the effective leaders and mentors whom I have encountered. To be a social work educator in a top-tier research university by definition involves the challenge of contrasts, as we are required to conduct meaningful research (including publication in top journals to contribute to the profession's knowledge base), to be effective teachers, and to participate in public service. The act of writing provides an example of the stimulus of contrast, as it can be a solitary or a synergistic endeavor through collaboration with colleagues. Similarly, leadership carries with it simultaneous communal and solitary experiences and responsibilities. The challenge is the visibility of decisions and actions as a leader and the perspective of the utility or destructiveness of those decisions and actions for those colleagues or constituents impacted, however proximate or far away. It is important to me to be the kind of social worker and administrator who does not jump to conclusions. I do not make decisions or take action based on initial impressions. Thus, when it is time for me to make quick decisions, I and my colleagues and constituents can more easily depend on the level-headedness of those decisions based on a history of having done my homework.

It helps that I am enthusiastic about and dedicated to the core goals of the social work and higher education professions. As a champion of these professions and their core goals, I have several personal characteristics that contribute to success in leadership, including the tendency to be collaborative, to read broadly, and to purposefully interact with a diversity of people to gain different perspectives. Having a sense of humor and an understanding of the importance of playing also enables me to consider a continuum of responses to leadership dilemmas. Every now and then we need to participate in activities that enable us to be grateful for the contributions our work makes to individuals and society in general.

I am proud to be a social worker! I look for opportunities to share this enthusiasm and to illustrate the depth and breadth of practice as I talk about my roles as researcher, teacher, administrator, recruiter, and motivational speaker. While the mission of universities is variously articulated, the core considerations common to my personal mission as a human being, a woman of color, and a social worker are those of transforming lives and contributing to the advancement of society through learning, discovery, leadership, and responsibility.

Further, as a result of my family's history, my life experiences, and my chosen profession, I am a proponent of social and economic justice, particularly for historically marginalized and oppressed populations. Social justice is a complex and often ideologically challenging concept to define. For the purposes of this discussion on women of color as leaders, I personally define my leadership as social justice work.

My development as a leader in social work education, then, includes a call for individual and collective responsibility for acknowledging, understanding, and transforming institutional perceptions and values, structures, and cultural practices that pose barriers to access and success in life, including higher education and the economic and social benefits that arise out of the pursuit of one's greatest possibilities.

Cultural Factors Affecting Leadership Style and Paradigm

My African American heritage has significant impact on my leadership philosophy and style. The liberation theology of the Black Baptist church is the cultural paradigm in which I grew up. In the Black church, liberation theology "takes the oppression of blacks as a point of departure for analyzing God's activity in contemporary America" (Cone 1986:9). I trace this theological underpinning as far back as the teachings of my maternal grandfather, Reverend Eli Cleveland Vester, who preached in July 1944:

> The youth must be our first care, our chief care. If we lose them, we lose all. . . . The youth express . . . all memories and achievements and hopes of the race down through the centuries. Without the conserving of the child today we lose tomorrow, for whatever you wish the coming generation to be must be implanted in the child. . . . The story of neglected children is a sad episode. We feel, as a race, we have some rights and feel that the other race ought to give it to us. It's ours. . . . It has a right to be properly born, a right to live and to be rightly trained for life. . . . There is no better tomorrow without a better today for the youth of our race.

This theology espouses confrontation of the structure of power and oppression and destigmatization and decriminalization of blackness. "The role of black theology is to tell blacks to focus on their own self-determination as a community by preparing to do anything the community believes necessary for its existence" (Cone 1986:15). Cone further suggests that discussions of, and interventions designed to accomplish, liberation from oppression must include a spiritual component to be meaningful to and successful in the Black community. This accounts for the influence of Martin Luther King, Jr., Jessie Jackson, and Al Sharpton. This also accounts for the influence of Black woman leaders including Sojourner Truth, Fannie Lou Hamer, Rosa Parks, Shirley Chisholm, and Barbara Jordan.

In this context, it is logical that I see my primary role and responsibility as a teacher and administrator as that of inspiring students and laypeople to understand the social work profession and to understand the power of higher education, particularly college and graduate education, and to lifting families out of poverty and despair.

Conversely, the patriarchal structure of the Black Baptist church was the leadership paradigm in which I grew up. Women have always been the majority of the membership of the Black Baptist church in which I grew up and the driving force behind the success of the church's financial resources, the education and spiritual training of the youth in the church, support of the ministry, and community outreach. Yet they yielded to male assertions of authority. In the more traditionally expressive roles, these women helped each other raise children, cared for aging parents and extended family, addressed the impact of poverty with tips on church and state agency resources, and prayed with and for each other through tough family situations, including the emasculation of their husbands and sons in the larger societal system of oppression. The model of female leadership that I witnessed did not include women as high-level church executives, ministers, deacons, or financial officers. Women, like my grandmother, mother, and aunts, took on traditional positions as the church secretary and secretary of the Sunday school, Sunday school teachers, and nurses aids, formed the bulk of the membership of the various church choirs, led the ladies' auxiliary, were missionary board members (visiting and caring for sick and shut-in members, for example), and served as the pastor's aide (laying out his robes and vestments, filling a glass of water at the table beside his chair at the pulpit, running interference when difficult members sought an audience, etc.).

Grounded in a philosophy that faith, persistence, and "right is might," the leadership model of Black women in my Black Baptist church was one of "the strength of the church manifested as the strength behind the pastor— the man." The power of women in the church was implicit, not explicit. There was this notion that a woman's position was legitimized through others and thus could go noticed or unnoticed, awarded or not, based on the pastor's wishes or the wishes of those who provided his counsel.

My perception of my own leadership style is that it tends to be very much in the direction of quiet persistence and behind-the-scenes strength of character and purpose that will, in the long run, win the day. I am often concerned that this aspect of my leadership style is interpreted by my bosses and those who report directly to me as weakness, detachment, or dispassion. This is a stylistic theme that I frequently write about in my multi-year journal entries. There is no epiphany nor resolution to this concern to report at this time.

Systemic Factors Contributing to Challenges and Strategies for Overcoming

As I mentioned earlier, as a junior faculty member and later associate dean I learned quickly that the biggest leadership challenge for me is effectively managing or supervising people. This has been the hardest lesson for me as my ability for team building, garnering respect, and gaining buy-in to an agenda and excitement for the cause have been my strengths as a clinical social worker and board member in nonprofit agencies.

Generally perceived as well respected, competent, committed, organized, and congenial, I believe, in hindsight, that as a new administrator of a team of three full-time staff, who were inherited from the former associate dean and were used to a totally different style of leadership, I was quickly perceived by my team as equivocating, unsure, and even weak as a leader. I began my tenure depending on my social work skills as I became acclimated to my new role as an administrator. Image management became an important and evolving strategy in my supervisory role. I began, for example, by making every effort to include team members in all decision making, soliciting their opinions along the way, and in some instances deferring to team opinion, acknowledging that they had been doing their specific jobs from three to eighteen years. On many occasions I pointed out how the wedding of our respective views resulted in new and exciting approaches to our work. This helped me highlight my belief that good leadership instills a sense of synergy and vitality in our work.

Strategies for Overcoming Challenges and Barriers

It did not take long to discern that my leadership style was not working for me or for the team. After reviewing my journal notes and talking with trusted mentors, I used the annual one-on-one employee evaluation meeting to engage each staff member in a conversation about what he or she viewed as working and not working related to my supervision style and how our program was running.

After listing the characteristics of my leadership and supervisory style, I volunteered that I had concerns that some aspects of my style were not in tune with their respective working styles:

- I do not mother or engage in frequent conversations and advice giving about the personal lives of employees.
- I work hard to motivate staff using praise and public recognition.
- I like to hold weekly staff meetings as a way to check in with where we all are on assigned tasks and duties as well as a way to help the team anticipate problems and celebrate successes.

- I trust that members of the team will follow through with assigned tasks, and I have a hard time with confronting them when they do not. My confrontation falls along a continuum of writing long e-mails describing in great detail exactly what I want done and why, to doing the work myself. Neither approach is successful in getting people to do what I want or believe should be done to achieve programmatic goals.
- I use humor to diffuse discomfort.
- I know that I am more self-effacing than is proper for a high-level administrator. Addressing personal factors that contribute to perceptions of my leadership abilities is an ongoing effort.

Tired of being frustrated and working long hours but never getting ahead, I began meeting with someone whom I perceived as a master at managing staff, Jennifer Luna-Idunate, director of the School of Social Work's Dinitto Center for Career Services. After reviewing the list of what I found to be most challenging as a manager and supervisor and my attempts to resolve these challenges, the first pieces of advice that I received from Jennifer included the following:

- Get to the point. No more long, detailed e-mails, especially after spending staff meeting time going over assignments and getting buy-in.
- Limit the amount of time spent justifying work requests.
- Use staff meetings as time to review task accomplishment and to emphasize and applaud accomplishing tasks and deadlines.

Just these adjustments resulted in my feeling and appearing more confident and purposeful as a leader and administrator. It was amazing.

Role of Leadership Programs

I cannot emphasize enough my belief that a good leader learns from other skillful leaders. Leadership programs are grounded in this philosophy. In 2005 the president of the university supported my nomination and subsequent application to participate in Leadership Texas, a yearlong statewide program of the Foundation for Women's Resources with the purpose of bringing together Texas women who have demonstrated leadership ability in their profession, community, or workplace for the purpose of sharpening skills and developing a network of women from diverse backgrounds.

The Leadership Texas curriculum is consistent with most programs focused on leadership enhancement, including opportunities for participants to hear perspective-broadening presentations by and interact with state and national experts. The program also includes on-site visits to major business, education, and cultural centers. The primary purpose behind these efforts is to expose participants to a diversity of information and ideas, thus increasing their "understanding of the challenges that leaders face in both the private and public sectors" (http://www.womensresources .org/LT.asp).

In my application to the Leadership Texas program, I referenced Virginia Gildersleeve, as she is among a number of woman leaders whom I strive daily to emulate. Virginia Gildersleeve earned a Ph.D. degree in English from Columbia University in 1908. A noted leader in women's education and dean of Barnard College for more than thirty-six years, she was also a cofounder and twice president of the International Federation of University Women. She was the only woman appointed by President Franklin D. Roosevelt to the 1945 U.S. delegation that established the United Nations and the first woman in the United States to sign a U.S. treaty. My professional creed evolves from a quote by Dr. Gildersleeve: "The ability to think straight, some knowledge of the past, some vision of the future, some skill to do useful service, some urge to fit that service into the well-being of the community—these are the most vital things education must try to produce" (http://www.enotes.com/famous-quotes/tag/education?start= 200). But, like most leaders, I have to make the extra effort to take care of my own learning needs. I need a way to rejuvenate my batteries after giving my all every day of the week. I look to opportunities such as Leadership Texas for the support and affirmation that I so readily give to others— and now adamantly require for myself as an important characteristic of a good leader.

Role of Professional Social Work Organizations

While often challenged with juggling competing demands of teaching, research, administration, and public service, I depend on the National Association of Social Workers and the Council on Social Work Education to keep me abreast of the perspectives of the profession on the crucial issues of the day. Further, just as I view my leadership role as an advocacy role, I depend on these professional organizations to provide written, workshop, national and local committee, and other opportunities to grow in leadership knowledge and skills.

Since joining the NASW/Texas chapter, I have gotten to know Vicki Hansen, the executive director and an example of long-term practical and committed leadership. Always available as a guest class speaker to undergraduate and graduate students, she provides an invaluable overview of issues in case management, medical social work, social policy, and social work licensure. An understanding of these issues is critical to me as a leader dependent on the skills of my leadership network.

The same is true for CSWE leaders such as my UT Austin colleagues, former CSWE and NASW president Dr. Barbara White; BSW program director and accreditation specialist Dr. Dennis Haynes; BSW program director Rosalie Ambrosino; and curriculum development specialist Dr. Roberta Greene. Through reports of their work with CSWE, each of these leaders in social work education has helped me gain greater understanding of leadership, including the underlying structure and philosophy of curriculum development and social work program accreditation.

Conclusion

My leadership style and philosophy are evolving, dynamic, and an emerging critique of power structures in relation to those who are marginalized and oppressed in society. My leadership style and philosophy are deeply influenced by my family's history in the Black Baptist church, and by the dynamic interplay of the church and Black liberation theology of the civil rights movement. The more I grow in my skills as an administrator, the more I can effectively use my clinical and teaching experience to set the context and experience for leading.

It is my hope that something said in this chapter helps future leaders, especially women of color, understand the challenges and the rewards of leadership. As a college and professional football fan, I liken my recommendation for current and future leaders to commentator comments about quarterbacks who have had one or more passes intercepted during a game. The leadership decision to throw the ball that was intercepted is usually viewed as a poor decision. The effective pro football quarterback cannot dwell on that mistake as he risks being distracted during the process of making subsequent decisions. He does not have time to throw dirty looks toward or be angry at or hold a grudge against the guy who intercepted his pass. He can ill-afford to take excessive time to blame others on his team for not being where they needed to be to avoid the interception. The effective quarterback goes to the sideline, talks to the experts in the skybox upstairs, looks at a few aerial photos, and talks with his coaching staff and peers about strategies to avoid falling into the same trap. He then returns to the field with informed focus and commitment to making good decisions. This is a concrete example of the process and stance of the effective leader.

Leadership in social work academia is as tough as it is rewarding. Time, patience, strong networks, a sense of humor, resilience when feelings are hurt, and a cadre of people to remind us of what is really important in life are among the most important resources in the life of the leader.

Note

Thank you to Regina Grant Biddings, my little sister and my best friend; a reader, and now editor, and confidante to the challenges of leadership as a woman of color.

References

Cone, J. H. (1986). *A Black Theology of Liberation*. Second ed. Maryknoll, N.Y.: Orbis.

Grant, D. (1994). "The Texas Addiction Training Center: Promoting the Recruitment and Training of Minority Chemical Dependency Counselors and Allied Health Professionals Using a University and College Based Consortium Approach. In *The Minority Student Today: Recruitment, Retention, and Success*, conference proceedings, San Antonio, Tex.. Columbia: University of South Carolina with Incarnate Word College.

—— (2006). "Resilience of Girls with Incarcerated Mothers: The Impact of Girl Scouts." *Prevention Researcher* 13 (2): 11–14.

Herrera, S., K. Murry, and D. Grant (1994). *Accepting the Challenge: A Plan for the Recruitment and Retention of Persons of Color for Careers in Chemical Dependency Counseling*. Austin: Texas Commission on Alcohol and Drug Abuse.

Leadership Texas, a Program of the Foundation for Women's Resources, Is the Premier Statewide Women's Leadership Program (n.d.). Available at http://www.womensresources.org/LT.asp (accessed December 26, 2007).

Lewis, G. (1996). "Situated Voices: Black Women's Experience and Social Work." *Feminist Review* 53: 24–56.

Robbins, H., and M. Finley (2004). *The Accidental Leader: What to Do When You're Suddenly in Charge.* San Francisco: Jossey-Bass.

PART TWO

Deanship in Multidisciplinary Schools and Colleges

[3]

Following the Call, Leading from the Spirit

DARLYNE BAILEY

The real story begins. It seems that I was destined to be a pioneer, a "first": first born; first in my family to go to college; among the first group of women to attend a formerly all-male college (Lafayette); first woman and African American to later receive that college's alumni award for "professional distinction"; first African American woman to be appointed dean at one college and within its university (Mandel School of Applied Social Sciences, Case Western Reserve University), dean and vice president at another (Teachers College, Columbia University); and now again dean and assistant to the president at the University of Minnesota. Our College of Education and Human Development is brand new—the result of a merger of several colleges in July 2006—so I am the *founding* dean. Yet, amidst all the joys and challenges of pioneering, it was only within the last several years of academic leadership that I realized what it really meant to be "a first": it is my responsibility to do all I can to make certain that I am not the last woman of color in my position.

Even more recently (in response to repeated questions about the "planfulness" of my journey in academia), with all due respect to my career-planning and executive-coaching colleagues, I have come to recognize my walk as a calling, disguised as a series of serendipitous events, with me as a follower on the path of faith. And so it is with these two epiphanies that the real story begins.

> To whom much is given, much is required.
>
> —Luke 12:48

My late colleague and friend Dr. Paulo Freire described education as a political act, one of the keys to personal freedom. While I am certain that neither of my parents had ever heard of Freire's definition, they raised my sister Dawn and me knowing that getting an education was required. Despite (or perhaps because of) my mom going through high school in the "business" track and my dad dropping out at age thirteen, they told us that education was something that "no one could ever take away." So we went to school, and we also watched our parents. I saw my mom spend most of her time caring for us and overcome her shyness when actively involved, volunteering in our community. Both of my parents sacrificed and invested much in our well-being (it is *still* not easy to find goat's milk, my dietary staple for my first three years, in Harlem, New York).

Like everyone else in my family and most parents, our mom and dad wanted more and better for us than they had been able to have. With that came their dream for us to live in a racially integrated neighborhood and have a backyard with grass. After much searching, we moved to Englewood, New Jersey, one of the first towns in our country to undergo racial desegregation in its schools. For me, this obviously meant pioneering again, as this courageous and committed city implemented many innovations that showed up in specific courses, in classroom designs, and ultimately in the reassigning of an existing building to become the new "Central Sixth Grade" building—all purposefully planned to bring together the different talents of this ethnically and socioeconomically diverse community. In short, both within and outside of our home, I learned what it meant to truly care about and care for others.

Graduating from high school with these foundational values in place, I joined with about four hundred other women to make Lafayette College co-ed, as one of nine women of color—all African American. After I received a master's degree from Columbia University's School of Social Work with a focus on psychiatric practice and completed the certificate program from Lenox Hill Hospital's Psychoanalytic Psychotherapy Program, it made sense for my first professional job to be in the outpatient center of a county mental health hospital in New Jersey. Joined by a psychiatric nurse, I started a clinic for young adults carrying the diagnosis of schizophrenia. *Service* had become as natural to my life as breathing.

Three and a half years later, a quarter-inch advertisement in the local newspaper caught my mom's attention, and I soon relocated to help start and provide the leadership for a community mental health center in my hometown of Englewood. With "Intake and Access Services" (also known as 24/7 crisis intervention) as my area of responsibility for another three and a half years, I was reminded of yet another touchstone in my life, *collaboration*. No matter what my title was or how well conceived my ideas, I discovered that the implementation was always more effective and the process just more fun when others came aboard and we formed relationships of mutual teaching and learning, respect, honesty, and a shared commitment to the goal.

Fast-forward through the next eleven years: realizing that I wanted more formal education; serendipitously entering into the Department of Organizational Behavior at the Weatherhead School of Management at Case Western (who had ever heard of "OB" without it being followed by "GYN"?); and then graduating and declining faculty positions in business schools to accept the challenge of creating courses for the "management concentration" in the Mandel School of Applied Social Science, one of our country's oldest schools of social work. Three months posttenure, I was asked to assume the deanship.

> When I dare to be powerful—to use my strength in the service of my vision, then it becomes less and less important whether I am afraid.
>
> —Audre Lorde

To be given the position of college leadership as a newly minted associate professor, as a woman, and as a woman of color, I experienced feelings of surprise, honor, ecstasy, and, yes, fear. By now I had grown accustomed to undertaking challenges, and as one just honored by being accepted into the W. K. Kellogg National Leadership Program (Group 13), I had been reaffirmed in my leadership capabilities by all the self-assessment tools that we were presented. But this felt like too much too soon, despite the reassurance of the very courageous, smart, and caring university president,

Dr. Agnar Pytte. The next eight years (with a deep desire to be known as a "scholarly dean," resulting in my promotion to full professor in the fourth year) were filled with every emotion known to womankind. Through the joys and pains of faculty meetings, collegewide retreats, successful fundraising jaunts, curricula restructuring, births, illnesses, deaths, and professional reaccreditations, we at the Mandel School together discovered the power of *true dialogue*, as had first been introduced to me early in my deanship by Paulo Freire.

You see, emboldened by the invitation to be a Kellogg fellow, one day I telephoned Dr. Freire at his home in Sao Paulo, Brazil. During this exchange—which he said was the first time that he had answered his own phone in over two decades—Dr. Freire, in both English and Portuguese, and I, in my very rough Spanish-English, connected. I asked if I (joined by other Group 13 fellows and an advisor) could come and visit with him. I explained that I had just been appointed to a very important leadership position and that I knew I had a lot to learn—fast. Dr. Freire did not hesitate. He immediately said yes and then added the words that I have always remembered: "I have a responsibility to share with you all that I know." These words provided the launch for our ten-day sojourn: a time in community with all of my new colleagues; the beginning of my friendship with many, including Paulo Freire; and the wellspring of my learning the true meaning of dialogue.

Freire saw dialogue as more than a conversation. In fact, he described dialogue as an act of creation—a process in which two or more people discuss a topic by sharing opinions and simultaneously being open to the opinions of the other(s) (Freire 1981). Dialogue requires positive regard (for self and other), trust (in self and other), and unconditional caring (of self and other). It is not an exchange where you talk and I listen, or I talk and you listen, and definitely not where everyone talks and no one listens. No, true dialogue is an open-hearted and open-minded exchange of thoughts and feelings that, as Dr. Freire taught us, can only come from the integration of humility, faith, hope, and love.

With the process of dialogue both as our internal and boundary-spanning vision, our school determined a new mission. At the core of our purpose, our reason for being, was service in the community, to be community-based. All our research initiatives were grounded in the needs of the local Cleveland neighborhoods. And the findings from these explorations were interwoven into our classroom teaching. Indeed, the president started to refer to us as the "university's link to the community." Despite all of these connections being made, in the third year I began to feel very alone. While my faculty, staff, students, and even associate and assistant deans were actively engaged with peers, as the dean I grew to understand why it is said that "it's lonely at the top." This feeling blossomed into a question that framed the next steps in my personal and professional journey: *What sustains women as leaders?*

> The future belongs to those who believe in the beauty of their dreams.
>
> —Eleanor Roosevelt

Having planned to ultimately retire from the Mandel School, I surprised myself when I accepted the vice presidency at Teachers College. But it was in Harlem, the birthplace of my sister and me, and where my parents were raised, so I would again have the opportunity to give back. Moving into this position was also a step closer to what had become a dream—to assume the right and responsibility of leading an entire institution of many disciplines to attend to the needs and further the strengths of its community—a college presidency. So, amidst many tears and, yes, still some fears, I returned to the East Coast.

Joining with faculty and staff colleagues first to uncover the natural alliances among the many disciplines in this college and then to bridge the divide between our college and the local community became the major visible foci of my work. What guided all of this, however, was the question about the sustainability of woman leaders and the growing belief that there was something very powerful in "connections." It sounded so easy to say, but it was far from easy to bring about: discovering ways to work with others to create an environment in which everyone felt safe and secure enough to risk engagement with others. How could I begin to use my position of leadership to provide the systems and structures necessary for a culture wherein all faculty, staff, and students recognized everyone's worth? I knew that it would only be our ability to come together that would ensure that we would not just survive, but truly thrive.

For just short of five years, I worked twelve- to fourteen-hour days, six-and-a-half days a week. While I was their academic leader, my faculty, staff, and student colleagues were great teachers. My earlier belief in the power of multiple disciplines coming together to attend to a common issue was reaffirmed. Despite their initial reluctance, whenever several colleagues from different professional schools of thought came together and engaged in true dialogue around a particular issue (closing the achievement gap, for example), both the process and outcomes were highly informative, productive, and memorable. Additionally, such interactions soon provided the necessary reinforcement for others to risk joining in.

It was also during this time that I began to fully understand that the most effective leadership required attending to both *change and continuity*—knowing why, what, how, and when to hold on and to let go. Most important, it was over this time that I was to seek out and join with other women leaders to go much deeper into the answers to my question about leadership sustainability.

In a series of four-day retreats over the next three years, we women (representing the worlds of multiple sectors in our society) wrestled with all our questions, sharing our joys and our pains, and creating a space that was safe for these conversations and our connection. During this time we also sought out other women in positions of leadership, and we were gifted with their stories in focused interviews. These stories are shared with others in our book, *Sustaining Our Spirits* (Bailey et al. 2008).

> When the women dance, they form a circle . . . they move with the Earth . . .
> to be a part of that circle is a great source of strength.
>
> —Joanne Shenandoah

We continue to meet. Our circle expands. We appreciate and cherish the reality that our retreats—the sharing of joys, challenges, and strategies—deeply enrich our lives as women leaders.

Based on our own experiences and observations, as well as through those interviews with other women leaders across multiple sectors—not-for-profit/social, corporate, faith-based, and public—spanning individual lifestyles and cultures, we have come to recognize and understand a phenomenon we call "spirituality" as a source of sustenance, both personally and professionally. For us, "spirit" refers not to religion but rather to the life-giving force that unites us all. In fact, the Latin root of spirit, "spiritus," means "breath" or "breath of life."

Here in the Western part of the world, the idea of spirit and even the valuing of connection often sound strange and unfamiliar. Not only in the academy but generally, we are taught to value individualism—the belief that each being is separate and can be classified as either complementary or oppositional to something else. Children are encouraged to strive for personal, individual achievement—to be the single best student of their class—and to compete against each other to get into the most prestigious high schools, colleges, and universities, and sometimes even preschools. Throughout our culture, this omnipresent labeling and ranking subsequently gives way to forms of domination and control.

In contrast, however, the focus on individualism sounds discordant to many indigenous and Eastern cultures. Instead, these cultures conceptualize life on Earth in a more expansive and interconnected way. In fact, distilling some of the principles of these cultures and integrating them with our own experiences in leadership has led us to a perspective that we are calling the Earthview (Bailey et al. 2008). Rather than in a linear or hierarchical fashion, Earthview order is circular or weblike, and each and every being is required and valued. Rather than considering life to be filled with either/or decisions, the Earthview approach sees "both/and," holistic possibilities.

I suspect that this concept sounds more familiar in the context of the growing efforts and conversations around becoming more "green" and ecologically conscious. We know that the devastation of pollution and deforestation not only affects the local areas of the activity but also weakens the greater whole of the Earth. This reality became apparent to me in the late 1980s when, on behalf of the organizational behavior department, I was traveling with a doctoral student. We were in Ghana, meeting with all the tribal chiefs in the southern half of that country. I still vividly remember one of the chiefs coming up to me after my address, very politely yet with tears in his eyes, asking me why America did not like them. Our time together so far had in no way suggested this, so I was shocked and asked him why he thought that. He answered by reminding me of the vast oil spill into the waters along the shores of Alaska. While many of us were stunned by this waste and angered and upset by the ecological impacts on plants and wildlife, my new friend knew that this "spill" was more like a flood. Because we on this planet all share the same bodies of water, these massive amounts of oil could result in the inability of his tribe (and all others along the coast) to get healthy, edible fish for their families.

My experiences and dialogue with other woman leaders have deepened my understanding of this interconnected reality to enable me to begin to discern and then embrace the *elements* of spirit, facets that can be readily seen but have been rarely acknowledged—a cluster of seven attributes unique to each of us yet, paradoxically, common to us all, about which I have written (Bailey 2006:298–302). While often considered to fall under "values," "beliefs," or "dispositions," these attributes can actually be taught and learned. We recognize them as the very essence of life only when we internalize them, however. Indeed, recent studies have shown that organizations that seek to recognize the spirit and even attempt to align their goals with the spirit outperform those that do not (e.g., Mitroff and Denton in Pink 2006). I believe that these seven attributes of leading from the spirit—leading from the inside out—are critical to fully utilizing our skills in transforming our institutions of higher education, in the words of the management researcher Jim Collins (2005) from "good to great." Let me share a bit about each of these.

First, *authenticity*. Authenticity has its roots in self-discovery. It requires that we take the time and space to be aware, to know who we really are, and to understand our talents and our areas needing attention. To lead authentically, we must have the strength and courage to honor the gift of life by being all of who we are with integrity—realizing that we show up in each choice, whether big of small, that we make each day.

Our second attribute of leading from spirit is *empathy*. Empathy is articulated by those in the "helping professions" yet best lived by all who possess authenticity. It is the self-knowledge that comes from the grounding and the space to be able to "hold" the perceptions and the emotions of another. To be empathetic, we must remain centered and true to who we are, opening our hearts and minds to genuinely know others. As leaders, we have learned that our only limit to being able to do this is our willingness to do so.

Humility is the third attribute critical to leading from the spirit. Originating from the word *humus*, or earth, humility is being centered and grounded in the world. It is understanding that positions of power are solely positions; true leaders know that who they are is much more than what they do. When we are grounded, we are secure enough to appreciate our uniqueness, realizing that all of us are required in life; we are all here at this time, together, for a reason. Going beyond our egos, we build character, which releases us from the need for approval from others. Somewhat paradoxically, humility allows us to have room to take in the ideas and feelings of others and even understand both praise and criticism as key components to life's journey.

Next is *courage and compassion*. For me, courage and compassion work best in combination because together they provide us with balance. Courage and compassion demand that we undergird our strategic decisions and actions with a reverence for life. The union of courage and compassion enables us to see opportunities in problems, to find possibilities in resistance, and to understand that most people in life are doing the best they can. The balance of courage and compassion reminds us not to become mired in the day-to-day small conflicts, but to risk seeing fully both the challenges and the joys of the larger patterns of potential synergy.

Leadership attribute number five is *patience*. I define patience as the ability to be secure and diligent as we attend to ourselves and to others—people and situations. It is welcoming the engagement through deep listening, understanding that timing is critical to know when and what to prune and when and what to build up, trusting wholly in the process.

Our next leadership attribute is *faith*. Faith is best understood by its opposite: it is not contrary to reason, it does not ignore people and situations that are harmful or untruthful, and it is not synonymous with religion. In leading from the spirit, faith is about living amid ambiguity and trusting that everything that happens fulfills a higher goal; that there is a lesson to be learned in every moment—good or bad—of our lives. Faith can indeed be a "leap." Organizational "vision" statements are grounded in this type of faith. Although most organizations tout vision statements rather readily, faith is one of the most challenging attributes to secure because it runs up against fear. Although some fear will always be present in our lives, we must not operate from that place. We must work hard to prevent creating—or even maintaining—a world in which fear is amplified. Tragically, we have plenty of others doing that for us. Our challenge is to stand on the ground of faith and move others toward being in a similar place in the world.

And, lastly, at the foundation of our leadership, perhaps also most challenging for us as women to publicly affirm, yet also most important, is *love*. Agape is a very special type of love: one that is greater than the love between partners or spouses and one that is even deeper than the love parents hold for their children. A real leader's love coming from the spirit can be found in the lives of the people that many of us consider as heroes— Mahatma Gandhi, Mother Teresa, Martin Luther King, Jr., Susan La Flesche

Picotte, Abraham Joshua Heschel, Grace Longwell Coyle, Desmond Tutu, and, yes, Paulo Freire, just to name a few. This type of love is *agape*.

Agape is a love for all beings simply because they exist. Agape transcends all of our learned prejudices (prejudgments) and emerges out of the interweaving of authenticity, humility, empathy, courage, compassion, faith, and patience.

Joined with the earlier-described values of service, collaboration, change, and continuity, these seven critical components collectively remain the cornerstones of how I lead . . . and live. And, these beliefs and ways of showing up in life wonderfully resonate with our social work ethos. The fortune of finding my personal values aligning with those of my profession supports my ability to go beyond espousing to enacting; even in settings that do not identify as social work organizations, but whose essence is truly one of a kindred spirit.

> Life's first imperative is that it must be free to create itself. . . . Life's second great imperative propels individuals out from themselves to search for community.

> —Margaret Wheatley

And then, just as the road opened up leading me to what I had thought was to be my dream job as a college president, once again what I was beginning to recognize as divine intervention took place. How else could I ever understand choosing to step off this path? My totally unforeseen move from Teachers College at Columbia to the University of Minnesota (and all the changes that came with it) was indeed a calling—a calling to discover a community.

After several months of deep reflection and conversations with family, friends, and wise elders, and many telephone conversations and e-mail exchanges with the incredibly tenacious folks at the University of Minnesota, I agreed to an interview for the founding deanship of the new College of Education and Human Development.

I must confess that I immediately thought of the cold: images of long underwear, lots of snow, and freezing temperatures. So, to "thaw those thoughts," when I came to the "U" for the public forum, I had two objectives in mind: first, to let folks know who I am, underneath the academic credentials and professional accomplishments. I wanted everyone to get a sense of my values, perspectives, and, yes, even my quite alive sense of humor. My other objective at that time was to ascertain whether the people with whom I would be working daily (meaning, beyond the president and the provost) were really prepared to roll up their sleeves and join me in doing the "heavy lifting" required to build a brand new college. I needed to be sure that foundational to all the rhetoric about "strategic repositioning" and "embracing change" was the organizational will. What I found was that I was seen and folks were ready. The magic within this connection was immediate and obvious. And so when I awoke at 3:00 a.m. the day after this visit and put together five single-spaced pages of ideas, I knew I was hooked, and blessed to have this opportunity.

> The place God calls you to is the place where your deep gladness meets the world's deep needs.
>
> —Frederick Buechner

Admittedly, my career has provided many incredible leadership opportunities, but joining the folks at the U to discover the connections at the foundation of our new college and to work collaboratively in a highly ranked public research university, and in a community and a state that place a very high value on education, was, and remains, compelling. So, driving over a thousand miles from New York to Minnesota with my partner and our dogs and cat in tow, I made my way to the University of Minnesota.

Everyone immediately asked me about my vision, hopes, and dreams for our college. Well, I had plenty. But there were three major themes that, as you now will understand, had their roots in my story and therefore continued to shape my ways of thinking and being. I referred to them as the "3Ms," but they were not the Minnesota company that invented Scotch tape and Post-Its. For me, the collective power of the 3Ms was what would, for many years to come, create the culture of individual and collegewide excellence by focusing our attention. They were multidisciplinarity, multiculturalism, and model for engagement. In a short time my 3M dream was embraced by my new colleagues to become the M^3 vision for our new college. A bit about each.

• Multidisciplinarity. We use this word quite purposefully and distinctly from "interdisciplinary," which reflects an admirable relationship between two and sometimes even among three different professional fields. In this relationship, each one—individual or group—shares his or her perspectives, and the result is ideally a well-informed combination of practices and beliefs. The multidisciplinarity that we are talking about also has folks working from their disciplines or perspectives, yet through a dynamic, continuously self-examining, and evolving process that actively engages and reflects all. Through spanning their fields in multidisciplinary relationships, they create *new* ways of seeing and enacting. This kind of exchange and knowledge production is essential to help us understand and address the issues of our globalized world; issues that are neither one-dimensional nor conveniently and clearly categorized but rather are messy, overlapping, and multifaceted.

Let me further describe this process through an example in teaching. Imagine a continuum of degrees of connection going from low to high between two teachers who have agreed to engage in a relationship of coteaching. With this already decided, at the interdisciplinary end of the spectrum, coteaching might look like "handing over the baton"—one person would teach one day, and another person would teach the next day. Or these teachers could alternate teaching within the same class period in a "tag-team" approach, each working from her/his discipline to bring the best, most appropriate content to this course. Midway along this continuum of connection is the process of coordinating the syllabus with each other's materials so that there is actually overlap and alignment. Genuine multidisciplinary education, however, takes us much further along. It is the act of standing in one's discipline, yet in this example with each teacher risking to create new ideas and ways of being between and among themselves and the students. True multidisciplinary education is most powerful because it has the capacity to give life to something new—an exercise, a course, a program—that far exceeds what either one of these two teachers could have produced alone. And this kind of creation can also occur in research and service—the latter being what we now only refer to as community engagement.

• Multiculturalism. Another core element of our new college's vision is multiculturalism. As you may have anticipated, we also use this word quite purposefully, and distinctly from "diversity," which, to me as a former diversity trainer, focuses largely on the *differences* between people. Multiculturalism refers to the reality of many cultures and cultures within cultures—the divergent *and* similar ways in which we process information and generate new ideas and form opinions, as well as the acknowledgment of our *many* identities, the visible and largely invisible ways that we show up in life, including race/ethnicity *and* culture of origin; gender *and* sexual orientation; intellectual *and* emotional *and* physical abilities; religion *and* spirituality; language/dialect *and* accent; and socioeconomic class *and* political *and* ideological perspective and position. As leaders, we must choose to embody an "us and we," not a "we and them," approach to life.

When we engage in a multicultural way of thinking and being, we move forward through life in unity with others. We open ourselves to listen and truly learn from seemingly disparate perspectives to be able both to honor our differences and to recognize, as was said back in 154 BC by Terentius Afer, an African slave who was sold to and then freed by a Roman senator to become a popular playwright in Rome: "I am a human being. Nothing human can be alien to me" ("Homo Sum").

When we (re)construct our organizational cultures to structurally and systemically live those words, our worldviews and conceptions of power begin to change. As our college's associate dean for community outreach and engagement, the scholar Heidi Barajas (2005:136), reminds us, multiculturalism in even our secondary schools seeks out "socially-just educational opportunities for all students." Teacher and author Deborah Meier (2002:4) details the psycho-social activities that must be facilitated to have truly multicultural environments in the academy, stating that "all children [and, I would add, teachers and administrators] can and should be inventors of their own theories, critics of other people's ideas, analyzers of evidence, and makers of their own personal marks on this most complex world." This process of socially just collaborative thinking and learning obviously has an impact on our decision-making processes, encouraging us to acknowledge and serve the needs of others in more inclusive, intentional, and (as most recent research shows) healthier ways (Ransom 2007). In short, for me, "multi" is more than a prefix; it is a life-changing process. Through our own relationships with others, we enrich the relationships between and among all.

- Model for engagement: our new college aspires to be a model for cultivating generations of leaders best prepared for and committed to mutually impactful, replicable, and sustainable local, national, and global engagement. This model requires that we first listen to (and for) the needs of our communities both locally and around the globe, learn from them, and then thoughtfully pull together and align all of our resources to work with those outside of our college to best meet those needs. Our work in the world is most impactful when it comes from our greatest talents and is in response to a current or anticipated need in our communities.

Working from our new vision of multidisciplinarity, multiculturalism, and model for engagement, my leadership beliefs required that an opportunity be given to *everyone* to help shape—even wordsmith—the purpose of our college. It had to be, in a sense, a calling for everyone. Our coconstructed mission, embodying our connections, needed to be broad and deep enough to safely hold us all. So together we developed our college's mission: a fifty-three-word statement that, as the late management guru Peter Drucker said, tells the world our reason for being and, *I* would add, reminds us why we work so long and hard:

> The new College of Education and Human Development is a world leader in discovering, creating, sharing, and applying principles and practices of multiculturalism and multidisciplinary scholarship to advance teaching and learning and to enhance the psychological, physical, and social development of children, youth, and adults across the lifespan in families, organizations, and communities.

Drucker always urged us to keep our mission statements short. He said that the best missions were those that could fit on the back of a t-shirt and be memorized by all. And yes, our first fall, all of our new students got their t-shirts!

As our mission flowed from our vision, so did our strategy stem from our mission. To live up to our vision and into our mission, our new college developed what I called "neighborhoods"—three multidisciplinary units that pulled together the college's many resources and strengths toward a commonly shared focus of action designed to exist within and across the college's departments and centers for faculty, staff, and students. One neighborhood is called Teaching and Learning; another, Psychological, Physical, and Social Development; and the third, Family, Organization, and Community Systems and Contexts. Neither restrictive nor proscriptive and with permeable boundaries, these neighborhoods collectively seek to foster multidisciplinary and multicultural scholarship through the synergies of our discoveries in research, teaching and learning, and authentic community engagement. Each of these neighborhoods has been well resourced (with talented faculty and staff leadership, space, and time), and together they serve to provide a vehicle for interconnecting and transcending the traditional, individualized silos of academia.

> Life is no brief candle to me. It is a sort of splendid torch which I have got hold of for the moment, and I want to make it burn as brightly as possible before handing it on to future generations.
>
> —George Bernard Shaw

It should now be quite obvious why I began my story acknowledging that despite my "firsts," I was actually a follower on the path of faith. Here at the U, all that I have done in my past has been called upon to prepare me for all that I am now doing. While I continue to learn much every day, throughout this process of being (and still becoming) a woman leader, three fundamental "must do's"—activities undergirded by the process and attributes I described earlier—have become apparent to me:

• Development of vision and mission as the "ties that bind." As a leader, you have the right and the responsibility to share your dreams and then stay open to those of the people around you to establish a common identity. Your first act must be to get folks on the same page to be able to discover or even re-create a college that "sings"—not flat or off-key, but in-tune—for everyone. And at our college, it is through our vision, mission, and neighborhoods that we are providing leadership in our university for work in our communities.

• Managing job-related dilemmas and other competing expectations of ourselves and of others. As leaders, our roles and responsibilities are fraught with many more dilemmas than problems. Knowing this enables us to avoid the trap of searching for "the right solutions" to the issues we are confronted with almost daily and instead, invest the time and careful thought to unpack these tensions, these bundles of competing needs, to better understand and then begin to ideally manage or even balance them.

An NSF ADVANCE Institutional Transformation Grant at Case Western Reserve University revealed our need as women to balance our amount and type of attention to and value of research, teaching, and community engagement with our work life and family needs, and with "the search for truth" nature of universities (Subcommittee on Faculty Engagement, Motivation, and Commitment and the Resource Equity 2004). I would add that we are also confronted with reconciling the rewards of individualism in academia with the reality that we *all* are (but even more so for women) relational beings. Our systems need to respect that, beginning with the papers we require in our classes, through our dissertation preparations and defenses, to our promotion and tenure processes.

All of this sits right next to a hard reality: everyone assumes that we women can do it "all." And we must own the even harder reality: we believe that we must do it all. Underlying this is the need to manage our own expectations that we can do it all. We often find ourselves working extremely hard to prove our worth within unreasonable timelines. We tend to feel "responsible," and others often help us to maintain those feelings.

As best put by the consummate leadership guru Frances Hesselbein, as women leaders, our biggest challenge is getting "our house" in order. Yes, for today and tomorrow, this requires making certain that the mission of our organizational homes stay compelling and relevant. Yet, we must also get "our personal house in order . . . reserving the time, building the psychic energy, for introspection . . . listening to the whispers of our lives" (Hesselbein 2002:73–74). We must make and take time for ourselves. Whether it is reading a compelling mystery novel or a romantic comedy, cuddling quietly with a loved one, cooking or going out to eat with friends, or even laying in the grass with one of our four-legged "babies" and watching the clouds play in the sky, it is critically important that we remember to keep our own spirits alive. While our work may be fun, it is not play, and healthy, meaningful, and joy-filled lives require both.

• Communicate, communicate, communicate! We must be inclusive and go beyond trusting that information, shared with those smart (you hope) experts (associate deans, department chairs, administrative directors, executive assistants) that you appointed and/or hired, gets fully shared with all. It is better to be a consistent "broken record," and while not everyone will necessarily agree with all you say, most will appreciate and respect systematic, clear communication and opportunities for their own dialogue with you and one another. Communication requires connection, and connection is requisite to community. And I believe a most productive, caring community requires a leader who embraces all the values and processes I have highlighted in my story, staying awake and following the call of leading from her spirit.

I am now solidly in my fifth decade of life, yet daily I learn more about this art and skill, this blessing of leadership. And, oh yes! I have learned that it does not matter what label or title is given to your call; whether, for example, it starts with a "p" (for president) or "d" (for dean), leadership is leadership. What does matter, what we are each required to do, is to stay awake for our very own call—the one that has the pitch, rhythm, and resonance and is perfectly composed for only us to receive. I am frequently honored by those younger in their careers by being told that I am their role model and being asked to be their mentor. And as Dr. Freire once said to me, I now have a responsibility to share all that I know. Engaging in these mutually impactful mentoring relationships and making the time to present my thinking through both the spoken and the written word with local, national, and international groups of women and men are now two of my major responsibilities. Together, these activities serve as my contributions to helping to keep the worldwide leadership pipeline filled with talented, passionate, smart, and courageous women of color.

Note

I dedicate this with love for my family, friends, and teachers—past and present—without whom I may not have known that "the call" was also for me.

References

Bailey, D. (2006). "Leading from the Spirit." In *The Leader of the Future 2: Visions, Strategies, and Practices for a New Era*, eds. F. Hesselbein and M. Goldsmith, pp. 297–302. San Francisco: Jossey-Bass.

Bailey, D., K. M. Koney, M. McNish, R. Powers, and K. Uhly (2008). *Sustaining Our Spirits*. Washington, DC: NASW Press.

Barajas, H. L. (2005). Creating Spheres of Freedom: Connecting Developmental Education, Multicultural Education, and Student Experience." In *The General College Vision: Integrating Intellectual Growth, Multicultural Perspectives, and Student Development*, ed. J. L. Higbee, D. B. Lundell, and D. R. Arendale, pp. 131–53. Minneapolis: Regents of the University of Minnesota by its General College and the Center for Research on Developmental Education and Urban Literacy, University of Minnesota—Twin Cities.

Buechner, F. (1993). *Wishful Thinking*. New York: HarperCollins.

Collins, J. (2005). *Good to Great and the Social Sectors: A Monograph to Accompany Good to Great*. New York: HarperCollins.

Freire, P. (1981). *Pedagogy of the Oppressed*. New York: Continuum.

Hesselbein, F. (2002). *Hesselbein on Leadership*. San Francisco: Jossey-Bass.

Meier, D. (2002). *The Power of Their Ideas*. Boston: Beacon.

Pink, D. H. (2006). *Why Right Brainers Will Rule the Future*. New York: Riverhead Books.

Ransom, L. K. (2007). "Shifting Strategic Paradigms: A Study Assessing the Determinants of Possessing a Global Mindset in a United States Based Diversified Transnational Corporation." Ph.D. dissertation, University of Minnesota.

Subcommittee on Faculty Engagement, Motivation, and Commitment and the Resource Equity (2004). "Report of the 2004 University Community and Climate Survey." Higher Learning Commission. North Central Association of Colleges and Schools.

[4]

Inclusive Leadership

Lessons Learned from My Journey

EARLIE M. WASHINGTON

There is something to be said about being born and raised into an incredible family, yet in the context of the "deep South," specifically in the state of Mississippi. History has its place not only in the lives of individuals but also in the community that supports those lives. Both family- and community-based strengths and barriers are realities that often either hinder or help progress. People say that hindsight is always 20/20. As I reflect on my experiences growing up, I recognize the struggles, challenges, and sacrifices that have led to resiliency and hardiness in my personality and way of being. Essentially, my upbringing as an African American woman from the South had major implications for my human experience and life course.

My education background includes a bachelor's degree in psychology from Tougaloo College, Mississippi, a master's degree in social work from Ohio State University, and a Ph.D. degree from the University of Chicago. Currently, I am a professor and the dean of the College of Health and Human Services at Western Michigan University in which I have stewardship over the departments of Blindness and Low Vision Studies, Occupational Therapy, Physician Assistant, and Speech Pathology and Audiology, and the schools of Nursing and Social Work. I have additional responsibilities that include oversight of the Ph.D. program in interdisciplinary health sciences; an undergraduate degree program in interdisciplinary health services; and certificate programs in substance abuse, holistic health, and gerontology. Likewise, I have oversight for the college's unified teaching/research clinics in child trauma and assessment, women health, substance abuse treatment, hearing, speech, low vision, and occupational therapy, and the center for disability services. Prior to this office, I held multiple leadership and administration positions in schools of social work at Western Michigan University and University of Southern Mississippi, and taught at Tougaloo College, Illinois State University, and the University of Chicago. My areas of expertise include administration and management, mental health, substance abuse treatment, gerontology (i.e., informal and formal care giving), and staff development and training. I have years of leadership experience with the Council on Social Work Education, the National Association of Social Workers, and my community.

The Journey

My journey to leadership and administration was not intentional, yet somewhat predestined in the sense that at a very young age in the 1960s I understood from my experiences at home and in the community that social and economic justice is the cause of great leaders, of which cause I wanted to be a part. A foundation for this life course was formed from my early experiences with leaders in my family and community who mentored and nurtured me together with other children. Truly, it takes a village to raise a child. Mentorship, for lack of a better word, was one of the greatest gifts I received from my family and community. I had informal mentors from church and the community. However, my greatest mentor and role model was from my home—my mother. She was not a college graduate, but she dreamed of being one. As valedictorian of her high school class, she looked forward to studying at a university and becoming a teacher. Unfortunately, her family was poor and every member of the family needed to work. Attending college was not an option. Although circumstances can alter our dreams, my mother realized her dream of a college education through her children. She sent all six of her children to college. She made many sacrifices to raise us, but she never sacrificed our education. As you can imagine, I learned a great deal from my mother: I learned to never give up and to face challenges with courage and determination. I learned to do for others what others have done for you. I learned to be generous with my time and with my knowledge, to take someone under my wing. Teach someone something he or she will need in the future, and that person will carry on this gift of wisdom. As many children probably experience, it was not until years later that I fully appreciated what my mother did to provide a better life for her children.

With a solid foundation built at home and in my community, I continued my journey into the universities where mentorship became formalized. Many men and women in the academy and communities in which I lived as an adult provided continuous mentorship and nurturing. All of my teachers and professors have positioned me well for leadership and administration, for which I will be forever grateful. In terms of my academic career, three mentors made great impacts on my life: my undergraduate professor Shani Brooks, my dissertation advisor Dr. Elsie Pinkston, and the social work dean who gave me my first administrative position in social work education, Dr. Beulah Compton. At age sixteen I graduated from high school and entered college with a scholarship and the intention of majoring in chemistry as a pre-med student. As the youngest child, I wanted to follow the footsteps of my siblings who were attending college so I studied hard and graduated in eleventh grade. Although I am a relentless planner, many of my plans consisted of microlevel goals and objectives. Fortunately, I was surrounded by people who saw me in the bigger picture and helped me redirect to bigger and greater directions. My route to earning the MSW was inspired by my first mentor, Shani Brooks, who taught me social change, social control, and social and economic justice. Likewise, Dr. Pinkston, one of my professors at the University of Chicago, encouraged my passion for working with older people and engaging in research about family care-giving for older impaired relatives.

In the beginning of my doctoral education, I had a vision to continue my teaching, research, and scholarship as a way to contribute to social work education and policy. I wanted to be a strong researcher. As I progressed in the program, my vision began to change and became refined. Dr. Compton hired me in my first administrative position in social work education and encouraged me to focus more on administration, and thus far, I have remained true to that advice. She was instrumental in securing my leadership positions. Again, another life experience happened where I realize that life is not linear, that it cannot be seen through microlevel lenses only, that multiple experiences must occur in order to lead me to the right place, and that there are multiple ways to contribute.

Drs. Bogart Leashore and Leon Chestang provided invaluable support to me as I transitioned into administration. Likewise, colleagues whom I met in my doctoral program have been my number one fans and have continued to support me for more than twenty years. Still, there are colleagues at various schools of social work who have been tremendously supportive and have listened to my woes for hours. There are also those whom I have mentored who have helped sustain and reinforce my commitment to social work. And finally there are all the chairs, directors, students, faculty, and staff with whom I have had the good fortune to work. It is because of your accomplishments and good work that I have been asked to write this chapter on leadership. To all of you, you have my heartfelt appreciation and gratitude. Thank you. Today, I continue to have many opportunities to grow and apply my experiences in social work in a broader context of the college and university.

Leadership Roots

The formative years were critical to my development as a leader. As a child growing up in Mississippi, I lived in a home and community that embraced a culture that valued people both old and young. Our community leaders were folks in the church, Southern Baptists. These leaders were not traditional leaders in the sense that many of them worked labor jobs, but they were deacons, deaconesses, and ushers who held positions of honor, respect, authority, and accountability in the church and community. My teachers were respected and held accountable by both children and parents. As a result, my leadership models and paradigms were formed from the day-to-day living experiences in my home and community. For instance, my home and community leadership paradigms valued the genuine recognition and appreciation of people. I learned from my mother how to interact with people regardless of venue—to acknowledge the existence of others, greet people as you pass them, respect people, be polite, listen, work hard, and give back. All of these were ingrained in me at home and in the community. I have fond memories of my mother's tendency to create opportunities that honed my leadership abilities, even if that was not the intention. Since childhood I developed a love for jigsaw puzzles because they challenged me. Through working on these puzzles I learned to problem solve, which has proven beneficial for me as a leader. Such activities also cultivated healthy competition and the drive to do it right and do it well.

I recall my exciting experiences with raising funds in elementary school through selling candy and treats. I was always passionate about these events because they provided opportunities to develop expertise and skills in organization, interaction with people, initiative, and presenting a case that is persuasive and convincing. I enjoyed the recognition and the challenge, which was often extrinsic. During high school I developed a knack for participating in competitions in my church. I was involved in many church functions but especially enjoyed the various speech and writing competitions. Again, I enjoyed the recognition and the challenge. As the youngest of six children, I often mimicked my older siblings. I knew that my older brother was leaving for college, so I decided to work hard and graduate from high school at age sixteen. As I entered college that year, I made it a point to continue developing my skills. I hit the ground running in college and learned an incredible amount of information about who I am as an African American person living in the United States. I was fascinated about the fact that Black people were major contributors to our society although they were not mentioned in mainstream history books. My eyes were opened to the world and all of the amazing things it offers. Consequently, in the summer after my freshmen year in college, I wrote and was awarded a grant to teach Black history to elementary school children in my hometown, giving back to my community. As one can see, my extracurricular activities were not the traditional sports and recreation. But, these experiences are markers in a predetermined course of leadership. I have found these skills and experiences timeless and transferable.

As I left for college, there was a paradigm shift from having models of leadership drawn from the community's day-to-day life into having models from academic and professional life. But the same principles of leadership transcended horizontally into this new environment, with a goal of strengthening them. I always made it a point to ensure that my interactions with people would last and that positive outcomes would transfer to other venues. In other words, every good experience would have longevity. Respect and genuine interest in others made this possible. I learned that when my personality solidly reflects my leadership principle, when I become it, what people will see as a leader is who I really am. Consequently, I became comfortable with both leading and following, moving from one place to another with little difficulty. As many others note, a leader has to lead but also follow. These two roles are common in any leader's life. The leader is as good as the people they lead. In fact, no great leader claims that he or she has done it alone.

Do's of Leadership

These are not what I did, but I want you to do!

- Be open to opportunities. Develop flexibility because opportunities do not come when you are ready for them. It is not easy; it involves moving, readjusting to new situations. Opportunities bring with them a set of challenges that require your best problem-solving skills.
- Early on, determine your interest in leadership and administration so you can prepare yourself for opportunities. Look for both formal and informal ways to test that interest. The next generation will need more formal ways of preparing for opportunities—for example, attending the various leadership and management academies and seminars. Some people are natural leaders and others develop into leaders. Once you have decided what you want to do, it is easier to deal with nature and nurture.
- Engage in strategic planning and develop a vision as to who you are and where you want to be. Be strategic about your next move toward your interest. Each time you move to a new job, you need to determine if that job will give you a piece toward your ultimate goal (e.g., being a director, dean, provost, or president).
- Build relationships and opportunities with people in leadership roles. This network will provide opportunities for learning, possible additional opportunities, and professional development. If you are pursuing something, you have to network with people. Do not minimize the fact that building these relationships can serve as references for you. Look for a wide spectrum of people across situations, broadly based, who can speak for you.
- Whether you pursue it or not, *do your best* in that role! Whatever your position in life, ideally, every place you have been, you should be able to go back to. Whatever the task you are working on, make sure you do your best because you can build on those successes. Work hard and establish a reputation of doing good work and striving to achieve excellence.

• Be reflective and continuously assess yourself. Take stock of where you are, tweak it, and be prepared for the next move.

• Somehow, through all of this, develop a balance. Find your own balance. Learn early how to balance what you want to do in life—how to balance your career with your life. Balance this pursuit with all of the other important aspects of your life. Do not be out of balance! Shift and adjust that balance as needed.

Leading and Administering Successfully

The topics of leadership and administration are well documented in the literature, nationally and internationally. In light of my life experiences and the abundant existing information on these topics, there are a number of significant lessons that I have found "tested and true" in my experiences as a leader and administrator. I have found that the bottom line of leadership and administration is that it is value driven: in this case, social work values of service, social justice, dignity and worth of the person, importance of human relationships, integrity, and competence (these core values listed are from the NASW Code of Ethics, which was revised in 2008). Based on these social work values, the following are general lessons I learned. The list is not exhaustive but supplementary to those that other leaders have provided.

1. People first. Recognizing and showing gratitude for those who have come before you and those who are here now helping you through the journey are important to being a successful leader. As a leader, I have experienced the significant impacts of recognition of and gratitude for what people have done for me. I always felt a responsibility as a leader to pass on the gift of knowledge to the next generation and celebrate those who passed on to me their own knowledge. Cultivate and hone human relationships, observe, listen and learn, and aspire to creating lifelong relationships that transcend space and time.

2. Participatory leadership. I consider myself a participatory and facilitative leader, in that I will roll up my sleeves and work with my faculty and staff. I lead by example, and I will not require anyone to do a job that I will not do myself. I value everyone's job and try to learn them not because I want to micromanage but because, if I need to, I will be able to do

them. Most important, knowing each person's job sensitizes me to their demands.

3. Problem solving. Whether it is solving a personal problem or helping another, acknowledging people's feelings but focusing on solutions is important. Every moment you interact or converse with another, let it be educational; serve as a mentor and role model. Facilitate civility in problem solving. Learn to cope not only with your own stress in a healthy manner but with the stress of others. Pay attention to both the details and the big picture. Work hard. Be fair regardless of the circumstances.

4. Staying grounded and open to change. As a leader, change is inevitable, particularly with technology and new inventions. Look to your foundation, beliefs, and values as the guide to your changing for the better. Become better developed in your sense of appreciation for others and yourself. You must be okay with complexities and complications as a part of life. You must learn to multitask, meaning, "being able to leap tall buildings in a single bound."

5. Power of one. Remember that you have enormous power to preserve what you hold dear and to change the world for the better. We need other people, but ultimately success begins with you. Take on this responsibility. Do not wait for someone to take the initiative. Make a difference, find success, and be true to yourself.

6. Humor. Have fun, laugh, and celebrate achievements by you and others.

Refining Fire of Race and Gender

Leadership is a human endeavor, and as such, there will be times when race and gender impact one's leadership either negatively or positively. Throughout one's career, personal identities based on race and gender will inevitably unfold; thus, the goal is to learn how to evaluate their impacts and influences on one's behavior as a leader. Such race- and gender-based influence must be evaluated from both the different stakeholders' perceptions as well as the perception of the leader herself or himself. It is important to evaluate how and when the variables of race and gender are salient in leadership relationships. For women of color, it is critical to lead in a way that others will perceive one's race and gender as positive contributions to one's leadership style and philosophy. Indeed, leadership of women of color, by virtue of possessing two significant personal identifies of race and gender, is different not deficient, strong not weak, progressive not outdated.

At my last two universities there were few women in academic leadership positions and even fewer women of color. It is part of human nature to identify with people who are similar to you. The absence of people of color in leadership may create situational isolation for women of color. Isolation and noninclusive environments are real challenges for women of color.

- Advice 1: Create networks of people of color within the university and in the community to provide the support to you and others that may be missing from the immediate environment.
- Advice 2: Encourage university administrators to hire more women of color. If you are in a hiring role, aggressively recruit and hire women of color.

Over the years as an administrator in higher education, I have observed that there are informal networks that I am not a part of due largely to my race. For example, I often would hear my faculty talk about some conversation they had with the president of the university at their church or at a friend's house for dinner. Given that they belong to the same church and share the same social networks, there were multiple opportunities for some of my faculty to interact with my supervisors who are the senior leadership of the university. On the other hand, my interactions with the same individuals tend to be through more formal channels (e.g., scheduling an appointment with the secretary for individual meetings, groups meeting with other deans and directors). While I place no value judgment on this situation, these are some of the privileges and benefits that are based on race.

Having a scarcity of women of color as leaders in the academy does not always provide opportunities for others to interact with them, and thus others may have biased attitudes due to insufficient interaction and exposure. But biases are not always based on race or gender. I recall an incident from years ago when I was leading a research meeting with colleagues. One colleague (who became a good friend of mine) asked me in the middle of the meeting, "How did you become so sophisticated coming from Mississippi?" And there it is—that old bias about people from the South. The lesson here is that throughout your leadership, you will experience bias behaviors of others due to your race, gender, and a host of other variables. I encourage you to choose which biases you will confront. There is no rule that says you must fight them. For those that you do decide to confront, try to create teachable moments. How can you create a learning opportunity so that it is a win-win situation for all parties?

Challenges of Academia

The academy is a system that has advanced specific groups in society, particularly white males. It is known that women of color in academic leadership positions lag behind other groups in both numbers and political power. Inherent in this disparity are the dual choices of creating an adversarial relationship or a collaborative relationship with those who are advantaged, to pursue equality and equity for those who are disadvantaged. Because women of color have been the most disadvantaged group in academia, there is a need for commitment to and diligence about ensuring social and economic justice among those who are currently in the academy and for future generations.

Multiple Ways of Developing Leadership Qualities

All experiences are important to a leader. There is a need for a wide array of skills and experiences in being an effective leader. Self-awareness and understanding of one's strengths and areas needing improvement are important to being an effective leader. But becoming a well-rounded leader is a lifelong goal—a continuous process of leading, assessing and evaluating outcomes, and making adjustments and modifications. Specific knowledge and skills are required of leaders. First, a leader must develop skills in communication, problem solving, planning and development, evaluation, budgeting, administration, and supervision. Reading books on leadership and great leaders is part of this education process. Observing those who are experienced leaders and critiquing their leadership behavior, those who are most or least effective, and understanding why they are effective or not, is an exercise that has built my repertoire of skills. As I mentioned earlier, enrolling and participating in formal leadership academies and seminars has great educational benefit and increases networking opportunities. Second, formal and informal mentorship can connect experienced leaders with those pursuing leadership roles. I encourage leaders to look for mentors both within and outside their home institutions. Although there are some variations, I have found that mentors within an institution are effective in providing specific context, direction, and guidance, whereas mentors from outside can provide broader context, direction, and guidance. With the advances of technology, access to a cadre of leaders in a particular field who can serve as mentors is just an e-mail away. Third, to become an effective leader one must have multiple opportunities to engage in the behavior, whether it is through chairing a committee or board, coordinating a program, or administering a department, school, or college. I encourage you to seek out those experiences that will provide the greatest opportunity to further develop leadership skills.

All I Needed to Learn, I Learned in Social Work

I am convinced that my leadership style as a dean and previously director has grounding in social work values and my experiences as a social worker and educator. Throughout the years, I have received responses from faculty and students that validated the critical role of social work values of service, social justice, dignity and worth of the person, importance of human relationships, integrity, and competence in my vision and goals as a leader. These leadership principles and values are applicable to all leaders. Box 4.1 is an actual example of how one social work faculty views the relationship between social work values and the leadership style of their director.

Furthermore, in relation to social work values, a few additional issues of leadership warrant discussion. Taking control of the situation and setting boundaries are essential for facilitating progress and productivity and preventing further problems. I have found that part of my effectiveness as a leader has been the ability to exert authority and assertiveness in regrouping, reframing, and problem solving. I experienced the importance of accountability as part of this process and humor as equally important in redirection.

Box 4.1

We appreciate your inclusive strength-based leadership style; the way you respect and show acceptance for all faculty. We are grateful for your high degree of integrity and for the generosity and appreciation that you show to each of us. You are a warm, gracious person with a great sense of humor. You are incredibly hard working and have achieved so many accomplishments for our School, about which you are so humble. In fact, you are so humble about your accomplishments that we don't even know the full extent of them. Instead of taking the glory you help us individually and as a School to shine. Just a few of your many accomplishments:

- Made shared governance a reality at the School.
- Dedicated to a quality curriculum that is current with the times.
- Kept the school vital by writing grants and extending the School's influence locally, nationally, and globally.
- Used your amazing national network for the School's benefit.
- Welcomed new ideas and ways of structuring the curriculum; you took action to implement them.
- Encouraged Historically Black Colleges and Universities (HBCU) students to attend our School.
- Mentored faculty on the tenure track.
- Promoted our School in the university and in the nation.
- Coached faculty to enhance their administrative skills.
- Recruited and filled an Endowed Chair after the School had searched for years.
- Problem-solved and advocated for just solutions to instances of prejudice and discrimination.
- Assumed extra responsibilities due to staff shortages so that the School did not suffer.
- Provided excellent representation of the School in the community and at School sponsored events.
- Assisted faculty members to write budgets; obtained research assistants.

- Increased the visibility of and support for our off-campus Program.
- Created a research committee to strengthen our research infrastructure.
- Helped obtain much needed technology.
- Gave your time and energy to support faculty in acquiring grants.
- Provided opportunities for students to travel and participate in social action and attend conferences.
- Enriched the diversity in our School.
- Made clear the roles of students and faculty members and their responsibilities toward each other.
- Prevented triangulation between students and faculty; you encouraged a direct and honest approach.

Thank you for these sample accomplishments and for so many others. Thank you for making our workplace a kinder and more compassionate place to be. We have a more productive, effective and efficient School because of your outstanding leadership.

With respect, affection, and gratitude,

2005 School of Social Work Faculty Members

Likewise, I have found that making tough decisions is an integral part of being an administrator. I have learned to be clear with the criteria upon which to make decisions and to make these criteria transparent for all, be fair, and consider all facts before making decisions, particularly decisions that would negatively impact people. I have also learned the importance of viewing people in their environment, and making sure that the environment supports success even if the person is not successful at the end.

Moreover, I have learned that positive reinforcements are necessary for leadership success and effectiveness. As I matured, the recognition I received became more intrinsic rather than extrinsic. The notes of thank you from students and faculty are sustaining through tough times. It is important for administrators to create reminders of why they are engaged in this task of leading and administering; that they are in it to make a difference and remove barriers so that people can accomplish their goals. Among the many techniques of creating reinforcements is to store those positive things mentally or physically. As such, when you walk in my office, you will see many plaques, proclamations, and awards of recognition. I keep them on display not for others, but as reminders to me of my motivations and commitment to the work that I do, especially on those days where "nothing is going right."

As a university administrator, I consistently have had opportunities to lead task groups. In facilitating these groups, paying particular attention to beginning and ending phases has proven beneficial. Beginning is used as a time for introductions and making the initial connections, and ending as recognition and appreciation. For me, the beginning ceremonies speak of engagement that is expected to be sustained throughout the life of the interaction. This is the social work process of building rapport and relationships. I have also learned that food is a great moderator regardless of one's cultural background. From experience, having an opening and closing ceremony is essential to unifying a university with diverse perspectives. It binds the group in solidarity of purpose and outcomes. As dean of a multidisciplinary college, I find that diversity in perspectives and values is more pronounced; thus, unifying activities such as these are important. As the director in the School of Social Work, because we have shared values and essential paradigms of social work, I used such activities to further strengthen the team.

Keeping the Movement Alive

There is strength in numbers, whether it is a group of individuals bound together or multiple systems and organizations. One of the most valuable ways I have found for me and perhaps others to keep the movement alive is to serve in professional organizations such as the National Association of Social Workers, locally and nationally, and the Council on Social Work Education. As a site visitor, chair, and commissioner, I learned skills that made a difference in my leadership career. These were powerhouses that happened early in my career and secured my role as a leader.

Likewise, two formal programs made an impact on my leadership experiences: I completed a certificate program in grant writing and a program to become a national certified trainer for mental health. Whether I was seeking external funding for research or designing continuing education opportunities for graduates, both skills have been invaluable to me as a leader in an academic institution.

As women in leadership roles, we have to help each other and share the process to keep the movement alive. We have to build opportunities for dialogue and recourse. We need to network locally, nationally, and internationally. About a year ago a few colleagues and I formed a group focusing specifically on leadership and administration. We meet at least three times a year, either face-to-face or via the phone. We discuss issues of career development and strategies to reach our administration goals. I mentor the other three women of color with a mission of pursuing deanship. In giving to these women, I am strengthened. So I have learned the importance of gathering and mentoring multiple women, groups of women. It sustains all of us. All of these issues of stewardship and legacy link back to my mother's early teachings.

There is a need to get to people early for leadership endeavors. We can connect with women through their churches, schools, communities, and homes. We need to encourage women of color at a very young age to start thinking about leadership and administration positions. We need to start developing young women of color in high school, start talking about and creating leadership opportunities in elementary school, high school, and of course college. We have to create opportunities for young women of color, finding ways to give them a "break" and having them do something with that break. We have to find a way to let people understand that leadership roles give you the right and opportunity to give others a chance, take barriers out, and so forth. Level the playing field. Understand that leadership is service.

Recognition

As I have already indicated, recognition is of tremendous value to leadership. I discussed the importance of recognizing and celebrating the accomplishments of others in many different forms. But it is also extremely important for those who are in leadership roles to be recognized for their accomplishments. Recognition, whether large or small, frequent or infrequent, when it is received, can sustain and restore one's commitment to effective leadership.

I believe that each milestone in our lives is a method of preserving and perpetuating the participation of women of color in leadership and administration positions in the academy. One of my proudest moments was when I received the Elizabeth Butler Award in 1998 in Chicago from the School of Social Service Administration at the University of Chicago and proclamations from the governor of Illinois and the mayor of Chicago, in recognition of my passion for and contribution to social work education, research, practice, and leadership. Returning to my alma mater and being recognized in this manner made me realize that I have reached a milestone in my career. Awards such as this help sustain and empower me to do better continuously. I wish the same for future generations of women of color in the academy—that your worth and work be recognized and celebrated by those with whom you share it.

In this chapter, I have talked very little about problems in leadership, the difficulties of being an effective leader, and the potential burnout that can occur in leadership positions where there are insurmountable barriers to achieving positive outcomes and where the daily hassles seriously outweigh the uplifts. In these final comments, however, I want to acknowledge that leading is not easy, especially in administration in social work education. It is time consuming, replete with a list of never-ending tasks and meetings. It is challenging, with barriers that are created by a variety of stakeholders. Sometimes you are effective and are able to accomplish your goals, and sometimes you are not. Even when you are successful, sometimes you receive gratitude, but most often you do not. And yes, there have been many times I have thought about leaving administration and returning to a position where I have more control over my schedule and consequently my time and activities. It is, possibly, this challenging side of the leadership equation that is responsible for the sage advice I received from colleagues earlier in my career to plan to spend about five to seven years in an academic dean position. Fifteen years later, I am still enjoying what I do every day.

So my advice to you is to be prepared, passionate, and ready to embrace opportunities with a strategic plan and a vision; build relationships of trust; consistently evaluate and reevaluate your personal and professional life and find some balance; live by the principles of people first and inclusive leadership; remain grounded in your family and cultural upbringing; be open to change; and have some fun along the way. Consider what Maya Angelou said: "If one is lucky [blessings, miracles], a solitary fantasy can totally transform one million realities." To all the women of color on the rise in leadership and administration in the academy, may we continue to transform realities of generations to come!

Note

I dedicate this chapter to the women of my community, to all those women who nurtured me! These are the women who raised me. They laid the foundation for me to walk on.

Reference

National Association of Social Workers (2008). *Code of Ethics.* Washington, D.C.: National Association of Social Workers.

[PART THREE]

Deanship in Schools of Social Work

[5]

Writing My Own Story

SALOME RAHEIM

Pursing Leadership and Academic Administration

My Journey

My journey in social work and social work education spans thirty years and covers diverse terrain—from a historically black college to a Big Ten university, from the East Coast to the Midwest, with forays into international territory. My experiences include psychiatric social work in community mental health, social service program administration, higher education administration, and national leadership in the profession. My story stands in opposition to dominant narratives that stigmatize those with my social identities—African American, female, first-generation high school graduate and child of a female-headed household supported by welfare. Those narratives write me out of higher education and leadership and into inescapable poverty and disempowerment. I am grateful for the many elders, mentors, teachers and colleagues who helped me write a different story.

The Early Years

Growing up with my grandmother and sisters in inner-city Baltimore, I aspired to become a postal employee. Listening to kitchen table conversations among my grandmother and her friends, I had learned that working in the post office was a sure path out of poverty. Although my grandmother's magic could turn powdered eggs, powdered milk, and canned meat into an edible meal, the possibility of life without government food, food stamps, and public assistance called me powerfully to economic self-sufficiency.

"Chile' you better get your education 'cause that's the only thing nobody can take away from you" was my grandmother's admonition that served as the value context for my educational pursuits. For her, education was the key to self-empowerment and getting *an education* meant graduating from high school, something my mother, father, grandmother, and my mother's twelve brothers and sisters had not achieved. The value of education was reinforced by other family members and early mentors, including Sunday school teachers, neighbors, and my uncle, who helped care for us. The message was consistent—education was the path to a better life.

During high school, mentors appeared in my life who expanded the concept of getting an education from high school completion to graduating from college. Going to college became an appealing but mysterious notion. These mentors demystified the path to college and served as early models of educational leadership and administration. This part of my journey began with my first formal job at the local elementary school.

The Harlem Park Elementary School was across the street from our rented house in Harlem Park, an economically depressed and racially segregated neighborhood of Baltimore. Through Neighborhood Youth Corps, a federally funded employment program for low-income youth, I was assigned to work in the school's main office during the summer before I entered high school. The staff at the school became significant mentors on my path to higher education and leadership. The principal was an African American woman, the vice principal an African American man, and the secretary—my supervisor—an African American woman. Nearly all the teachers were African American as well. I was surrounded by African American professionals and was in a different relationship with them from the one I had as a student in school. Being in close proximity with the principal and vice principal and learning they had graduate degrees made an impact on my perception of possibilities.

I worked in the same position after school and during subsequent summers until graduating from high school. After a day at the predominantly white, upper-middle-class high school I attended, where I often felt marginalized and insignificant, I retreated to the elementary school office where I was nurtured and affirmed. Early in my senior year, the principal inquired about my college plans and found I had little knowledge about how to identify colleges, apply, or seek financial aid. Although my middle-class classmates and their parents had made college visits beginning early in their junior year, I was clueless about how to make such arrangements and manage the travel and related costs. My mentors guided me through getting an application from Bowie State College, a historically black college (HBCU), and completing it. They contacted the admissions director, who they knew, and arranged for him to visit our home to provide my grandmother with the information and acknowledgment she needed to grant permission for me to attend. Prior to his visit, she had refused to sign the application because she had been left out of the decision-making process. My application was accepted, and I applied for and received a Maryland Senatorial Scholarship. I was poised to enter a new chapter that forever changed my life.

The HBCU Experience

Bowie State College provided a welcoming and nurturing environment in which I blossomed. The faculty and administrators were predominantly African American, and many had doctoral degrees. I was inspired by and proud of their achievements. Resident students were all African American, and many were like me, first-generation college students from working-class and low-income families. I felt comfortable and at home. At this 115-year-old, small HBCU, faculty, staff, and administrators came to know me and showed interest in my progress. Among them was the college president, Dr. Samuel L. Myers, Sr.

The president regularly invited groups of students who had distinguished themselves through leadership and academic achievement to dine with him in the private room of the college dining hall. After making the dean's list during my first semester, I was invited to one of these dinners, along with nineteen other African American students. President Myers told us that we were among the "talented tenth," the W.E.B. Du Bois construct of the best and the brightest who would improve conditions for African American people. Having attended a predominantly white high school that did not integrate African American writers and intellectuals into the curriculum, I was unfamiliar with Du Bois, and the "talented tenth" concept seemed elitist to me. Nevertheless, President Myers's invitations were welcomed, and I enjoyed hearing that I was "special," a potential leader, and could have a positive impact on the future of "our race" by my choices and achievements.

Professor Charles Stallings, dean of faculty, was another significant influence during my years at Bowie. Although he was never one of my course professors, Dean Stallings requested a meeting with me, during which he asked if I had considered attending law school. The idea was so foreign to me that I thought he had confused me with another student. He assured me that he knew who I was and that I had come to his attention because of my academic performance. He had a law degree, as well as a doctoral degree, and spoke confidently about my ability to be successful in law school and find funding to attend. Our twenty-minute conversation planted an idea that grew into a new sense of possibilities and perceptions of myself. Before our meeting, I saw law school as inaccessible, something that could be done only by people who were "different" from me. Subsequently, I began to consider the possibility that graduate/professional education was within my reach. The seed of expanding possibilities that Dean Stallings planted was nurtured by countless conversations and words of encouragement from social work and other faculty and administrators during my college years. I began to make decisions from an awareness of a wider field of possibilities.

College student government was one of my early formal leadership experiences, made possible by my sense of belonging at this small, largely residential campus. There were many leadership opportunities. Information was widely distributed and easily accessible. Unlike in high school, I felt no sense of marginalization because of race/ethnicity or socioeconomic class. I was not one of the "poor black students" being bused in from the inner city. I was a student among fellow students. I was elected student government secretary in my second year of college and vice president the following year. With two years as a student government officer, I developed new interpersonal and administrative skills. I graduated from Bowie with a growing sense of agency and a clear sense of myself as a leader. Feeling hopeful about earning a master's degree in social work in the near future, I considered the possibility of becoming a social work professor "one day" in the far distant future.

My career as a social work educator began much earlier than I could have imagined. After earning an MSW and practicing social work in community mental health, I learned about a faculty opening in Bowie's social work department. A former professor encouraged me to apply, and I was surprised when offered the position. Although I was daring enough to apply for the position, I was not fully confident in my readiness to teach. After receiving the call from the dean who appointed me, I thought, "If they think I can do it, I guess I can."

Leadership opportunities were plentiful as a faculty member at Bowie. The college (now university) is a teaching- and service-intensive institution. With only three, sometimes four, faculty in the social work department, everyone's effort was needed to implement our undergraduate program. During my seven years in this position, I had major responsibilities for committee leadership, curriculum development, preparation of the accreditation self-study, and organizing student services. I served as field coordinator for four years and was actively involved in community service. My desire for continued professional growth inspired me to seek broader administrative experiences and pursue doctoral education. My pursuits led me to a federally sponsored, summer professional development program for HBCU faculty in the Midwest, where I subsequently moved and enrolled in a doctoral program in communication studies at the University of Iowa.

Starting Over

After earning my doctoral degree, I joined the faculty of the University of Iowa School of Social Work as an assistant professor. During my four years of doctoral study, I had taught at the school, first as an adjunct instructor and later as a full-time visiting instructor, and had become well acquainted with my faculty colleagues and the school's environment. Still, the culture and priorities of this predominantly white, midwestern university were a sharp contrast to the HBCU where I had become a social work educator. The focus on scholarship and the subtle message that teaching and service were less important created dissonance for me, given my prior experience in Bowie's intense teaching and service environment. Striking a balance among research, working with students, and service was my first critical challenge.

At the University of Iowa, I was in the delicate position of being an experienced social work educator, a junior scholar, and the only person of color on the tenure track. My knowledge and skills were recognized and respected, and I was appointed to many leadership positions. Prior to tenure and promotion, I chaired the graduate admissions and affirmative action committees as well as the practice sequence, and I served on the curriculum committee and most search committees. Outside of the school, I served on college and university committees, including the graduate college affirmative action committee and the coordinating committee for an interdisciplinary degree program. In the community, I served on agency boards, conducted training for local agency staff, and made presentations at community forums. My teaching and service contributions were outstanding, while my research progress was slow.

During my pretenure years at the University of Iowa, I established a reputation as a leader in my school, on campus, and in the community. During my annual reviews, I was often cautioned to do more scholarship and less service. Nevertheless, requests for my participation in service continued from the school, the university, and the local community. My service was excessive for a probationary faculty member and could have been my undoing had I not sufficiently developed my research program. While I could have done less service, making a contribution in this way kept me grounded in my sense of professional competence while I grew in my new role as a scholar. My service also assuaged my concerns about being at an institution with so few students of color, when my efforts could have been devoted to working with students whose lives and stories were more like mine. Working on affirmative action initiatives, making presentations about diversity, and bringing a cultural competence perspective to organizations were strategies for increasing the professional and personal meaning of my work.

The Turning Point

Despite the energy I was investing in leadership activities, I had no aspirations to be director of the School of Social Work. My interest in the position began to shift when I attended a Council on Social Work Education annual program meeting's panel of women deans and directors at the invitation of my faculty mentor, who was then my school's director. The session was designed to encourage women, who were underrepresented in social work education leadership, to pursue positions as deans and directors. Panelists shared stories of their journeys and advice for women aspiring to leadership.

Some panelists had developed five-year plans to attain their positions. Others had come to their positions more serendipitously, responding to their school's or institution's need for their service, rather than their own deliberate, self-directed career plan. Their narratives demystified the paths to these positions, helped me see that those who occupied them were not completely unlike me, and left me with the sense that I could make an important contribution to social work education in this way.

While I did not leave the session with a commitment to become a dean or director, these women's stories illuminated new possibilities and lit in me a spark of interest. The stories of all of these women were now available as I developed the plotline for my own story. Gradually, I began to aspire to the directorship. I observed the three individuals who held the position over the next several years and made mental notes about their leadership styles and initiatives. What approaches were effective? Which ones were not? At the same time, I reflected on my leadership style and ways I might further develop my knowledge and skills. I envisioned ways I could promote change as the school's director—in our physical facilities, our level of collegiality, and our effectiveness working with issues of human difference, that is, our cultural competence. Still an untenured assistant professor, I imagined being the school's director in the distant future.

Entering my first year as a tenured associate professor, I was appointed as associate director and MSW program coordinator. The same year, the director announced she would be stepping down at the end of the school term, and the school launched a national search. Although the search was not successful, the director stepped down as planned. With full support of social work faculty, the dean of the college appointed me as interim director while we resumed the national search. The search was again unsuccessful, and the dean appointed me as director with considerable faculty support.

This set of events created the opportunity for me to lead the school while still an associate professor, which a move conventional wisdom

Each CSWE leadership position enabled me to pursue my passion for social justice and commitment to make a contribution. Each position expanded my knowledge of national issues in social work and higher education, strengthened my administrative skills, and enabled me to work with social work leaders across the nation whom I respect and admire. These experiences enormously expanded my leadership capacity.

Blueprint for Pursing a Leadership Position—Do's and Don'ts

There are at least two approaches that one might take to consciously and deliberately prepare for a formal or broader leadership role. The first is service on one's own campus. For example, participation on committees within one's department or school facilitates development of valuable knowledge, skills, and leadership experiences. Equally important is participation on college- and university-wide committees, which provides opportunities to learn the operations of the larger system and understand the multiple perspectives and values of those outside of social work. For example, participation in university-wide faculty governance committees increases understanding of the passions, priorities, and perspectives of non–social work colleagues. These understandings enable us to develop a wide network within the institution and be more effective in leadership positions and interdisciplinary contexts. Whether within the department/school or the university, volunteering or accepting service assignments when asked is excellent preparation for larger leadership roles.

In tandem with activities on one's own campus, engaging in professional service outside of the academy at community, statewide, and national levels is a second approach to preparing for and securing a leadership position. Typically, opportunities abound for volunteer service on agency boards and committees. Participation in human service and other organizations also fosters development of relationships with a wide network of people and facilitates learning different perspectives and keeping abreast of practice and policy issues. Such participation counteracts the insular tendencies of academic institutions and promotes being informed about what is important locally and regionally. Participation in professional organizations can accomplish similar objectives. However, involvement at the national level broadens opportunities for interacting with colleagues around the country and developing a broad information and support network.

While the path to leadership is unique for each person, five elements provide a solid foundation for moving forward—competency, credibility, connection, contribution, and cultural competence.

• Competency. To become a respected and effective leader in the academy, it is vital to demonstrate excellence as a social work educator. Mastery of the essential components of your current position creates a clear sense of empowerment and provides the foundation of self-confidence needed to engage in a more formal or expanded leadership role. Effectiveness in your current role demonstrates that you are a valuable contributor to the mission of your school, institution, and profession.

Beyond your current position, identify the additional knowledge and skills the position to which you aspire requires and seek formal and informal opportunities to acquire them. Will you need to deepen your understanding of your institution's administrative structure? Budget and finance? Personnel policies and procedures? Issues in social work and higher education? Workshops, online seminars, books, and higher education periodicals (e.g., *Chronicle of Higher Education, AAC&U News,* and *Black Issues in Higher Education*) are valuable sources of news and information. Additionally, consulting individuals in similar positions can be a source of insider knowledge of positions of interest and the skill sets required.

• Credibility. Demonstrations of competence and excellence provide the foundation for gaining the credibility one must have to become an effective and respected leader. Integrity and professionalism combine with competence to establish credibility. Developing a reputation for value-driven, ethical behavior and consistent follow-through on commitments is essential.

• Connection. Establishing and maintaining good collegial relationships within and outside of your unit is crucial. This can be accomplished through the application of the social work value of treating all with dignity and respect and using the basic practice skills—listening, genuineness, and demonstrating unconditional positive regard for all, not just those whose politics we like.

• Contribution. Clarify your vision for the contribution you will make in the leadership position you seek. What will this position enable you to do to enhance the mission of your unit, institution, and profession? How will you be a contribution to your colleagues, to students, to the broader community, and to the profession in this position? How will the position enhance the purposes you have for your life and career? The answers to these questions will propel you forward, keep you focused on your aspirations, and help you decide what positions are right for you.

• Cultural competence. Women of color are uniquely situated to understand the importance of working effectively in the context of human differences. By virtue of our experiences in the academy, we have likely developed a high level of biculturalism. However, our effectiveness working in the context of differences in ethnicity, sexual orientation, disability, religion, and other diversity requires ongoing professional development. Understanding the operations of power and privilege in the academy and in social work practice and the standpoints of those with marginalized identities is fundamental to our effectiveness as leaders. Increasing cultural competence enhances competency in our current position, credibility and connection with a wide range of people in the organization, and the contribution we can make in any leadership position.

Finally, when pursuing a leadership position, the advice of mentors is invaluable. They can help you assess your readiness and identify the advantages and disadvantages of pursuing a specific position or type of position. They can also provide valuable information regarding the application, hiring, and appointment process. Seeking the perspectives of several mentors may be useful. Still, all advice you receive must be measured against your vision and sense of purpose. Your decisions must make sense and feel right to you once you have weighed all the information and advice you have solicited.

Leading and Administering Successfully

Cultural Leadership Paradigms

Effective leaders transform organizations by developing a clearly articulated and compelling vision that is broad enough to encompass the visions of others. Vision guides organizational goal setting and enables us to attract and recognize the people, resources, and opportunities needed to achieve those goals. Vision is central to my leadership style, which is a blend of the transformational leadership and servant-leader paradigms. As a transformational leader, I work collaboratively with others to develop a shared vision. As a servant-leader, I work to cocreate an environment of support and encouragement and the resources needed for people to attain their individual goals, while contributing to the collective vision.

Immediately after my appointment as interim director of the School of Social Work, I led the faculty and staff in a strategic visioning process. We began the process at our annual retreat and continued the following year with developing our strategic plan. At the end of the process, we had consensus on our vision, core values, and goals and the strategies to achieve them. The process was as important as the document we produced because we had created a common sense of direction and clarity about our goals and how to accomplish them. Once the strategic plan was complete, my primary role was then to secure the resources and provide encouragement to support the success of faculty, staff, and students. The role I played in this process illustrates transformational leadership and the servant-leader approaches.

The knowledge, skill, and value base of social work has been vital to developing and successfully implementing my leadership style. Through my early graduate studies and microlevel practice experiences, I developed a strong knowledge foundation of human behavior, skills in problem solving, and excellent interpersonal skills, including listening and communicating genuineness, empathy, and unconditional positive regard. Subsequent graduate studies and macropractice experiences helped me to develop an advanced knowledge of group dynamics and organizational behavior and skills in facilitating organizational change. Viewing my administrative roles as my practice encourages me to mindfully draw upon my professional practice base to support my leadership efforts.

Personal Factors

Like other aspects of professional practice, effective leadership requires ongoing self-assessment and evaluation. The insights and self-awareness gained from systematic data collection about others' perceptions of the nature and quality of one's administrative skills are invaluable. An evaluation process that I have found particularly useful is 360-degree feedback, which provides data from multiple perspectives. This process involves completing a self-evaluation instrument and using the same instrument to collect data from several individuals, specifically a supervisor, a peer, and someone whose work I supervise. The 360-degree feedback process revealed how others perceived my effectiveness in managing projects, interpersonal communication skills, and level of organization. Comparing the perceptions of others to my self-perceptions deepened my self-awareness, allowed me to identify or affirm areas of strength, and clarified capacities that required further development.

The DISC Profile is the second valuable evaluation tool I have used. This self-scored, personal assessment tool classifies one's behavioral style within a four-dimensional model (Dominance, Influence, Steadiness, and Conscientiousness). My preferred DISC Profile style is Influence, which is associated with being people-oriented, optimistic, expressive, encouraging, and persuasive. Learning my primary style and its attributes increased my awareness of my preferences for dealing with people, problems, and data. My strengths and areas for continued growth became clearer to me. The DISC also helped me to understand those whose primary styles are different from mine and how to work with them more effectively.

The power of a leader's self-knowledge cannot be overstated. The self-awareness gained from the 360-degree feedback process and the DISC Profile has enabled me to plan professional development activities to augment my skill set. This knowledge also guides me in consciously building teams of people that bring diverse styles to complement my own. I have attracted and been attracted to leadership positions where my leadership style and personal characteristics were of particular value for the organization at that point in the organization's development.

Cultural Factors

As early as high school (1966–1970), I recall wanting my life to make a positive difference in the world. Although I did not know the meaning of the term "existential questions," I was asking them: *If the world is no better after I leave than when I came*, I asked myself, *what purpose will my life have served?* My Christian upbringing had instilled in me the value of service to others. My grandmother's kitchen table stories linked our poverty to the history of slavery, lynching, and segregation and the discrimination she and her mother had faced working as domestic servants. The kitchen radio blared news of unrest across Africa as liberation movements struggled to overthrow colonial rule, and my awareness grew of the worldwide subjugation of people of African descent. I did not have the power and privilege analysis I would later develop. However, from my marginalized position, I clearly saw an urgent need for social change. This personal history served as the backdrop for developing a collaborative and inclusive leadership style, focused on a vision of social justice as the process and outcome of our work.

As an African American, two cultural messages heavily influence my leadership style:

• Message #1: Striving for individual achievement is important because there are many who have sacrificed much for the rights and opportunities available to me. I have an obligation to pursue these opportunities. My individual achievement is a contribution to the collective.

• Message #2: While individual success is important, it is never to be accomplished at the expense of others. I have a responsibility to help others succeed. The adage "Don't forget where you came from" conveys this sentiment.

Both cultural messages are reflected in the Colored Women's Club Movement motto, "Lifting as We Climb." These messages easily translate into social work education and higher education leadership. They have encouraged me to strive for personal and professional excellence, while nurturing and celebrating the individual accomplishments of others and connecting those accomplishments to the collective good.

Systemic Factors

My biggest leadership challenge came at the outset of my tenure as director of the School of Social Work. The school's two-year unsuccessful national search for director came on the heels of the departure of several faculty during the previous few years. The college had not granted permission for faculty searches to replace these losses. Moreover, the college had taken a keen interest in the school's financial operations and was exercising an unprecedented level of oversight of our affairs, including placing a college staff member in the school to observe our operations. There was an air of suspicion and resentment. Faculty and staff were angry, demoralized, and disempowered.

To respond to this difficult set of circumstances, improving dynamics within the school and between the school and the college was imperative. As previously described, our strategic visioning and planning process created a sense of shared direction, which contributed to improving internal dynamics. To further support this positive shift, I created mechanisms for faculty, staff, and students to become aware of, appreciate, and celebrate individual and organizational contributions and achievements. We were like many academic units in which faculty and staff work independently of each other, with no systematic methods to know or appreciate each other's work and accomplishments. I developed a "Director's Report" to publicize the contributions and accomplishments of faculty, staff, and students as well as schoolwide projects and initiatives. Distributed at monthly faculty meetings, the document celebrated recent publications, presentations, funding awards, honors, and service appointments. At the beginning of each meeting, I highlighted the content of the report and encouraged enthusiastic applause for the achievements it detailed. The process generated a culture of collegiality, support, and celebration for each other's efforts, as well as a sense of being informed about our collective accomplishments.

To further promote awareness of faculty scholarly productivity, I had a wall-mounted display case installed in a highly visible location with each faculty member's picture and the cover page of their most recent publication. The display was a powerful tool to communicate the contributions of faculty members to each other, to current and potential students, and to visitors to the school. These information-sharing and celebratory efforts brought a new sense of appreciation for the school and for each other. External funding and faculty scholarly productivity increased substantially as a result of these efforts, combined with strategic planning and allocation of resources in alignment with our strategic goals. Principles of strengths-based and empowerment practice informed these interventions.

Improving the relationship with the college to garner more resources and regain our autonomy was my second challenge. I enrolled the school's administrative team in working cooperatively with the college to improve fiscal procedures and satisfy concerns about the efficiency and effectiveness of our operations. I created opportunities to communicate faculty and staff accomplishments to the college, broader university, and community through announcements of funding awards, faculty honors, and collaborative community projects. I articulated the school's achievements in the context of the college and university strategic plan, emphasizing ways we were making a contribution. I unabashedly promoted the school's projects and achievements and faculty accomplishments whenever and wherever possible. The college subsequently withdrew oversight of our fiscal affairs and approved searches to replace faculty the school had lost.

An ongoing challenge is prioritizing time, resources, and opportunities. In most leadership positions, especially in higher education, there is no end to the demands of work. There are more innovative projects to launch than time and energy to launch them. There are more calls for university and community service than are humanly possible to accept, and there is always a need for more resources, particularly funding. For public institutions, reporting requirements continue to increase as legislators and university governing bodies demand evidence of the value of higher education to taxpayers. A clear vision and strategic goals, informed by the broader social, economic, and political context, are the best guides when making decisions about how time and resources will be spent and which opportunities will be pursued.

Mentorship, Collegiality, and Networking

Relationships are vital to my successful leadership. They are the medium through which ideas are generated, information is exchanged, support is given and received, and commitment to the collective is generated and sustained. Within the School of Social Work, collegial relationships have cultivated an inclusive and welcoming environment where members of the community can thrive and are inspired to contribute to each other's success. They have created the space for developing and pursuing a shared vision. Outside the school, I have developed relationships with a wide network of people—on campus, in the local community, across the state, nation, and world. Through these relationships, I keep informed about the broader environment, gain diverse perspectives on current issues, and learn new strategies for addressing challenges. Many of these relationships are an important source of emotional and psychological support as I face the challenges and demands of leadership.

Within these networks are my mentors, whose guidance, support, and encouragement have helped me navigate unfamiliar territory. What are the pros and cons of pursuing a position for which I have been nominated? Is this the right time in my career? How do I negotiate my hiring package? What salary, administrative supports, and commitment of resources do I propose? How do I implement a strategic-planning process? How do I sustain it? Mentors have given me sage counsel on these questions and raised others that I did not know to ask. Mentors have helped me prepare to assume leadership positions and make strategic decisions once I attained them.

Role of Formal Education and Training, Institutional Strategies, Policies, and Supports

In tandem with mentorship, two academic leadership programs provided valuable support for my professional development and successful leadership in higher education. The university-sponsored Administrative Leadership Institute was a four-day training program designed to acquaint participants with central administrators, the university's administrative structure, and budget and issues in higher education. The institute introduced me to the DISC Profile and 360-degree feedback assessment process described earlier.

The Committee on Institutional Cooperation (CIC) Academic Leadership Program was my second formal leadership program. This program is designed to develop the leadership and administrative skills of faculty on CIC campuses. As a program fellow, I traveled to other CIC campuses for seminars, heard presentations by CIC provosts and presidents, and met others in leadership positions in higher education. These seminars broadened my knowledge of theories, ethics, trends, and issues in higher education administration. For me, this leadership program was an excellent knowledge- and skill-building experience.

Role of Professional Social Work Organizations

Professional social work organizations play a vital role in leadership development in at least three ways. First, organizations can identify promising social work educators for volunteer positions and prepare them for greater leadership roles. Professional organizations can systematically create service opportunities and broadly recruit members to participate, especially women of color and others who are underrepresented in leadership roles. Second, organizations can proactively provide professional development experiences for volunteers and those in leadership positions. Including a leadership development component in regularly scheduled business meetings and conferences or systematically sharing current issues in higher education are two ways to accomplish this. Finally, professional organizations can also sponsor programs designed to encourage women to seek leadership positions, such as the National Association of Deans and Directors of Schools of Social Work panel of women deans and directors that inspired me to consider a greater leadership role in social work education.

Keeping the Movement Alive

The cultural principle "Lifting as We Climb" motivates and obligates me to be a contribution to the achievement of others, especially those who may have limited access to information, resource networks, and opportunities. For undergraduate students and practitioners who may believe that master's level or doctoral education is beyond their reach, encouraging their pursuit of graduate studies reach is of critical importance. *"Continue your education. You have so much to contribute. You can do it"* is my message to them. Being available as a mentor to students and junior faculty is a second critical strategy for being a contribution. Serving as a guide to those who may need support to navigate the unfamiliar terrain can be an important contribution to their success. Encouraging those who are underrepresented in leadership positions to pursue them and supporting them once they are chosen are essential to changing the face of social work education and higher education leadership. I serve as an encourager, mentor, and guide whenever possible.

The Journey Continues

Early in my journey, I did not have a clear sense of my potential for leadership. While on faculty at Bowie State College, a trusted advisor told me that

I might well be a college president in the future. The idea was appealing, primarily because it was a bigger vision than I had for myself. The possibility was fascinating. Still, I did not approach my career with a five- or ten-year plan to become a leader in social work or higher education. Instead, I engaged in leadership activities that would advance social work's mission and challenge me to grow professionally. Only after attending the CSWE annual program meeting's panel of women deans and directors did I begin to think proactively about gaining the knowledge and skills needed to enable me to be the director of my school. Prior to this time, my mentors and others held the vision for me, affirmed my capabilities, and called me forward to consider possibilities that I had not yet been able to imagine. Once I came to a fuller awareness of my competence, capacities, and agency, I no longer relied on others to envision an expanded future for me. I had developed my own vision for my future and plans for realizing it.

After nearly eight years of serving as the director of the School of Social Work, I was nominated to apply for a newly created position at the University of Iowa, senior associate to the president. While I felt torn about leaving the directorship, I applied for the position, feeling ready to pursue academic leadership in a broader context. The university president selected me, and I enthusiastically brought my social work practice perspective to the president's office. I served two presidents over a period of eighteen months. At the conclusion of my tenure as senior associate, I returned to my faculty position with invaluable knowledge of higher education from the vantage point of central administration. Subsequent to completing this narrative, I was appointed dean of the University of Connecticut's School of Social Work.

Moving forward to the next chapter in my life, I do so with the clarity that I am authoring my story, and I can write it as I choose. My desire for all who have been marginalized by dominant narratives is a similar awareness of agency and authorship.

References

Bass, B. M., and B. J. Avolio, eds. (1994). *Improving Organizational Effectiveness Through Transformational Leadership*. Thousand Oaks, Calif.: Sage.

Burns, J. M. (1978) *Leadership*. New York: Harper and Row.

Du Bois W.E.B. (1903). The Talented Tenth. Available at http://www.teaching-americanhistory.org/library/index.asp?document=174 (accessed January 12, 2008).

Greenleaf, R. K. (2002). *Servant Leadership: A Journey into the Nature of Legitimate Power and Greatness*. New York: Paulist Press.

[6]

An Unplanned, Though Predictable, Pathway to Leadership

PHYLLIS IVORY VROOM

Pursuing Leadership and Administration

The Journey: A Context

When I think of the irony of being a dean, I cannot stop smiling. Not a broad grin, but rather a wry sort of smile of self-recognition. Leading or administering was the last thing I ever thought I wanted to do. And yet, somehow, throughout my career, I have always ended up in leadership and administrative positions. It is that "somehow" that the first part of this chapter addresses: the unplanned but, in retrospect, inexorable journey.

As a second-year graduate social work student—a very young one at that— I asked my advisor for permission to substitute direct practice courses for supervision and administration courses. I had always imagined myself as a practitioner only and emphatically expressed my lack of interest in pursuing supervision and administration. But my wise advisor let me substitute other courses. My aspiration was to join the Merrill Palmer staff, where I had had a field placement, to work with poor children and their families and help find solutions to problems such as autism, schizophrenia, emotional disturbances, hyperactivity, childhood depression, and speech disorders. However, I knew that I needed to get a doctorate to get a position in such an organization and that I needed much more "seasoning" before getting a doctorate.

I had another compelling reason for wanting more practice experience. I had difficulty reconciling the psychoanalytic theoretical orientation used to make diagnoses in my field placement with my family background in social action and social change. My parents were active members of the National Association for the Advancement of Colored People (NAACP), and my father was a union organizer. We attended two different Baptist churches, one of which had a long, colorful history of fighting slavery, being part of the Underground Railroad, and many other activities supporting civil rights. Most important, we were allowed to attend NAACP meetings at our home and union meetings with our father. Later, I joined the state NAACP youth group and strongly identified with the union movement. My parents always examined the social, economic, and political forces that shaped behavior and the impact that discrimination had. We heard the often horrendous stories of racial injustice and of the fights against injustice and inequality locally and nationally. These experiences shaped my career choices, my beliefs, and my behaviors as a social work practitioner, as a faculty member, and in leadership roles later on. However, it was the civil rights movement, the Black Power movement, and the unrelenting activism of the National Association of Black Social Workers (NABSW) that brought a critical mass of Black social work practitioners into faculty positions in Michigan. In response to NABSW's demand to make the social work faculty and student body more reflective of the diversity of the communities served by social work, I was recruited to serve on the faculty of an urban school of social work.

Two faculty positions were available. One was a highly paid, grant-supported post related to promoting health among low-income populations; the other, a much more modestly compensated position to support the development of undergraduate education in social work—the school's response to the perceived need for creating a human service workforce trained in social work. I was offered a choice between the two. I sought the advice of an African American faculty member who counseled that, though the former position was more highly paid and had higher visibility, he thought undergraduate education might be a better match with my work experience and, most important, was probably the wave of the future. After much thought, I took his advice. This choice set me upon an academic adventure and, ultimately, a journey toward leadership and management.

Lessons from an Unplanned Journey to Leadership

Exhilarating, exhausting, wonderful, and challenging are the terms that characterized my experience as a new member of the faculty in the late 1960s and early 1970s. Three tasks faced me as a new professor: learning my craft, learning the culture, and learning the role expectations of the faculty.

LEARNING THE CRAFT OF TEACHING

For me, learning the "craft" of teaching meant immersing myself in the literature, fastidiously preparing lectures, illustrating each concept with practice experiences, and using group work skills to actively involve students. It also meant being responsive to students, particularly to students of color who expected African American professors to be a kind of natural resource. Many had never had an African American professor and were eager for mentoring. In addition, African American faculty members were expected to help make the curriculum relevant to prepare students to work in African American communities, and to bring the African American perspective and presence into the school and the university. I learned early that to be an effective professor required study, discipline, determination, hard work, setting priorities for use of time, and learning from mistakes.

Teaching also had a social element, requiring a degree of collegiality, which meant being honest with everyone and building a network of friends, as well as coaches and mentors among the faculty. Engaging students created a fount of goodwill, which later served to bring back alumni who were willing to be tutors, mentors, and scholarship donors.

LEARNING THE CULTURE

The culture was to value teaching, focus on the needs of students, develop excellence as a classroom teacher and faculty-field liaison, and support the excellence of others. This is still true.

In addition to the teaching role, we were expected to serve on ad hoc and standing committees in both the school and the university, even those of us who were new to the faculty. I agreed to take on service roles that, in retrospect, were well integrated with my faculty roles of teaching and scholarship. That integration is even more important now, when faculty members are expected to be excellent teachers, have heightened expectations for scholarship, and provide service.

Taking on service roles was both fun and hard work; it also provided an opportunity to take the measure of my colleagues and them of me. Service roles also socialized me into the language and norms of the school. Those who come into social work education after earning their doctorate learn these things in the course of their education, but those, like me, who enter academe from practice need to learn a language and culture that are quite different from those in practice.

Because I taught primarily undergraduates, I served on the Academic Senate. This proved fortuitous. I learned much about the cultures of the several disciplines within the university and the current and historic issues in higher education, and thus I could place our curricular and ideological issues in a broader perspective. It also gave me and the school valuable information about the pathway for gaining university approval to offer the BSW degree at the school. The heavy teaching and service responsibilities of my faculty role required discipline and strict time management. The multiple roles of wife, parent, and new assistant professor left little time for self.

LEARNING THE FACULTY ROLE

These multiple expectations of a faculty member in the roles of teaching, scholarship, and service, combined with those of being an African American, were being newly articulated in the school and university communities. They propelled me into university service much earlier than most assistant professors and, I found later, placed particular additional expectations on the few tenured African American females. Most social work faculties then were predominantly male. For me and other female faculty members, our academic lives exemplified the cliché that being Black and female was "triple jeopardy," with expectations that we would represent all of those statuses. Negotiating these multiple expectations as a faculty member prepared me well for the leadership and management roles I would later assume.

Moving into Leadership and Quasi-administrative Roles

After three years, I was promoted to associate professor without tenure. The head of our program retired unexpectedly, and the dean asked me to be BSW coordinator, a position I held for eight years. In those years I learned major lessons about leadership. As a lead teacher, committee chair, and program head, I learned to lead by doing, reflecting upon my actions and those of others, and my and others' mistakes.

Lessons Learned

1. Be a student of the social work curriculum. I worked assiduously to learn about curriculum content and design as I had to learn my craft as teacher. We defined the liberal arts base, developed a foundation curriculum, and determined the content in each course. We also offered a "pre–social work" curriculum through the Sociology Department. Teaching in the pre–social work curriculum while designing the undergraduate professional curriculum allowed us to learn more about those students who would seek admission. The Undergraduate Committee looked to me to bring the perspectives of undergraduate education and minority content.

2. Strive to be the best. Minority members from my epoch grew up with many strictures: "Be a credit to the Race"; "You must be twice as good as anyone else to be considered 'just satisfactory.'" My parents also emphasized that "You may be smart, but there will always be someone smarter, so don't be arrogant," and "Be humble," as well as "Look 'them' in the eye when you're talking to 'them.'" I cannot say that those admonishments were a driving force for me consciously. However, I do know that I always pushed to read "just one more" article or book, preparing my lectures and planning meetings to the nth degree so they had productive outcomes, and I strove to be well prepared as a faculty-field liaison.

3. Work effectively with a team. Successful leadership involves "doing the homework" (Bolman and Deal 1997), by becoming a student of curriculum, but also putting the right people on the team and making sure the "wrong" people are not (Collins 2001). The "right people" were committed to undergraduate education and to developing a high-quality curriculum and field expectations. They put the program first and egos second. Each was strong in subject area and in intellectual convictions but accepted my leadership role as "the first among equals." Leadership was not about charisma but rather about guiding the group to articulate the vision and goals and harnessing their thinking and actions to pursue the vision and goals in a disciplined manner. Working with a group of talented,

superior people was both exhilarating and exhausting. Remarkably, there were no power struggles, in spite of our heated discussions. As coordinator, I saw that my role was to bring the latest thinking to the group, to complete work on my portion, and to forge an agreement about what the BSW program would look like. This work required understanding group and individual dynamics, as well as the political processes of building alliances and coalitions and of compromises and trade-offs.

Not all faculty members accepted the idea of an undergraduate social work program, fearful we might "water down" the profession and encourage employers to hire BSW graduates, rather than MSW graduates, for leadership and advanced practitioner roles. And the liberal arts and science faculty, particularly in the Department of Sociology, fought to retain the pre–social work students in liberal arts, asserting that sociology was the intellectual base of social work. The undergraduate Social Welfare Program, as it was called, was located in the Department of Sociology, even though the graduate School of Social Work was an autonomous unit. Wresting the undergraduate program from Sociology and gaining approval for the professional baccalaureate social work curriculum was a pedagogical and political feat, both within the school and in the university, requiring us to serve as emissaries of the school and exercise a great deal of patience, persistence, determination, and interpersonal, communication, and political skills.

4. Be an emissary and build linkages. Knowing your craft and being able to guide colleagues while demonstrating expertise and submerging ego are key characteristics of leadership. However, they must be complemented by the ability to serve as an emissary for the school and program (Edwards and Baskind 1995) and the skill to "build relationships and networks" (Bolman and Deal 1997). An emissary is constantly presenting and representing what we stand for, what we prepare students for, and our vision, core values, and goals. We also need to build linkages to the program within both the school and the university by reaching out, making personal contacts, and serving on committees.

5. Program first, self second. I have been fortunate to have a career that has provided great intrinsic rewards: developing a program that I care about and believe in, working with people whom I admire and respect, and being paid to do what I love. And I learned early that focusing on achieving the goals of the organization also leads to tangible and intangible rewards. Our curriculum team was energized and motivated to do whatever it took to make our program excellent, get it accepted in the school and the

university, and earn accreditation. Ultimately, the school received some visibility because of the program's quality. Our team's self-motivation, clarity of purpose, and passionate pursuit of excellence resulted in the development and implementation of a program that now has been ranked number one by the Gourman Report for six consecutive years.

6. Be decisive. Leading is always a balancing act. When a decision has to be made, it is important to listen, ask the right questions, consult, and involve important stakeholders. However, at some point, a decision must be made. Sometimes decisions evolve from the best thinking of the task group. At other times, the task group looks to the leader to identify options and state a preference. At still other times, the leader has to make a decision without qualifications, equivocation, or ambiguity. The balancing act is knowing when to decide and when to evoke a decision from others. Because I had earned the trust of colleagues and built working relationships upon mutual respect, my solitary decisions were rarely, if ever, met with a contentious reaction from my colleagues.

7. Understand and value using political processes appropriately. Political processes need not be covert dealings, include superficial nonreciprocal relationships, or contain unsavory behaviors. It is important to form alliances and coalitions to win support for your programs. Academic organizations have diffuse power structures; faculty must be persuaded that a particular program or activity is beneficial to the organization and to them. Knowing when it is time to move from process to outcome is also a political art.

8. Know your values; they are your guide. As I reviewed my values, I realized they came from my parents and the institutions of my youth. Some of those core values are reflected in points 2 and 5.

After serving in and leading the BSW program for eleven years, I saw that expectations of faculty as well as our school and university were changing. The university's vision was to become a preeminent research university, built upon the strengths of each academic unit in research, publications, and external funding, while continuing strong teaching and service missions. Both the school and the university had excellent reputations for teaching and actively embraced the urban service mission. In response to seeing these changes, I resigned from my leadership role to pursue doctoral training in higher education administration, with a focus on research, which I thought was imperative if I wanted to remain relevant to

- Develop an excellent scholarly and teaching record.
- Select mentors who will help you advance your scholarship, enhance your teaching, and link you with leadership opportunities.
- Get to know your chair and dean, particularly through your "works" (terrific teaching, publications in respected venues, grant funding to support your scholarship, volunteering for service).
- Creditably perform service roles within the school, the university, the profession, and the community.
- Operate autonomously, but also contribute as a team member.
- Demonstrate an ability to work collegially.
- Put the program first; if it is successful, you will be too; if it fails, the failure will not be attributed to you.
- Be realistic about what you take on and what you decline; when in doubt, consult with trusted colleagues.
- Earn tenure before taking on heavy service assignments.
- Seek service assignments in your strongest areas.
- Be a trustworthy colleague; keep others' secrets and confidences.
- Eschew office gossip and align yourself with those who are positive and want to advance the organization.
- Avoid whining about how hard it is.
- Don't be a prima donna. Everybody is smart in academe.

Having completed a five-year term as dean and recently signed a contract for another five years, and having helped achieve many of our strategic goals, I also have some ideas about what it takes to lead successfully. These observations are based on the personal, cultural and systemic factors that support or present barriers to successful leadership.

Leading Successfully

Early in my deanship, I became aware of Collins's (2001) study of what factors propel business organizations to transform themselves from "good to great." I thought Collins's work had merit. However, some components of his framework, which I will describe shortly, and interpretation of his research findings did not match the realities of the university or the nonprofit sector. But when Collins followed his book *Good to Great* with a companion monograph written for the social sector, it was a better match to my beliefs and actions as dean. I consider it a blueprint for leading successfully, and it will serve as a guide for me during the rest of my deanship. The framework has five components (Collins 2005:3):

1. Defining "great." Collins defines a great organization without using business metrics. He writes that a great organization is "one that delivers superior performance and makes a distinctive impact over a long period of time" (5). Each organization assesses performance, based on outputs, "even if those outputs defy measurement."

2. Level 5 leadership. This level of leadership blends humility *with* professional wills (perseverance, determination). "Level 5 leadership is not about being "soft" or "nice" or purely "inclusive" or "consensus-building" (11). It is about being disciplined in focusing on the "right" decisions for the organization, and bringing in the "right" people to determine the focus.

3. First who, then what. This means "getting the right people on the bus within social sector constraints" (e.g., tenure and/or union contracts may constrain getting the "right people" or terminating the "wrong people" as one's leadership group or within one's organization). However, over time level 5 leadership is able to maximize the number of right people in critical spots in the organization.

4. The hedgehog concept. Collins describes the hedgehog as a persevering animal, without flash or charisma, that works consistently, in a disciplined way, toward achieving its goal. The three interrelated components of the hedgehog concept are (1) pursuing what the school is passionate about, what it "stands for," its raison d'être; (2) pursuing the unique contribution to the people the organization touches ("what you can be best in the world at"); and (3) pursuing the resources needed to drive the organization ("understanding the three parts that are the resource engine of your organization: time, money, and brand").

5. Turning the flywheel. This involves building momentum by building the brand (all members of the organization are clear about the identity and foster the identity of the school by working to enhance and maintain it).

Collins's framework has great power for me in explaining the personal and cultural factors that have helped make the school successful under my leadership and the systemic factors that have presented barriers to that success.

Personal Factors

I call myself a "realistic optimist," blessed with high energy and the ability to persevere and be determined and disciplined. My energy has always been intense but quiet. I have always believed that most people have an innate goodness that, if tapped in the right cause, could allow them to accomplish much. I enjoy diverse people whose personalities, gentle to assertive, may be quite different, but who are driven to excel and achieve for the group, the program, or the organization. The realist in me informs me that it may not be functional to invest energy and resources on naysayers, and recent scholarship on organizations supports this view (Collins 2001, 2005). Though I believe in the innate goodness of people, I know that one is hard pressed to peel away the layers to find it in some.

From my parents and our community, I developed a clear sense of identity and a heightened sensitivity to the needs of others and the importance of understanding those needs when examining any set of human interactions. I have also learned not to take dissent personally. Understanding the perspectives, motivations, and needs of others does not mean being unable to take a stand based on your own perspective. It does remove the tendency to view people unidimensionally and lets you examine the complexities of working with others. My personal characteristics are suited to leadership and managing in the academic organization that I lead. Ours is an urban school of social work, within a unionized research university in a diverse community with a strong union tradition and a history of African Americans in leadership positions. My school has a long tradition of shared governance. I am more likely to be broadly inclusive, patient, and nonhierarchical in decision making, but I believe in the responsibility of a leader to guide and, when appropriate, make the decision. I believe that most major decisions, such as budgeting, hiring, termination, and tenure, should be based on appropriate but limited consultation. Academic tradition places curriculum decisions with the faculty.

Most decisions lend themselves to a mix of leadership styles, a small part of which is "executive"—the "concentrated" power to make decisions individually—but most of which is "legislative," making the things happen by creating the conditions for the "right" decisions to be made. Academic organizations emphasize the "legislative" style (Collins 2005: 10–13). Certainly this is true of social work education; our accreditation standards measure how students and faculty share in governance. I prefer that approach, working with groups, forming coalitions, using persuasion, mixed with a use of "executive" functions, such as appointing one's leadership team and rewarding exceptional performance through merit raises and bonuses. In addition, I try to use my executive power to surround myself with a team that shares my values and work style. When I think it might be good for the school, I will at times try to include people in the leadership team who do not share my style. Studies of "nurture vs. nature" suggest that my innate temperament has probably contributed to my leadership style (Gardner 1995).

Women have played key leadership roles in our school for more than twenty years. At present almost all of the major leadership roles are held by women, recognizing their leadership abilities, commitment, and drive to be the best. To me this was only natural, having grown up in a milieu that recognized and rewarded the leadership abilities of women.

Cultural Factors

Throughout this chapter I have reflected on the contributions to my leadership style made by growing up in an African American family and community. As Gardner (1995:chaps. 1–3) notes, the stories we hear throughout our lives inform our identity, our understanding of the group to which we belong, and our values, including our spirituality. My parents and others told tales of how their survival depended on dogged determination, togetherness, community cohesiveness, and mutual aid. These stories have guided me since childhood.

The leadership style that had the greatest impact was the enlightened political leadership of my father and other union leaders. They were tough but fair; quiet but effective; power brokers rather than power seekers. My father always wanted to do the right thing, assembling a skilled team, being disciplined, and maintaining his principles in a harsh political environment. My mother was determined to earn a college education. She attended college part-time while working, sometimes in factory jobs, as a maid, and finally (hallelujah!) in a civil service job as a bookkeeper, and taking primary responsibility for raising three children. She earned her bachelor's degree when she was in her mid-forties and her master's in her fifties, and she rose to the level of assistant principal in the public school system. She was always driven to learn more, to be innovative and to excel.

While we were aware of the impact of discrimination on our parents' lives and in our African American community, we always believed that we could achieve. The models of leadership in the Baptist church and in the NAACP also informed my own leadership style. Though men were the nominal heads of these organizations, we had many female role models who had extraordinary leadership abilities. Watching these leaders illustrated the importance of collective commitment to a vision. It also provided important lessons on effective ways to overcome personal and organizational challenges.

Systemic Factors: Leadership Challenges and Barriers,
and Strategies to Overcome Them

In the first two years of my leadership in the school, I was interim dean. That temporary status led a subgroup of faculty to attempt to realign the school's power structure, highly circumscribing the dean's role. This press for change was partly ideological: some faculty fancied the idea of a faculty-run school; a subgroup of the faculty had always been antiauthority. Another factor was to test my resolve as a female of color. My own hypothesis is that the combination of my being both "interim" and an African American female signaled to that subgroup that I might be weak and that, therefore, now might be a propitious time to effect a radical change. All the previous deans had been strong male leaders who did not hesitate to assert their authority.

The faculty spokespersons were pressing for "shared governance." However, in reality, the proposal was for "faculty governance." The dean would become a group leader and facilitator of group decision making. Faculty would control budget, the executive leadership team, and the curriculum and develop strategic plans. The dean would have the options of accepting or modifying the plan.

I stayed out of the power struggle, determining when to compromise and when to stand pat, using my authority, albeit "interim," as vested in me by both the collective bargaining agreement and the school's bylaws. The faculty opted to engage in its own strategic planning. I negotiated with them a process in which strategic planning occurred in two phases, one participated in by the faculty and the second schoolwide. I pointed out that, as interim dean, I was both a part of the faculty and a part of the school, and therefore strategic planning would not be complete without my input. Furthermore, I had responsibility for the budget—a major tool for implementation of a strategic plan—and had veto power, according to the collective bargaining agreement, over school bylaws. I was not about to give away my authority, delegated by the Board of Governors, the president, and the provost of the university and accorded to the dean I replaced, a male, by the faculty. On the other hand, I was not about to change my character and become autocratic. We ended up with an excellent strategic plan—one with a clear vision, a definition of our identity as a school, and a set of goals that gave us direction and a sense of hope that the organization could achieve distinction. Together we crafted a renewed organization. Over those exhausting and exhilarating two years as interim dean, I worked with a leadership team that was remarkably selfless, hard-working, and committed. In addition, my persuading the faculty as a whole, dealing with subgroups that moderated the more strident members of the faculty, being clear on the content of the collective bargaining agreement, and shifting judiciously between the executive and legislative styles resulted in our emergence from the interim period as a much stronger organization. As the interim period ended, the provost stated his intention of appointing me dean and sought an advisory vote of the faculty, which strongly supported my appointment. In January 2002 I became dean.

Collins's characterization of the challenges facing leadership aptly echoed the challenges and barriers I faced. Other challenges, I believe, grew out of my being a woman of color.

First let me speak to the leadership challenges that come with taking on the leadership role. After selecting the right leadership team, the greatest challenges involve what Collins calls being disciplined in thought and actions. This means facing certain issues head on: who we are as an organization, what it will take to achieve our vision and goals, and how can we pursue them with perseverance. It also means holding fast to core values and mission. And it means seeking the counsel of colleagues, past and present.

The role of mentors and the counsel of colleagues are critical in every phase of one's leadership and certainly of utmost importance during transitions. Being able to call on deans in other schools of social work to seek advice and counsel and to think through strategies for addressing critical problems has been invaluable. At one point, I remember wrestling with the issue of a school of social work in our state moving into our traditional area for recruiting students. At a meeting of deans and directors of social work programs, I consulted with an experienced and creative dean in an urban school of social work with outreach programs similar to ours. This dean strongly recommended that we expand our extension programs. I brought this idea back to our executive leadership team and to our faculty, who were persuaded that a focused approach to extension would maintain our viability. As a consequence, we have selectively expanded our MSW program and strengthened our enrollment. It has also been important to call upon the talents, skills, and wisdom of our former dean. He agreed to write the first draft of the proposal to offer a Ph.D. program in the school and played a key role, along with several faculty members and me, in gaining approval for the program, achieving one of our strategic goals. He also played a major role in the school's self-study for reaffirmation of accreditation.

Listening to the advice of faculty has been beneficial to the school and, consequently, to my successful leadership and administration. Several years ago a faculty member suggested that we strengthen our presence in the state in the area of continuing education. He had heard that the state legislature was close to passing a bill mandating licensure for social workers. Following up on his information, we initiated a survey of alumni to determine the kinds of workshops we should offer. The legislation was enacted, and now our continuing education program is thriving, bringing in revenue that we are using, in part, to provide summer salaries for new faculty who are just developing their scholarly agenda and to support other school priorities.

Within the university, a small network of women of color is another informal source of mutual aid. We call upon each other to do "reality testing," seek advice, commiserate, and get a "heads up" on information important to our roles. I am the only African American dean in the university.

A number of other systemic factors help me function effectively as dean. Both my MSW education and training in social work with groups (as well as group work practice) and my Ph.D. program in higher education have informed my leadership and administrative roles. I have already noted how invaluable it has been to have theoretical and practical understanding of the dynamics of groups, the importance of group process, and the role of leadership in various types of groups. Doctoral study in higher education directly informed my leadership and administrative roles. It involved being immersed in the study of models of leadership and administration; organizational approaches to advancing faculty development, productivity, and satisfaction; finance and budgeting; the role and use of technology; and the history and philosophy of higher education. The discipline needed to successfully complete doctoral education underscores my belief that professional school and advanced degrees foreshadow one's professional career.

Other Sources of Support

The Council on Social Work Education and the National Association of Deans and Directors of Schools of Social Work both are committed to encouraging, supporting, and nurturing women of color who aspire to leadership positions and providing training for them. The leadership seminars and matching of mentors with individuals who desire mentoring that these organizations provide are good beginnings. However, professional development could be expanded through systematic leadership training, beginning with helping aspiring leaders among women of color to identify pathways to leadership, presenting ongoing series of workshops on models of leadership, finance and budgeting, development and fundraising, faculty development, and the like. This training should complement that offered by some leading universities and those offered by American Council on Education. These organizations will need to present programs that reach out to women of color and be highly visible to them, since throughout the country there are still elements that continue to suppress the aspirations of women of color who aspire to leadership roles. I am told by a number of these women that if they are assertive on their own behalf and on behalf of students of color, they find themselves isolated, sometimes demeaned, and their contributions disparaged. Professional social work organizations alone should not bear responsibility for keeping alive the movement of promoting women of color into leadership roles. However, the roles of the CSWE, NADD, and NASW might be expanded to offer a mechanism for these women to voice their concerns and advance their careers.

Keeping the Movement Alive

Some of my own efforts toward keeping this movement alive have been to appoint women of color to academic and staff leadership and management positions and mentor them. I have appointed women and, more particularly, minority women to almost all of the key leadership positions in our program. In addition, I eagerly serve on dissertation committees of numerous women of color in other disciplines within our university and have been vigilant to ensure that they are treated equitably and fairly. I actively support adherence to equal opportunity and affirmative action policies in my own school, always requiring that the university's EEO/AA officer give a mini workshop for each search group. And I am vigilant about attending to the selection of candidates for junior and senior positions to ensure that qualified women of color are not overlooked. At an institutional level, I have agreed to be one of the university's American Council on Education institutional representatives. This will give me an opportunity to support, advance, or reinforce programs and policies to keep women of color in the pipeline for leadership and administrative roles.

Some Parting Thoughts

To survive, grow, and sustain energy to fulfill the requirements of my role as dean, I have had to build important coping mechanisms, in addition to seeking mentoring, collegial support, and a network of supporting relationships. For me, such coping mechanisms involved being engaged in activities in church, including regular attendance, singing in the choir, attending Sunday school, and volunteering to teach a class of adolescents in vacation bible school. I serve on several boards and task forces that remove me from the university and the school but keep me engaged with the community of practice. During my first five years as dean, I avoided taking leadership roles in any other organizations (except for agreeing to be treasurer of both choirs); I felt that being a dean was an all-consuming position and therefore chose to take on only follower roles away from the job. Recently I have allowed myself to be elected to a leadership role in my church and find, ironically, that being dean has prepared me well for this role. And I continue the rewarding and challenging roles of wife, mother to adult children, daughter, sister, and now grandmother, a role that I have not yet had time to fully explore, beyond occasional babysitting. My husband, our sons, and particularly my sisters have been primary sources of support and succor during my days as dean. Furthermore, I maintain my favorite pastime of eclectic, nonprofessional reading.

One must be prepared, however, to devote considerable time and psychic and physical energy to being dean. It is a role that commands disciplined thought and actions and can be a major preoccupation during every waking hour of every day. But the rewards are great: though I was initially reluctant to assume a leadership or administrative role, my career as BSW coordinator, MSW coordinator, associate dean, and dean has provided me with opportunities to shape programs and policies, to set the conditions for dramatic organizational change, and to work with people of great talent and commitment. For these reasons, in the words of Maya Angelou (1993), I "wouldn't take nothing for my journey, now."

Note

Dedicated to Bessie Ivory; in memory of Marcellius Ivory; Frank Vroom, Phillip Bagley, and Ernest (Jojo) and Ebow Vroom.

References

Angelou, M. (1993). *Wouldn't Take Nothing for My Journey Now*. New York: Bantam Books.

Bolman, L.G., and T. E. Deal (1997). *Reframing Organizations: Artistry, Choice and Leadership*. Second ed. San Francisco: Jossey-Bass.

Collins, J. (2001). *Good to Great*. New York: HarperCollins.

——— (2005). *Good to Great and the Social Sector*. Boulder: Author.

Edwards, R. L., and F. R. Baskind (1995). "Providing Leadership." In *The Administration of Social Work Education Programs: The Roles of Deans and Directors*, ed. F. B. Raymond. Washington, D.C.: National Association of Deans and Directors of Schools of Social Work.

Gardner, H. (1995). *Leading Minds: An Anatomy of Leadership*. New York: Basic Books.

PART FOUR

Chair/Directorship in Social Work Departments and Programs

[7]

Living with a Purpose

One Woman's Journey

CAROL MINOR BOYD

There have been many days when I questioned my sanity about choosing to pursue a career as an administrator in social work education. Serving in an administration or leadership role can be very rewarding and fulfilling yet challenging, stressful, and frustrating. I have often pondered whether my being African American and female played a part in any of my frustrations, challenges, and stresses as an administrator. There is literature (Howard-Vital 1989; Singh, Robinson, and Williams-Green 1995; Zamani 2003) that discusses the challenges, frustration, and stresses that characterize the experiences of African American females in higher education, which has major implications for administration and leadership roles. These challenges are often outcomes of discriminatory treatment of African American females in predominantly white institutions. There are times when I am sure that my race and gender worked negatively against me; however, there are times when I am quite sure that my race and gender had nothing to do with my challenges, frustration, and stresses. Yet I love what I do and I am quite certain, after all these years of serving in administrative positions, that I made the right choice. In fact, I have encountered more rewards and positive challenges than negative ones. I absolutely love the administrative work.

I had many role models who influenced my desire to become an educator because teaching was one of the few professions that I had the opportunity to observe while growing up. I grew up in a time when teachers all seemed to love their work. Most spent countless hours in the schools beyond the usual teaching day. I am sure that their dedication had a great impact upon me and influenced my love for academics and my desire to further my education beyond high school.

I attended college immediately after my high school graduation, but I dropped out in order to get married. After working for five years, however, I decided to return to college. I started to discuss degree options with those in my workplace and became fascinated with social work through talking to one of my colleagues who had a social work degree. She expressed that social work is one of those professions designed to assist people in resolving some of their problems. I liked the idea of helping others; although I must admit that I had never heard of social work prior to my conversation with my colleague. Thus I completed a bachelor of arts degree in social work and forged on directly toward completing a master's degree in social work. While in graduate school, I realized that administration was the field of practice that best suited my personality.

I recall having conversations with a few of my graduate school classmates about my interest in administration. Some would make comments such as "don't you think working directly with the client would be more fulfilling than administration?" They seemed to think that because I wanted to be an administrator, somehow I did not want to be a social worker. Initially I felt a lot of guilt about my decision to be an administrator because of such comments. Then I spent the rest of my time thinking and reading about administrative roles in social work and affirming my decision to pursue this route regardless of my colleagues' feedback. Peterson (1992) stated that as Black women we believe that no other human being should define who we are. I agree with Peterson; no other person has a right to define who I am. So, I pursued my dream of being a social work administrator. I came to understand and appreciate that clients need committed and competent people who are able to influence and make policy decisions just as they need individuals who provide direct practice. The social work profession needs individuals at all levels of organizations and systems (direct practice, supervision, and administration). I have come to know that I can have as positive an impact on clients in my leadership and administrative roles as those who work directly with them on a day-to-day basis. My social work career began over twenty-nine years ago. There are so many more career options available to women—especially women of color—today than when I began my career in social work. Yet I believe that I would still choose social work academic administration as a career if I were just starting out today.

Pursuing Leadership and Administration

My journey to leadership and administration was planned—it did not happen by accident. After studying in the MSW program, I knew that I wanted to be a social work administrator. During my graduate field placement, I was assigned an internship in child welfare. I had an excellent agency field supervisor who asked me and the other students under her supervision for our vision regarding our career paths in social work. My vision was one of working in social work administration. She never questioned my choice, as had others. She assisted me in mapping out a plan that would help me obtain some administration knowledge while completing my internship. The plan included interviewing other women who worked in administrative positions in social work. My agency field supervisor and I brainstormed the names of women who would be good for me to interview, and we discussed the settings where they worked. We also discussed what knowledge and skills I could gain from the interviews with these women. After careful discussion we narrowed the choices to two women. My supervisor and I decided that I would ask only a few key questions: What led them to leadership and administration? What skills did they need? Did they enjoy it? What advice would they give me for entering this field of practice? My interview with one of these two women led to my first social work administrative job immediately after graduating from the MSW program. This administrator was reassigned to another position within her organization, which left her former position as a project director in a public health agency vacant. She recommended me for the job based on my interview with her and my strong interest in social work administration. As it turned out, the position was in my hometown, so I interviewed and was hired to work for the agency immediately after graduation.

My MSW program offered a few social work supervision and administration courses but not an administration concentration. I completed the courses, which laid the foundation that equipped and started me on an extraordinary journey into social work administration in academia. These courses were very helpful to me as a new administrator.

In my first social work administrative job in public health, I learned that working with people as a supervisor required great management and administrative skills. The agency did not provide additional supervisory or management training, but I learned from my experiences the critical nature of listening carefully to others, documenting everything, and staying on task.

Leading and Administering Successfully

My career as a social work educator began while I was employed during my first social work administrative job in public health. I received a telephone call from the social work program director of the undergraduate university I had attended. She offered me the opportunity to teach as an adjunct at my alma mater. At the time I had no idea that I would make a career in academia. I did know that I loved the administrative work, but I was so excited that I was teaching. I served as an adjunct for two years before leaving the program, but this same professor would offer me another opportunity to teach on a full-time basis, and this opportunity led to my current career in social work academic administration.

Personal Factors

A. Williams did a survey of Black women administrators in which she asked them to identify those characteristics that they associated with successful college administrators. "The descriptors that came up often were intelligent, well organized, hardworking, ability to stay calm, well respected by peers and subordinates, well groomed, dedicated, self-confident, a good leader, ability to recognize job-related talent, ability to give clear directions, concerned about the welfare of her staff, able to delegate responsibility, and willing to take risks" (1989:110). I agree with their perceptions and believe that possession of several of these traits has contributed to the success I have achieved in administrative positions. I think I am successful only because others have allowed me to serve as an academic administrator for the last seventeen years. I was also given the honor of receiving the Baccalaureate Program Director of the Year Award in 2006 from the Association of Baccalaureate Social Work Program Directors. Being awarded this honor confirmed for me that perhaps I am doing a good job. Of those traits identified by Williams (1989), I believe good leadership skills, hardworking, well organized, ability to see the big picture, skills in delegation, determination to succeed, and self-confidence are the most characteristic of who I am. I would like to provide some illustrations of how I have displayed these traits as an administrator and leader.

First, good leadership skills can be beneficial regardless of the situation. I took three supervision and management courses while I was in the MSW program, completing them prior to my first administrative position. Since then I have obtained a doctorate in educational administration, taking a number of administration courses while in this degree program. When one is in a leadership role, it is a bonus to have some knowledge acquired through education and training. This additional training provides administrative knowledge and skills and can assist one to think quickly in crisis situations and respond appropriately under pressure. Receiving training through courses kept me from making possible career-ending mistakes because I knew how to appropriately respond to most situations.

Second, one way to gain the support of the individuals with whom we work is to work very hard. I strongly believe in delegating tasks, but I also believe that part of my role as an administrator is to be an active participant in the work of the department. My experience has shown me that faculty will do their share of the workload as long their perception is that they are assigned work responsibility fairly and that the work is shared appropriately by all.

Third, being well organized helps me to keep my sanity. It is extremely helpful for me to plan my workday and workweek, and to keep an organized list of the projects with priorities and deadlines. Planning prevents stress and makes a person appear as if she knows what she is doing. This is important if an administrator is asking people to trust that she can lead them. The director of my undergraduate social work program gave me my first planner as a graduation gift while I was her work-study student. Since then I have always used a planner to keep organized. Now I use an electronic planner that is small and easy for travel and has alarms to remind me of all my appointments. Without it I would easily lose track of those important tasks that I have to do.

Fourth, employees will not always see or want to see the big picture of the organization. They do not necessarily have to, but an administrator must have the ability to do so. The administrator's job is to communicate to the staff how everything fits together, and to create a vision for others to follow. One skill in creating and developing one's vision is the ability to delegate responsibilities appropriately to others so that the vision is implemented. In academic settings there are professionals with many talents and skills; if their talents and skills are used properly, we can have much success. I believe this process assists them in buying into an administrator's vision and helps them to understand the big picture when they are appropriately involved. I have bought into the philosophy of Blanchard and Hershey (1977), whose work I studied in graduate school. Their Situational Leadership Model is based on the idea that managers use different leadership styles depending on the employee's skills and the work responsibility. This model allows for matching employee skills and talents with job tasks and support. Some of what Blanchard and Hershey have proposed has stuck with me. For example, I work hard with individual faculty members to provide them with the tasks and support to meet their needs. Since administrators are leaders of a team (employees), we are only as strong as the team players.

Finally, I believe that success starts in the mind, and if one makes a determination to succeed, one will succeed. I have a motto, "A woman has to do what a woman has to do." I do not let obstacles stop me from doing what I need to do. I do not believe in succeeding at the expense of others, but I believe one must see oneself as a winner. If an administrator does not believe that she can be successful, then no one else will. I must admit that I gained more self-confidence and determination to succeed over the years. Administrators should be confident in their abilities because they are not always appreciated, supported, or treated as if they know their job. This treatment may not have anything to do with the lack of skills or expertise. As an administrator, I do not let how I feel about myself come from my job. An administrator needs to have high self-confidence when she arrives on the job.

CONTRIBUTION OF NATURE AND NURTURE

I grew up the eldest of five children, so I was given responsibilities related to supervising my siblings. At the time I did not realize that I was learning leadership skills that would be useful to me later in life. In addition, in high school I recall running for different class officer positions over the suggests is unadvisable. It is well documented that moving into a major leadership position can slow one's progress toward promotion to full professor. There is also the concern that, in higher education, a disproportionate service burden frequently falls on women and people of color. I understood that taking on the directorship would limit the time and attention I could devote to scholarship and retard my progress toward promotion. However, I recognized the opportunity to make a contribution to the school and to further develop my knowledge and skills. While many felt the timing for my career was poor, I decided that the potential risk was worth the benefits.

Going National

My leadership journey within my institution paralleled my experiences in leadership through national professional service. My scholarship on self-employment and microenterprise as an empowerment and self-sufficiency strategy for women resulted in invitations to join several journal editorial boards, as well as appointment to the CSWE Commission on the Role and Status of Women. Before that appointment, I knew little about CSWE beyond its accreditation role, although I had attended the annual program meeting for many years. After being appointed to the commission, I became more familiar with CSWE and committed to serving the profession through volunteer service in the organization. After I had served two years as a commissioner, the CSWE president appointed me as chair upon the unanimous nomination of commission members. As my tenure as chair was concluding, CSWE changed the commission structure and created the Commission for Diversity and Social and Economic Justice. The decision created apprehension among some of the membership, as all social justice commissions (e.g., commissions on the Role and Status of Women, Disabilities and Persons with Disabilities, Sexual Orientation and Gender Expression) were to be amalgamated under the new commission. The president asked me to convene a working group of social justice commission representatives to implement this new structure and later appointed me to chair the new commission. By virtue of the new governance structure, this role placed me on the CSWE Board of Directors. About the same time, the general membership elected me to the CSWE National Nominating Committee.

years and winning a number of those elected positions (president, vice president, and student body representative). I do not believe that we are born leaders, but I believe that we have certain qualities or traits that are developed over time through experiences, training, or mentors that can guide us to be great leaders.

I had a number of experiences from childhood to graduate school that prepared me for leadership, yet I do not recall having anyone whom I can identify as having served as my mentor. I do not believe that I was ever nurtured. I had the opportunity to observe the African American dean of the graduate social work program I attended. I also have observed other women in leadership positions, and I believe that I learned a great deal from them—especially from the social work program director of my undergraduate program. You can learn a great deal by observing others.

RELEVANCE OF PERSONAL LEADERSHIP STYLE

I served in different administrative positions for over ten years before completing an assessment of my leadership style. While I was in my first social work academic administrative position, during an administrative retreat offered by the university, I responded to a leadership inventory that had a number of questions asking how I would handle each situation. Scores were assigned to different leadership styles. I do not recall the model that was used, but the exercise was helpful in getting me to think about how I functioned as an administrator. I have completed other leadership assessment scales since that time, which led me to the conclusion that I have a participatory leadership style with a delegation style as my alternate. (One such survey can be found at http://www.nwlink.com/~donclark/leaderstl .html.) There are many leadership scales that can be found to help determine your leadership style, and doing so is important if you are interested in serving in an administrative position. After I discovered my leadership style, I reexamined each question on the leadership inventory to ensure that I was satisfied with my responses and to determine whether I had appropriately identified my style. I considered what impact each of my responses would have on how I actually performed in my job.

I consider the identification of one's leadership style as an important self-assessment tool. One step in being successful as a leader is the ability to work well with other people. This ability is reflected in our leadership style. I believe that some administrators are not successful because they do not have a leadership style that is suited for working with others. Administrators could benefit from knowing their leadership style and using this knowledge to make adjustments based on whether or not their style or styles of leadership are working. People can possess more than one style of leadership; one style can be the dominant style and the other less so. I strongly believe that receiving the input and involvement of others in the department is a wise investment. I do not believe in an autocratic style of leadership (Kahn 1993). People give you permission to lead them, and no one wants to be told what to do, especially professionals. I do not intend to imply that my style of leadership is the only style or necessarily the best style, but I believe that others can benefit from this type of assessment.

I involve the faculty in all of the departmental decisions. They really appreciate having the opportunity to share in the decision-making process of our department. When my faculty is involved in making decisions, I hear fewer complaints and they trust me more, knowing that I value and seek their input. I believe that seeking the counsel of many is wise. I have found that when people are allowed to participate in the decision-making process, they are more likely to volunteer and complete the tasks that come from those decisions. As an administrator, I try to distribute the workload appropriately and responsibly among the faculty. However, I make sure that the faculty sees that I will work just as hard as they will in completing all tasks and job responsibilities.

Cultural Factors

As an African American I am always sensitive to how I am perceived by others. Over the years I must admit that I have become less sensitive than when I began my career as an administrator. I believe my success as an administrator and my ability to form positive relationships with my peer faculty and upper administration have led to an increase in my self-confidence. When I am faced with a situation where I believe that cultural factors may be a problem for how I am viewed by others or for how I view others, my approach is to work with those individuals to overcome the cultural biases on both our parts and create an atmosphere of collaboration. I always believed that I had to work harder and be very well educated in order to succeed, more so because of my race than because I am a woman. I cannot think of any particular cultural leadership paradigms that have contributed to my success in leadership and administration.

Systemic Factors

I have alluded to the challenges, frustrations, and stresses that I have faced over the years as a social work administrator. I have spent most of my administrative years in academic settings. There are three challenges I want to discuss: isolation, lack of acceptance, and the occasional feeling that I have all of the responsibility and none of the power to do what I was hired to do as an administrator.

1. Isolation. I felt isolated more often during the beginning of my career in social work education than later on. It seemed as if I was in a bubble and isolated from others mainly because I did not feel that my colleagues at the university (not so much in social work as outside of social work) were reaching out to me or accepted me as a new employee. For example, I started my social work academic career in a predominantly white institution. It appeared that no matter how many times I met people, they did not remember who I was. I would remember them and the conversations that we had, but they would deny ever meeting me each time. I felt like a nonentity. Collins (1990, 1998, 2002), as cited in Howard-Hamilton (2003:19–27), would call this feeling "outsider within" status. Collins describes the outsider within status as part of Black feminist thought and refers to "black women who have been invited into places where the dominant group has assembled, but they remain outsiders because they are invisible and have no voice when dialogue commences." I had two choices in how to deal with what I was feeling: remain at the university or leave. I decided to stay because I was an alumna and was working near the city where I grew up. I also decided that I had responsibility for my life and that I had to make the best of my situation. Thus I built my own alliance, network, and support systems. I started to attend every function that I could on campus, making sure that I met as many people as possible. I began to participate in professional social work organizations (academic and nonacademic) until I believed that I had enough support systems in place to provide the mental and professional support I needed. My participation in professional social work organizations was very helpful in developing relationships.

2. Lack of acceptance. I have always believed that I had to prove my competence as an administrator to some of my colleagues, at least initially. I based this on the insensitive comments I heard, although I am not sure that the individuals making them understood the impact of what they were saying. I do not know if all women in leadership feel this way at one time or another. I have had conversations with other women of color in administrative positions who believe that regardless of the fact that they have strong academic and work credentials, people somehow manage to question their ability to do the job. Hughes and Howard-Hamilton (2003) also believe that there is an assumption in our society that the African American woman who is high achieving and competent is an exception to the rule, rather than an acceptance that there are many African American women with the intellect and abilities to do a broad range of work and do it effectively. I believe that we must overcome any negative feelings and situations, whether they are real or imagined. Over the years I have come to have less of those feelings, either from gaining skills in how to deal with people who have doubts about my ability to perform my job or from gaining more work experience that speaks for what I can do. The way that I dealt with these feelings was to work harder to prove my ability to do my job and to remain calm in the face of any opposition. In remaining calm, I decided to work on changing negative attitudes and behaviors one person at a time.

3. Lack of trust in my ability. I have had to work past administrators who failed to trust me to do my job. It is my perception that I was held to a higher critical standard than my peers. I felt like I had all of the responsibility but none of the authority. An example was when my administrators made decisions regarding my department without including me in the decisions. This practice undermined my autonomy and relationships with my faculty. Over the years I believed that my assertiveness and decisiveness were seen as aggression by administrators. I am not sure if this was due to my race or my gender. Zamani (2003) and Hughes and Howard-Hamilton (2003) would say that such treatment would be due to both my race and my gender. I felt as if certain constraints were placed upon my ability to make decisions, yet I had responsibility for the programs or department. How did I handle the situation? I knew that my support and base was with my peer faculty, so I developed close personal relationships with them. I wanted them to view me as a person, a colleague, and an administrator. Once I received their support, it made a world of difference in

getting administrators to release their restraints. Our faculty is our greatest resource and support system. They have so much to offer.

MENTORSHIP, COLLEGIALITY, AND NETWORKING

I define mentoring as the process of assisting individuals in understanding their hidden potential and serving as a support system in helping those individuals to reach their fullest potential. I have known many individuals over the years who affirmed my ability to serve in a leadership role. I was very thankful for those positive individuals. My first department chair saw potential in me to lead the department after she had made a decision to move to another position, and she recommended me for the job. Her support was very helpful to me because she allowed me to learn and grow from my mistakes. She was also a positive role model for me to emulate. Her emotional support meant a great deal. If we have good administrators as our supervisors, we can be better leaders and become successful in our roles.

Collegiality keeps the burden of all of the responsibility from being on my shoulders. I am thankful for my faculty members who worked with me in sharing the responsibility and creating a great atmosphere in which to work. As the chief academic administrator, I am ultimately responsible for the department, but working with others makes my job so much easier. However, the faculty is such a valuable resource; they are experts in certain areas and can contribute much to our academic departments. I am also very grateful for my relationship with other social work administrators whom I have met over the years. My current administrator is female, and I have much to learn from her leadership style. Other administrators have served as great support systems of people who can relate to my experience as a social work academic administrator.

Networking has been very important to my success. I have done so much networking through professional organizations and consider it critical to surviving as an administrator. Through networking, I have the opportunity to normalize my situations by discussing them with administrator colleagues and realizing that many of them share the same experiences. We learn from each other. I have been a listening ear to other female administrators, and they have listened to me when I needed to vent. When we network, we share in each other's success too. I enjoy time with my colleagues in the state and from around the country. We generally network most at conferences, but now we get to network through a listserv as well. It is a different approach but very effective too.

FORMAL EDUCATION AND TRAINING

I received my formal education first and then moved into leadership positions. During my formal education and training, I had the opportunity to become self-confident, mature, knowledgeable, and skilled about different areas of administration and leadership, including professional behavior and dress. I had my MSW degree when I first became employed in social work administration twenty-seven years ago.

Now I have a doctorate in education administration (Ed.D.). There were many administrative courses in the education curriculum that I chose. Unfortunately, I pursued this degree later in my career, having completed it in 2003. I believe that this training has improved my administrative skills and that the knowledge I gained from it could also have been useful earlier in my career. Prior to my returning to school for my doctorate, I wanted to pursue a master of business administration degree. I believed that the business course would strengthen my administrative skills. I do not think that one has to have an MBA to be successful in social work administration, but taking administration courses—whether in business, social work, or some other profession—would be most helpful. I decided that the doctorate would be a more useful degree for me in academia than pursing another master's degree. The doctorate is the degree that most universities require their academic administrators, including those in social work, to have completed prior to employment.

INSTITUTIONAL STRATEGIES, POLICIES, AND SUPPORTS

There are a number of universities that offer programs designed to assist women and people of color to move into leadership and administrative positions. In these programs, participants are assigned administrative responsibilities within a certain department to gain additional leadership and administrative skills. These programs are great for individuals who want to gain new skills and experience, and they are a way for women and people of color to demonstrate to others that they are capable of doing administrative work. I have never been asked to participate in one of these programs, even though this type of program was available at one of the universities where I worked. I obtained my first social work academic administration position through promotion. I have to admit that when I was offered the position, seventeen years ago, I did not believe that in a predominantly white university I would be allowed to be promoted to the position of program director. I was not concerned because of any resistance from the social work faculty, but I was aware that the university did not have any African American program directors at the time, and I was unsure of why this was the case. I had served in nonacademic administrative roles in the past but never thought that I would be considered for this position. With the support of the faculty and my supervisor, I was considered and the rest is history. I remained in that position for thirteen years.

Three years ago I assumed my current administrative role as department chair at a large research university. My previous social work academic position had been in a small liberal arts institution. Feeling somewhat stagnant, I desired a greater challenge, which led to my current position. I was told that I was hired because of my previous work experience, knowledge of social work accreditation, and reputation with social workers in my state. I know that in the past, many women of color were hired in administrative roles because of affirmative action programs.

Affirmative action programs have been under attack lately by individuals and groups who believe that we no longer need them. There are many people of color and women who would not be in their positions if it were not for affirmative action programs, in spite of their great credentials. Gregory (1999) reports that African American women still occupy the majority of the lower academic ranks, such as instructor and assistant professor. This being said, it still seems that we need affirmative action programs. Affirmative action became associated with something negative because some believed that positions were given to unqualified individuals based upon their race or gender and not their qualifications. Do I think we still need those programs? Absolutely. No one has ever said to me that I was hired under an affirmative action program. I was promoted into my first social work academic position with support from the faculty and the program administrator. However, I believe that my minority status has not been overlooked by the upper administration. For example, I had the opportunity to participate in the African American First program at the university where I am employed; this program acknowledges the accomplishments of African Americans who were the first to serve in their positions.

Many universities have leaders who are committed to diversity in their workforce and encourage their program administrators to be diligent in hiring women and people of color. Yet administrative roles and faculty positions in higher education are still dominated by white males. The role of affirmative action and equal opportunity programs is to make sure that all candidates who apply are equally considered and are excluded because they lack one or more of the qualifications required, not because of race, gender, or other such factors. I hope we will be able to maintain the affirmative action process in some form.

Leadership programs can be a great way for anyone to develop administrative skills. Many universities have these programs. They are designed to assist mostly women and people of color in gaining the experience and training they need to become academic leaders in administrative positions. I have never participated in any of these programs, and I do not think that I necessarily need to at this point in my career. Yet these programs can be very useful in helping one to move beyond a mid-level administrative position. These training programs offer the chance to be seen by higher-up administrators so they can recognize one's talents and skills. Without them one may never be noticed and considered for higher administrative positions.

PROFESSIONAL ORGANIZATIONS

I strongly believe in being active in professional social work organizations. Anyone who wants to become employed in academia and serve in an administrative position should join and become active in the professional organizations associated with their disciplines. I have learned so much from my participation in these organizations. Serving in leadership roles in professional organizations gives you the opportunity to meet many different people, gain leadership skills, travel, network, and learn from the wisdom of others. I belong to several professional organizations: the Association of Baccalaureate Social Work Program Directors, National Association of Social Workers, Council on Social Work Education, and Mississippi-Alabama Social Work Education Conference. Being a member of these organizations has helped me identify with the profession, meet other social workers, and take risks because I feel that my colleagues will work with me in reaching my goals.

The Association of Baccalaureate Social Work Program Directors has been instrumental in my success as a social work program director. BPD is a very important organization to undergraduate social work education. I have been a member of BPD since 1991, when I became a department chair. I have never missed a yearly conference, and I have been very active in this organization. I believe that most of what I learned about effective program administration in social work education, I learned from the different educational sessions and networking offered at BPD. It is a great organization. I cannot say enough about it.

Another organization that has played an important role in developing my leadership and administrative skills is the National Association of Social Workers. I joined NASW in 1981 and have kept my membership active since that time. I have served as chair of several different committees at the state and national level since 1981. I learned so much about people and leadership by serving on these committees and attending three NASW leadership training sessions while serving as president and president-elect of the Mississippi chapter.

The Council on Social Work Education is another great organization from which to gain leadership skills. I have served on its Commission on Accreditation and as a site visitor, and through these positions I was able to assess other social work academic programs. I have also been able to improve my leadership skills through service in this organization.

Life Experiences

My favorite extracurricular activity is reading. I developed a love for reading as a child. During the summer months when I did not have much to do, I would check out a number of books from the library and read them all. I have always had a love for reading mysteries. My love of reading meant that I was willing to read just about anything that was of interest, including both academic and nonacademic material. Reading serves as a way to relax and unwind after work, which is important for relieving stress. As chair of a social work department, I find it essential to have time to unwind at the end of the day. Some people exercise and I do sometimes, but not nearly as often as I read. If I am more relaxed, I function better in my job.

There are several pieces of advice I would like to extend to those seeking to become effective administrators. First, regardless of major, take courses that will prepare you to become an administrator beginning with the undergraduate level. Sometimes in social work there is a tendency to think that because we chose this profession, we do not want to work in administration or are not prepared for work in this field of practice.

Second, let others in higher authority know that you want to work in administration. This could include your professors in college, too. They may steer you toward leadership programs, training, courses, mentors, or people who can help you develop the skills needed to become an effective administrator.

Third, participate in social work organizations and take advantage of participation in leadership positions by running for office in these associations. The National Association of Social Workers provides a leadership forum every year to those who are leaders of state chapters (president and executive directors). The Council on Social Work Education has started to focus on training leaders for the twenty-first century. The Association of Baccalaureate Social Work Program Directors provides great training at its annual program. I am sure that there are other social work organizations that are also effective.

Fourth, act like a leader. People will notice your leadership ability. Take advantage of every opportunity to demonstrate your skills.

Finally, take risks. This involves being confident about who you are and your ability to do a great job and reach your goals.

Keeping the Movement Alive

I could do more, but I have encouraged several women students over the years who have great leadership potential to further develop their skills and to continue their education, which includes getting a doctoral degree. I am currently mentoring two individuals. Both are African American, one male and one female. The male is new to social work higher education administration, and the female is not in higher education. I have allowed her to serve as an adjunct instructor and to guest lecture in my classes.

Each year adjuncts are hired to teach a few courses in our department. These are usually individuals who are very excited about working in academia, but very few have the doctorate that is usually necessary for full-time employment within the department. They are young and could serve as a pool of individuals who may be ready to return to school if someone is willing to mentor them and provide a nurturing environment in which to learn. I make a point of talking with them about their career goals and whether they are interested in a career in academia.

Graduate students are another group of individuals who could be mentored and directed into academia. Many are still deciding what they want to do with their careers. We have just started a graduate program in social work that is designed to serve the needs of these students.

Note

This chapter is dedicated to my husband, Leroy Boyd. I am always working on one project or another, and you have always given me the space that I need to complete them. Thanks.

References

Blanchard, K., and P. Hershey (1977). *Management of Organizational Behavior: Utilizing Human Resources*. Third ed. Englewood Cliffs, N.J.: Prentice Hall.

Gregory, S. T. (1999). *Black Women in the Academy: The Secrets to Success and Achievement*. Second ed. Lanham, Md.: University Press of America.

Howard-Hamilton, M. F. (2003). "Theoretical Frameworks for African American Women." *New Directions for Student Services* 104 (Winter): 19-27.

Howard-Vital, M. R. (1989). "African-American Women in Higher Education: Struggling to Gain Identity." *Journal of Black Studies* 20 (2): 180–91.

Hughes, R. L., and M. F. Howard-Hamilton (2003). "Insights: Emphasizing Issues That Affect African American Women." *New Directions for Student Services* 104 (Winter): 95–104.

Kahn, U. A. (1993). "Types of Administrator Differences in Work Satisfaction of Secondary School Administrators." *Education* 113 (4): 574–78.

Patitu, C. L., and K. G. Hinton (2003). "The Experiences of African American Women and Administrators in Higher Education: Has Anything Changed?" *New Directions for Student Services* 104 (Winter): 79–93.

Peterson, E. (1992). *African American Women: A Study of Will and Success*. Jefferson, N.C.: McFarland.

Singh, K., A. Robinson, and J. Williams-Green, J. (1995). "Differences in Perception of African American Women and Men Faculty and Administrators." *Journal of Negro Education* 64 (November 4): 401–8

Williams, A. (1989). "Research on Black Women College Administrators: Descriptive and Interview Data." *Sex Roles* 21 (1–2). Available at http://www.nwlink .com/~donclark/leaderstl.html.

Zamani, E. M. (2003). "African American Women in Higher Education." *New Directors for Student Services* 104 (Winter): 5–18.

[8]

Leadership from an American Indian Perspective

Leaving a Path for Those Who Will Follow While Walking in the Footprints of Those Who Came Before

PRISCILLA A. DAY

Pursuing Leadership and Administration

"Where are your women?" This was the question posed by Cherokee chiefs when they met with colonial leaders in the eighteenth century (Mankiller 2004:98). In traditional Native American cultures, women always had a presence in leadership, either in a formal or an informal manner. While colonization has impacted our communities greatly, the inherent value of women persists and can be seen in the way in which American Indian women lead.

Leadership is both intuitive and creative. Learning about it is truly a journey that is part of the overall journey of life. Looking back over my professional career, I can honestly say that I could not have predicted or planned for the many leadership opportunities that have been put in my path.

Like many American Indians who end up in leadership positions, my journey was unplanned. Raised in a supportive family environment, I was encouraged and always planned to attend college even though neither of my parents had the opportunity to do so. For most American Indian children, high school is a challenge, and many drop out.

According to Harvard University, the recent national high school graduation rate for American Indian females is 51.4 percent compared to 77 percent for white females (Orfield et al. 2004). In some regions, the high school drop out rate is even higher.

My experience was different in that, unlike what happens to many Native children, my school counselor actually encouraged me to attend college. My husband, who attended the same high school and had the same school counselor, was told that he had a "one in a million" chance of succeeding in college. Fortunately, he did not take the counselor seriously and went on to earn bachelor's, master's, and doctoral degrees. Unfortunately, many Native children become discouraged and do not graduate. The lost potential is staggering.

Opportunities presented themselves early in my life. I participated in college preparatory programs such as Upward Bound, for first-generation college students, and Indian Circle, which exposed American Indian children who lived on the reservation to the larger world. Both experiences helped to shape my very limited views of higher education, leadership, and administration. This speaks strongly to the important role of adults in education in encouraging and directing young women of color into programs designed to expand their worldviews. This is especially important for young women who do not have role models within their family who have had the opportunity to go to college. This number is high given the large numbers who do not graduate from high school.

One of the most important people in my leadership path was my maternal grandmother. Raised in an extended family unit (my parents, grandparents, and four brothers), I saw the challenges that she navigated through and how she managed our family on a daily basis with less than ideal resources. We all lived in a small two-bedroom house with one bathroom and a wood stove that took up a quarter of the living room. My family ran a small resort, and all the adults also worked outside the home. Needless to say, it took a lot of juggling to keep our extended family functioning effectively. My grandma was the matriarch of this extended family and continued to be so up until her death three months before her one hundredth birthday. Seeing a strong woman and having her as an everyday role model shaped me in ways that nothing else could have.

While my grandmother never held an official leadership or administrative role, she utilized many of the skills that are necessary to be successful in those roles. For instance, she was a very determined person—some might say stubborn. This enabled her to survive in a time when women, especially American Indian and other women of color, were not valued or given a voice. She lived through huge shifts in the way Indian people lived, from leading an interconnected seasonal life to living on an independent homestead and being forced to attend boarding schools for the purposes of assimilation. She was able to navigate through difficult times with a sense of integrity and a positive outlook on life. She loved people and had a terrific wit and sense of humor. At the same time, she was a staunch advocate for herself and her family. Being a leader means being able to take a stand and looking out for those for whom you are responsible. Portman and Garrett (2005:285) describe American Indian leadership as being characterized by "patience, listening, contemplating the situation, and developing innovative strategies to accomplish the needed task." My grandmother was especially good at these traits and taught me, through her example, to be a good problem solver.

Some of the best leaders often have had difficult experiences that they have learned from, and they develop a sense of empathy for others who have had similar experiences. My grandmother was a boarding school survivor. She was four years old when she was sent to live in a dormitory and forced to march to and from classes and work. She had to learn English and endured leaving her family with no understanding of what was happening to her. In spite of this, she had a positive outlook on life and toward people. It is essential for a leader to have an optimistic attitude and a sense of humor. An important component of leadership is having compassion and courage (Portman and Garrett 2005).

My grandmother was also very relationship based. In American Indian culture, who you are is defined by your family, clan, reservation, and tribe. She knew all those connections, and they helped sustain her. One of her primary roles was to keep our family intact and connected. She was really skilled at making connections with others and was good at staying connected through letters (this was before the invention of e-mail). She acknowledged the little things that really are the big things in life, such as people's birthdays. It was not unusual for someone to receive a birthday card from my grandmother with a dollar in it on his or her birthday. Great leaders acknowledge the little things in life and make important connections with others. This establishes a sense of community and makes people more likely to support you if you need them in the future. Inherent in the ideals of American Indian women's leadership is concern for the future and an understanding of the importance of nurturing others and caring about future generations to ensure the survival, not only of your family, but of the culture (Portman and Garrett 2005).

Leadership Aspirations

In American Indian culture, most people are given a name in their Native language. This is sometimes referred to as a spirit name and is used in ceremonies. My spirit name is translated as "Thunderbirds Circling in the Sky Woman." In Anishinaabe culture Thunderbirds are powerful beings. It was told to me that I would "circle" back to places throughout my life because there was great need and my assistance would be needed. This has indeed been my experience. Another core value central to American Indian leadership is spirituality (American Indian Policy Center 2002). Having a strong spiritual connection is seen as critical to being a leader who has the best interests of the people at heart (Gipps and Gipps 2003; Portman and Garrett 2005; Mankiller 2004). These connections also help one to stay balanced and strong during difficult times (American Indian Policy Center 2002).

Because I "came into" leadership rather than pursuing it, I do not think that I have a conventional leadership self-assessment tool. Rather, I continuously solicit input from those around me about how it feels to work in the environment for which I am responsible. Of course, not everyone can be happy all of the time, but listening to your staff, creating opportunities for them to learn and grow, utilizing their strengths, and engaging them in the meaningful activities of the program all help to increase satisfaction and productivity. If those who work with you are relatively satisfied, then you are going to be more successful as a leader. Leaders are part of the environment, not separate or above others, and they work for the betterment of the whole rather than personal wealth or stature (Gipps and Gipps 2003). True leaders are those that show concern for others and practice generosity and kindness (American Indian Policy Center 2002).

Today, I would suggest that any woman of color wanting to pursue a leadership position ask herself about areas of strengths and areas that need further development. There are many leadership assessment tools available for evaluating one's strengths and limitations. I would suggest finding one that solicits feedback from your colleagues and/or people who know you well. This provides you with valuable insights about yourself that you may not be aware of or validates strengths that you have but may not fully acknowledge. I have had the opportunity to utilize these instruments through my doctoral studies and leadership programs. The information these instruments revealed strengthened what I already knew by providing outside validation from people I respected. It also gave me the opportunity to become more aware of areas for improvement.

It is crucial to remember that leadership has a cultural and gender component. Women often underestimate their leadership capacity, not because of humility, but from internalized oppression. Being a woman of color often means having learned to be strong over the course of your life. We learn early that life is not fair. This can either make you hard and insensitive or strong and compassionate. Developing the ability to let go of things that don't work out and go on with a positive perspective is critical to successful leadership (McLeod 2002). As an American Indian woman, I am aware that what is seen as strong leadership practice in academia or in a mostly male setting may be seen as inappropriate in tribal settings. Most of us have already learned how to change our behavior depending on where we are and whom we are with, but it is especially important to acknowledge this difference when it comes to leadership. This is, of course, not an easy task as it is never an either/or situation but rather requires an ability to make determinations more on a continuum. This is where our own cultural competence and the intuitive part of leadership come into play. For example, when I was the director of mental health for my home reservation, my supervisor, an American Indian female, said to me one day while we were having lunch that I was the most "normal American Indian with an advanced degree" that she knew. I laughed but knew what she meant. Many Native people who go to college, especially graduate school, come back to their reservation with a new, mainstream way of interacting viewing the world. Joy Harjo states, "Colonization teaches us to hate ourselves." She describes what she calls an "over culture," which is based on material values and overt power that is "transitory and violent" and separates people from one another (Mankiller 2004:62). Some Native people, through no fault of their own, either have been raised outside the culture or return to the reservation from higher education with mainstream ideas and values and find that they do not go over very well. While there is valuable learning in higher education, how you use such learning in cultural settings must be considered carefully. Because most colleges do not know or appreciate this cultural component, they do not teach how to actually implement leadership in one's own cultural community. Nonetheless, some people are naturally gifted in this practice or have great intuition; others have to learn the hard way.

In her article "Keeping the Circle Strong," about successful female tribal college presidents, McLeod (2002) describes the characteristics of what made them successful as possessing a clear vision, focusing on the articulated mission, understanding their leadership influence and using it to be a positive role model, soliciting and promoting the groups ideas and values, and encouraging others to work to their highest capacity.

In traditional Native culture, being a true leader is about your concern for the greater whole, not what leadership brings to you as an individual. Wilma Mankiller, the first woman to be a principal chief for the Cherokee people, wrote, "Cherokee traditional identity is tied to both an individual and a collective determination to follow a good path, be responsible and loving and help one another" (2004:50).

Leadership and Administration Blueprint: Do's and Don'ts

Even after I realized that I had leadership skills and had success in being a leader, I cannot say that I actively pursued leadership and administrative roles. For most Native people, leadership is situational with the person who has the set of skills most appropriate to the task emerging in a time of need. That has been my experience. I always give myself time to consider what I am being asked to do. According to Basil Johnson, Ojibwe leaders always took time to consider all aspects of a situation before making an important decision because of the impact it could have on future generations (American Indian Policy Center 2003). I try to objectively weigh what I know are my skills against what the job entails. I also try to honestly look at my deficiencies. By this I mean areas that I do not enjoy or in which I do not have skills (and may not want to develop those skills). I have turned down what others have seen as "wonderful opportunities" because I did not feel it was the right fit for me. Several years ago I was offered the opportunity to become an administrator and be mentored by our dean. While I was flattered by this offer, once I thought about it, I realized it would take me away from work that I am deeply committed to doing in the American Indian community. It also would have been a loss to the tribal community as my focus and energies would not have benefited tribal people. While the job offer was a definite "promotion" and may have benefited me personally at many levels, it would require me to give up something for which I have great passion. I have not regretted this choice; to me it was not worth the cost.

In addition, when asked to take on leadership roles, I limit the length of time I am involved in a particular role. For example, several years ago I was asked repeatedly to consider the position of department head, but I really did not want to leave teaching and community research. After a failed external search, I agreed to accept the department head position for three years. That allowed the department to go through reaffirmation of its accredited status and for less senior faculty to gain more experience. After this period of time, I stepped down even though many people wanted me to remain in the position. I used that time to learn more about the university and administration, which has been helpful to me in my various other academic roles. A common theme in looking at literature on American Indian leadership is that leaders seldom maintained that role forever; rather, leaders emerged in times of need when their skills matched what was needed and then receded when the need was met (American Indian Policy Center 2002). This rotation of power served several functions, including utilizing the skills of many people, allowing opportunities for others to learn to lead, creating a broader investment in the community by decentralizing power and sharing responsibility, providing leaders with breaks from the constant demands of leadership, and helping to create empathy for leaders as others discover the difficulties of leadership (McLeod 2002).

In terms of "do's," I encourage you to be inclusive, listen, keep a sense of humility, understand that you need those who work with you to be happy and to feel valued, build on strengths, provide opportunities for growth, acknowledge the contributions of others, and share the accolades. Laugh at yourself and with others. Take responsibility for, and be open to learning from, your mistakes (we all make them; do not be too hard on yourself).

Regarding "don'ts," do not leave others out of important decisions—you may need to make the final decision, but at least you will have considered their input. Do not criticize unless it is constructive and done with compassion. Do not give someone something that you know they cannot do unless you provide support. Do not consistently underutilize someone's skills. Don't take yourself too seriously!

Leading and Administering Successfully

Personal Factors

The topic of leading and administering successfully is a complex issue. What I learned through my family has influenced my life choices, which in turn influenced my leadership style. As the only girl in my family and a middle child with four brothers, I learned to interact with men and to get along with others. I also learned not to be intimidated by men. I can read people pretty well and know when I have to adapt my behavior to be more or less assertive. While I like everyone to get along, a common female and middle child trait, I have learned to be okay with conflict if it needs to happen. Sometimes women shy away from conflict at any cost. This is definitely not a good leadership trait. On the other hand, if one goes into every situation on the defensive, one will not get far either as no one likes to be in conflict with someone all the time. Sometimes women who are inexperienced or insecure take that approach.

I used to keep a picture of a bridge painted by Monet in my office to remind me to build bridges both within my own tribal community and between Native and non-Native cultures. Faith Smith says, "Women build more bridges and try to find connections instead of confrontation. Women have to negotiate all the time, from the moment we get up until we go to bed at night. We may not like everyone, but we can build a long-term agenda without camps or factions" (Mankiller 2004:115). Good leaders have this ability.

It is probably a common developmental trait, but it took me until sometime in my twenties to realize that I often see things from a different perspective than others, especially white people. I did not know that most non-Natives do not see the world as I do. From this knowledge, I have learned to pick and choose my battles; to try to articulate issues in ways that others can "come to understand." My own ability to acknowledge and appreciate the developmental process of "coming to understand" has increased my tolerance for others. Sometimes you plant a seed, water it, and wait until the plant comes up. From that point, it may still take a long time to see a flower bloom. Working in academia is a lot like this; we often spend a lot of time talking and planning before something comes from it.

If you enjoy doing new things that require you to problem solve, you are a perfect fit for leadership and administrative positions. In taking personality tests, I have learned that while I can do many different tasks required of leaders and administrators, I most enjoy the earlier stages of getting things going. The danger of this is that, as a leader, one also has to be a finisher. I sometimes find this process tedious but necessary in order for projects and programs to be successful. This is where working with a good team that includes task-oriented people is important. In Indian culture we learn that we all have gifts/roles to play in life. A good leader is able to bring diverse people together to create an effective whole.

It is important to have clear boundaries and be able to advocate for others and yourself. This includes being able to take a stand that may not be popular or understood by others. It is so important to have a sense of yourself and recognize that others "give" you positional power that comes and goes. Personal power remains, regardless of what formal position you acquire.

Bring passion to your leadership! I get truly excited by new projects, directions, and ideas. Long ago I was given a plaque for working on a statewide sexual abuse training project. The saying on the plaque was, "My work is my passion, pass it on." I have always felt like this—what I do is not just a job, although some aspects are not as exciting as others. I always tell my students, "You are going to work with people that could be my family. I need for you to be good." I expect excellence in myself and others. That is not to say that we do not make mistakes. Mistakes keep us humble and provide an opportunity to learn. Being excited by your work is contagious and leads to others being excited. Working in an environment where people enjoy what they are doing creates energy and is really rewarding and stimulating.

Sometimes women become apprehensive in situations where they are the only female because of gender role issues. Learn to not be easily intimidated —this is important when sometimes the strategy is to intimidate and make you go away quietly. Those who know me know I am tenacious and not afraid to speak out. On the other hand, I like to work collaboratively and am able to compromise. The reality is that sometimes you just are not going to get what you want, and you need to be able to go on without damaging relationships. This is a part of picking and choosing battles. Sometimes you have to strategically plan for the long term if in the short term the answer is "no." I also tend to have my grandmother's stubborn streak of "I will do it in spite of you," which generally serves me well. However, I also believe in the Alcoholics Anonymous saying of "attraction rather than promotion." Doing things well makes others want to join in the success. That is often more effective than continuously arguing or asking for support. Even if you never end up getting all the support you want, you still have a successful program that is meeting an important need.

I have learned that how I react greatly impacts how those who work for me react. Sometimes you just "act as if" it is going to be okay and keep on working to make it so.

I am endlessly optimistic and have seen things come about because I believe that they will and I work to make it happen. This is where creativeness comes into play. I see connections between projects that most others do not see. Once it comes together, it makes sense to others. As I have done this repeatedly, most of my colleagues have come to trust that I have a vision that will make sense at some point even if in the beginning it is somewhat murky. This attitude also fosters and creates a synergy that in turn leads to more creativity and optimism. This is the kind of environment in which it is fun to be a part.

Relevance to Leadership Development

Find a place to work that generally shares your values and supports you in your goals. Working in academia is a good fit for me, especially in social work education, leadership, and administration; there is always something new to get involved with or to problem solve. I enjoy the autonomy of academia and at the same time the opportunity to work collaboratively. Portman and Garrett (2005) write about academia as a good setting for those who embrace empowerment because it promotes harmony and opportunities for all to be successful. It is the antithesis of competition. Being in leadership and administrative positions enables me to impact those areas I feel most passionate about—working with tribal people and cultural competence. I believe and try to practice the ethics of social work in my leadership positions. This includes treating people with dignity and respect, inclusiveness, and so forth (NASW Code of Ethics, 2008, available at http://ncsss.cua.edu/Docs/NASWCodeofEthics.pdf, accessed July 12, 2008).

Because I have been in academia for a while, there are opportunities to mentor others. Being in a more senior position has enabled me to create opportunities for women of color within my department and in the student body. While I sometimes feel a twinge of "I wish I had that when I started," I do try to support these women in a way that I would have liked to have been supported. Sometimes that means taking time to talk with them, inviting them to collaborate on some activity or publication, or simply providing a friendly person with whom to have lunch. Other times, it means reminding others in the department, institution, or profession of our commitment to cultural competence and being a place where everyone feels included and welcome. There is no such thing as a perfect workplace. Challenges will always be present. Recently a world leader was asked if his position was a burden; he said that "it depends on how you frame it, it can be either a burden or an opportunity, I see it as an opportunity." You will always have struggles—the politics of resource allocation, the bureaucracy, and feeling invalidated or unappreciated within the institution may occur. Because of these ongoing struggles, it is important to develop strong support within your department or unit to help weather these outside forces. It is also important to frame these challenges as opportunities.

While we are not perfect, our department is a place where we have these difficult conversations and are committed to creating an inclusive environment. My role has evolved over time from being the only one to raise issues to now having others for whom issues of inclusiveness are also important. This has taken repeated efforts on my part but is paying off in now being joined by other like-minded people. While people and organizations never really "get there," women of color in academia are slowly but surely changing the color of the "ivory tower" in many ways, like shaping teaching and research methods, providing unique leadership styles, and, most important, creating future pathways for those who will follow.

Cultural Factors

I have touched on cultural factors that require further discussion. Situational leadership is one of those areas. In talking about community leadership, Simms (2000:638) describes leadership as "doing what you have to do." She goes on to say, "we don't put people on levels. Momentarily, we rise to the occasion," but when we have played our part, we "sit down" and let others take the lead.

The concept of service is another important concept. Audrey Shenandoah states, "One of our traditional (Onondaga) laws teaches us we are supposed to make things as good as we can" (Mankiller 2004:52). To be on this earth is to seek to find our role in making things better. A leader rises to this challenge.

People often make themselves the center of attention. As a Native person, I have learned the importance of understanding humility. An elder was quoted as saying, "if humans were to drop out of the cycle, the rest of the world would go on and become healthy again" (Mankiller 2004:52). For me, this says it all.

A story that illustrates this is when I became the chair of my department, a Native woman on our social work advisory committee said to me, "Congratulations, you've become a piece of furniture!" These kinds of comments, said in jest, are also a way to keep one humble. Simms (2000:643) says, "In the Indian world, the spirit of the community neutralizes individual power." My grandmother always told us to "never act too proud." What she meant by this is to understand your role as a humble human in this great and wondrous world.

In Native tradition, all work is good work if it serves the common good. A true leader believes this and practices it by being willing to do whatever it takes to make something successful and create a sense of community. Sandy White Hawk stated in an interview that "Indian people look at a leader as someone who does not put themselves above other people but is equal with and equal to and even puts themselves below other people or even behind other folks. . . . status is not achieved by gathering things or having people recognize you for your status as an Indian. . . . if someone is a good leader, you might not recognize him if you were from outside of that community" (Simms 2000:641).

American Indian people laugh a lot. Laughter is a great release when you are stressed. At the end of her life, at age ninety-six, my grandmother moved in with us. A few weeks later, on April 1, we were having breakfast when she said excitedly, "Look, there's deer in the backyard." We all turned to look and she started laughing, saying, "April Fool's Day!" She chuckled about that for a week. Humor can also be useful in the workplace; just remember, humor is culturally based, and sometimes what is funny to one group is not funny to others.

It is an American Indian belief that all Indians have a spiritual connection to the world. Some people would say that all humans have this connection, but our fast-paced lives keep us from acknowledging it. For American Indians who practice their beliefs, spirituality is part of everything, including work and leadership. According to the American Indian Policy Center, American Indian leadership has a spiritual component. Traditional leaders are expected to have a strong spiritual connection. Values, ethics, integrity, honesty, hard work, respect for self and others, and generosity are all spiritually based. As an American Indian leader, it is important to acknowledge and practice spiritual beliefs in all we do. The value of treating others with respect is critically important to leadership, and its core is about honoring the spiritual nature of one's self and others.

Systemic Factors

Portman and Garrett (2005:286) suggest that American Indian women in academia have an "opportunity to develop an insider perspective of the organization and institution where they are employed" to improve their leadership and then have a responsibility to mentor other women who will follow. As mentioned earlier, the role of helping those who come behind you is deeply embedded in Native belief.

One of the biggest areas you may encounter in academia is gender or racial discrimination. When I was hired as a faculty, my dean, who was a woman, told me that as a woman and a person of color, I would have to be better than other faculty when I went up for tenure. Remember that life lesson that life is not fair? Rather than file a grievance, I chose to do my best to insure I would get tenure.

One of the differences I have encountered is in what is seen as important. I am not too into appearance, degrees, status, and the like, but I am into working with my community. When I first started I was told that I would have to focus on research and not be available to the community because it takes time away from other things. In most academic settings, community service and outreach is not valued except if it results in publications. I refused to let my community and cultural connections go. For me, they are the source of my grounding and my strength.

Most American Indian women in academia do not have the support of other Indian women. I was fortunate to start in a department with another American Indian woman who was a tenured faculty. She laid a solid foundation for me to walk upon. I knew that if I needed support, I could count on her. In department meetings and across the university, she provided a role model of standing strong and speaking up on behalf of yourself and others. Portman and Garrett (2005:287) offer that developing American Indian leadership from a traditional perspective includes supporting others through a developmental process of "self-mastery, inner strength, and the development of individual abilities that contribute to the well being of the tribe." Her presence allowed me to learn, grow, and gain confidence.

I also came into a department that had embedded American Indian content into the curriculum and had a commitment to hire Native faculty (28 percent of the department faculty). Those institutional commitments made a huge difference in my experience and opportunities for leadership and administration. Coming into a department that knew something about American Indian history and had institutionalized this commitment made a good path for me to walk upon. This support came about because at one point the social work program was under attack and in danger of being eliminated. The American Indian community came forward and advocated continuing the program's existence as a graduate program. Without this support, the program might have been abolished. It was written into state legislation that the program would have a focus on rural and American Indian communities, which it continues to do. While I doubt that the intent was to provide opportunities to American Indian people for leadership and administrative roles, it has in fact done so. Because of legislation and policy, our program has a "legitimate" focus and therefore structure to require that faculty and department leadership have experience in working with Native communities, again providing opportunities for the leadership advancement of American Indians. If this were not the case, our Equal Opportunity program would not really make a difference in providing those opportunities. One of the most powerful things a leader can do is to institutionalize change. People come and go, but when something is policy or law, it is harder to ignore.

Leadership programs can play a pivotal role in supporting women of color to move into leadership and administration. My doctoral program was run through the Leadership Academy at the University of Minnesota. Because of this focus, we had speakers come in and talk with us about the realities of leadership in higher education. It provided insight into the inner workings of higher education. I also had the opportunity to interact with others in leadership positions who were pursuing advanced degrees. There is great benefit to talking with and interacting with other women of color in leadership and administrative positions. These opportunities also exist by participating on boards in national organizations such as the Council of Social Work Education and National Association of Social Workers.

Life Experiences

There has not been one experience that resulted in my having an epiphany about leadership, but rather a pattern of being in situations where I had ideas that either others expressed before me or were not expressed because I was too uncertain to voice them. Eventually, I found my voice by being around other women who were in leadership and administrative positions. As I began to dare to state my opinion, I found validation. Through this I learned that I could make a difference. American Indians, for the most part, do not seek positions of authority but rather come to leadership and administrative positions in different situations and as their skill set is appropriate.

Leadership is a developmental process. Over many years I developed the skills to lead, and as people started looking to me, I came to believe that I could make a difference. Most women have to learn to be comfortable seeing themselves as a leader and an administrator. For some it is a natural role, based on a personal sense of power, whether in an official position of leadership or not. As an American Indian woman, I believe I have been given and further developed these gifts, and it is my responsibility to use them to assist others. I tell my students that privilege is to be used in the service of others.

Fortunately, I have seen the benefits of good leadership. By that I mean leadership that empowers others; that builds upon the strengths of others. This leadership is transformational and can create change and improve organizations. I believe some leaders are born with natural talents that can be further developed, and that other people have to work hard to develop effective leadership skills. Therefore, if one has natural leadership talent, learn to enhance it by observing others and being patient in developing your own skills. Some things only come with time and experience. While natural talent is a good starting place, we all can learn to be better leaders by observing others and allowing ourselves to take risks and to make mistakes from which we can learn.

Keeping the Movement Alive

It is the obligation of those of us who are in leadership and administrative positions to open paths for those who come behind us, just as those who came before us opened paths for us. To keep this movement alive, I share my experience and provide suggestions or historical context about my own leadership journey to other women and women of color, so that they do not have to repeat some of my mistakes. When I can, I refer women of color to opportunities so that they can get experience and create relationships with others who may be of assistance to them.

Here are some of the ways in which you can create a path for those who will come after us.

- Advocate for women of color to get into positions of leadership and then to support them.
- Take opportunities to include women of color at all levels of social work education—national, regional, state, and local.
- Sit on master's and doctoral committees of women of color and encourage them to pursue leadership positions.
- Recognize your responsibility and be a positive role model for other women of color.
- Network with other women of color and support one another in leadership positions.
- Share your leadership story, including challenges and ways that you kept pursuing your goals in spite of those challenges.
- Stay approachable and share your experiences with generosity.
- Advocate for positions specific to American Indians and other women of color.
- Advocate hiring women of color in faculty positions and support students of color.
- Bring in women of color as speakers/visitors to serve as role models for students.
- Embed cultural competence into curriculum, policy, and the overall environment of your program.
- Take on new challenges in leadership/administration.
- Stay true to your culture and support other women of color to maintain their cultural connections.

While I was talking to a staff person the other day on campus, a white male faculty member from another department came up to me. He put his arm around me and said, "I am so glad to see you—you represent stability in a time when so many people I know are leaving." He is a man who has always been supportive of me and is well respected by Native people. It made me realize that sometimes just the presence of someone over time can make a difference in how women of color are viewed in academia. Sometimes we have to just keep showing up.

Note

Dedicated to my husband, from whom I learn something each day about leadership with dignity; to my children, who are coming behind; and to my mentors, colleagues, and, most of all, my grandmother, Emma (Shawanosekwe)—"Lady Going South"—who left a good path for me to follow.

References

American Indian Policy Center (2000). "American Indian Leadership Report," St. Paul, Minn.

Gipps, D., and G. Gipps (2003). "Chiefs and Visionaries," *Tribal College Journal* 15 (1) (Fall).

Mankiller, W. (2004). *Every Day Is a Good Day: Reflections by Contemporary Indigenous Women.* Golden, Colo.: Fulcrum.

McLeod, M. (2002). "Keeping the Circle Strong." *Tribal College Journal* 13 (4) (Summer).

Orfield, G., et al. (2004). *Losing Our Future: How Minority Youths Are Being Left Behind by the Graduation Rate Crisis.* Cambridge: Civil Rights Project at Harvard University.

Portman, T., and M. T. Garrett (2005). "Beloved Women: Nurturing Leadership from an American Indian Perspective." Invited publication for the *Journal of Counseling and Development: Special Issue on Women and Counseling* 83:284–91.

Simms, M. (2000)."Impressions of Leadership Through a Native Woman's Eyes." *Urban Education* 35 (5) (December).

9

Leadership from an Asian, Christian Perspective at a Small, Private, Rural University

SHARLENE B.C.L. FURUTO

Pursuing Leadership and Administration

Before my thirtieth birthday, with MSW in hand and one year of teaching experience, I found myself the chairperson for the social work program at Brigham Young University Hawaii somewhat by default when my partner in academia left the university. This unplanned opportunity for an administration position occurred without aspiring, pursuing, or "politicking" at a small, faith-based, liberal arts university in a rural setting. Since the mid-1970s I have been the department chairperson more years than not.

In reflection, if I were to draft a blueprint for pursuing a leadership position, I would probably summarize the do's as follows:

1. Start now if you are a student. Do well academically, run for office, lead informally, volunteer and participate, get to know your professors, gain broad experiences, and join social work or university organizations. Keep your grades up so you can get a doctoral degree from the best university you can; meanwhile, be actively engaged and contribute to your social work program so that faculty and students will miss you when you graduate. Then go out and practice social work to the best of your ability—again

doing such a great job that your supervisor and colleagues will miss your leadership and support when you apply for and secure a full-time, permanent teaching position at a university that shares your personal and professional values. Prepare yourself academically and with those experiences that lead to the leadership positions of your dreams.

2. Start now if you are a faculty member. Learn about your status, campus needs, faculty members and administrators, and resources. Again, exert your supreme effort while volunteering for or accepting tasks, being an active team member and supporting others, participating meaningfully in department meetings with innovative ideas that could breathe life into the department (Hess and Cameron 2006), all the while demonstrating basic characteristics such as timeliness, responsibility, dependability, and organization in addition to caring and kindness.

3. Engage with mentors and other successful administrators. Learn from them as much as you can about your university and faculty, how to be promoted, how to fit in and succeed, as well as what leadership positions might be right for you. Ask for their recommendations, referrals, ideas, and opinions.

4. Tentatively identify several leadership positions that interest you and that seem to be right for you. Learn the requirements for those positions in terms of education, experience, skills, years of experience, etc. What else are required for the positions? Are there any personal characteristics or behaviors, such as introvert-extrovert or thinker-feeler, that seem to fit the leadership position? Sometimes when these personal characteristics are manifested during the interview, they could help push your application above the others.

5. Secure job descriptions for those positions from the Human Resources Department or School of Social Work. Assess the "goodness of fit" between the requirements and job descriptions and your extant and potential strengths. What "dormant" strengths do you need to work on?

6. Develop a detailed plan of action to bridge the gap between the requirements and your readiness for that leadership position. Be sure to include specific ways in which to gain the necessary requirements, including a realistic time frame and rewards. For example, if you need more proficiency on the computer, consider enrolling in two computer classes before the end of the school year, and then be sure to celebrate! You may also want to learn about leadership and how to be an effective leader by

attending workshops, reading books, and consulting with others. Or you could sharpen your leadership and organizational skills by being a leader through volunteering to help with fund raising, campaigning, or organizing and advocating for an issue about which you are passionate.

7. Resolutely pursue your plan of action. Keep a copy of your plan of action near your computer, tell others about your plan, use your support system and resources as needed, and work steadily and diligently on your plan. Consider completing your "career mapping" by reflecting on your values and standards, thinking about what you want to do with your career, and planning for your professional legacy.

8. Be the leader you would want to follow. While preparing for that preferred administrative position, actively participate in meetings, introduce innovative ideas, support colleagues, pursue excellence, display visionary characteristics, be a personable team member, use your initiative, and volunteer for tasks and assignments. Continuously assess the situation and select the right style of leadership at the right time for the right situation.

9. Always display your personal best self (Hess and Cameron 2006). While working on your plan of action, keep forming relationships (Hess and Cameron 2006; Joiner and Josephs 2007) and networking with both women and men, learning from mentors, pursuing general knowledge such as sports and technology (Center for Asia-Pacific Women in Politics 1999), and communicating with those who can help you and whom you can help. Two characteristics that can be quite useful while doing daily tasks are resilience and flexibility, keeping in mind that your mode of operation may need to be flexible as the situation warrants. Remain vigilant to what is happening in the department, school, university, state, nation, and world since events near and far impact people, programs, and leadership positions on campus. Whatever you do, do well.

10. Engage in formative evaluation and change! Be rigorous in your regular and frequent self-examination. Determine reasons for limitations but not excuses. Identify changes to initiate, and make these changes in your behavior or beliefs to support your movement into the leadership position (Carter 2007). Be the change you wish to see (Gandhi 1913, Carter 2007). Continue to display your best leadership and make proactive efforts to become an even better administrator. Engage in summative evaluation when the leadership position has been filled. Celebrate if you get the position—celebrate and march on if you do not!

Leading and Administering Successfully

There are a number of personal characteristics that would facilitate successful leadership and administration, many of which are stated cogently by Si Kahn (1991). Several characteristics that I have found to be especially effective include:

- Remembering clearly policies and decisions. If memory is sometimes fuzzy, then record what needs to be remembered and have an administrative assistant who helps you stay on track.
- Networking regularly and frequently with decision makers, non-supporters, and stakeholders. Spend a good part of your time where the movers and shakers gather. If you don't play basketball with the boys at lunchtime, then you will have to find other places where you can informally discuss, debate, and learn. Meet monthly with your boss and have an agenda of achievement and issues on hand.
- Enjoying the opportunity to lead by learning from others, making some decisions alone and others as a team, committing to a position, and following up on issues and decisions.
- Reflecting on staff strengths, status of operations, department limitations, ongoing progress, potential resources, and another perspective on issues.
- Reading and talking with colleagues at other schools about how they address common problems your departments are facing.
- Knowing how to use technology to facilitate administration, communication, research, and teaching.
- Being passionate about your students, faculty and staff, university, and community to keep you going onward.

For some administrators, all of the above come naturally—they seem to have been born leaders—while others they may struggle with some of the characteristics. Certainly nature and nurture both contribute to our makeup; however, generally speaking, I believe that most of us can probably learn well to do the above with practice. It may require some stretching and readjusting for a "quiet" person to speak up and be an active participant in crowded department meetings, but even that can be done with commitment, patience, and practice.

I believe my personal leadership style is relevant for my department as a leader in social work education. My department consists of four full-time Christian social work faculty members, including myself, and the other three members are Caucasian men, one of whom is my age while the other two are young and new to academia. I believe my leadership style, which can probably be described as being more "inclusive, low-keyed, caring delegator seeking consensus" than "singular, center-stage, lukewarm, micromanaging decision maker," fits well with my department members. Rather than usually giving orders, I generally bring order, and rather than grasping for power, I prefer to generate power. I believe in being gentle but firm and brave but prudent. I recognize not only my default preference for a more feminine style of leadership but also my flexibility to include a more masculine style as well.

Being a devout member of the Church of Jesus Christ of Latter-day Saints also impacts my leadership style. I believe that Christ was both the perfect leader (Kimball 1979) and the ideal leader (Lesson 29 2007). As such, I pattern my leadership style after His by basing my leadership on fixed principles, understanding others through patience and love, being selfless, involving others, being accountable, using time wisely, garnering personal potential and the potential of others, and emulating Jesus Christ (Kimball 1979). I also try to follow Him as the ideal leader model by preparing myself, loving the people I lead, basing my leadership on the freedom others have to choose, guiding others by asking them questions, and obeying the ancient and modern commandments (Lesson 29 2007). I have also used the spiritual powers of prayer, revelation, and personal righteousness (Harris 1984) in the workplace. The Latter-day Saint leadership style is readily accepted and even expected on this Mormon campus by both genders and all ethnicities and cultures.

Cultural Factors

There are a number of ways in which my ethnicity and culture impact my leadership style. I am third-generation Japanese and Chinese. My grandparents migrated from Japan and China to Hawaii, and my parents were both born and raised in Hawaii as U.S. citizens. I was born in the middle of the twentieth-century knowing only the English language and being very proud to be "all American and made in Hawaii"; however, it was not until I was a young adult that I realized how Asian I still was on the inside. Many of my behaviors and beliefs were based unknowingly on Confucian philosophy, which is the root of the Chinese culture and later on the Japanese culture as well. For example, one of the four major virtues in Confucianism, *renqing*, refers not only to being kind, benevolent, righteous, or respecting the feelings of other people, but also it is related to a sense of shame that keeps behavior in check. In addition, *renqing* indicates the emotional responses of an individual confronting various situations of daily life (Chhokar, Brodbeck, and House 2007). Chinese are expected to control our anger, hatred, and desire because *renqing* is reciprocal and the golden rule applies. Also, if emotions are uncontrolled, one person if not both will lose face—an absolutely cardinal sin.

My leadership style is more harmony oriented and sometimes indirect. If I must confront someone, I notice that I do so gently at first, to get a reaction, and if that is ineffective then I exert more firmness. Nevertheless, manifesting *renqing*, I leave space for the other person to have an excuse for the missed deadline because this allows him or her to save face—an act we both know is occurring—but with the body language that encourages the other person to honor future deadlines.

Having been born and raised in Hawaii, a state with perhaps the greatest ethnic diversity per capita, I unobtrusively learned the Hawaiian culture during my formative and teenage years. I learned the American culture more openly at church and when attending university. Fortunately, the Hawaiian and Asian cultures are quite similar, but these cultures seemed less congruent with the American culture. As I reflect on my culture, then, I am a product of not only the Hawaiian and Caucasian cultures but also the Church of Jesus Christ of Latter-day Saints and island culture. All these ethnicities and cultures have enriched my life and broadened my leadership style. On a campus that is predominantly Asian–Pacific Islander from both Hawaii and abroad, my mixed ethnicity and cultures has prepared me well for working with these students and faculty members. Repeatedly, I see my group orientation, inclusive and supportive nature, and quiet but effective leadership style generally in focus.

On the other hand, I have had to develop characteristics opposite to the above and have used them as needed. Some situations require the above characteristics while other situations may necessitate different leadership characteristics.

In summary, the cultural leadership paradigms that I feel most comfortable with and that have contributed to my successful leadership and administration would have to include the following:

- From leading and delegating to micromanaging
- From facilitating to giving orders
- From inclusive to exclusive
- From low-keyed to aggressive
- From caring and loving to being cold
- From seeking consensus to being a solo decision maker
- From empowering to limiting
- From Christian to less Christian
- From Confucian to less Confucian
- From being group-oriented to being individual-oriented
- From serving and supporting to being less involved
- From asking the right questions to knowing all the answers
- From being harmony-based to being confrontation-based
- From flexibility to rigidity

Like Pande (2007) and his Six Sigma leadership, I believe a truly effective leader and administrator should have the ability to choose the right approach at the right time, keep in reasonable balance, and avoid putting too much emphasis on either side of the range. I also agree with the Characteristics of Women's Leadership model (Aburdene and Naisbitt 1992) and its six components: empower, restructure, teaching, role model, openness, and questioner.

Systemic Factors

In the last thirty-plus years that I have been on this campus, I have noticed some improvements for women administrators as well as ongoing challenges. In 1975, 13 percent of the seventy-three faculty were women. Of those eleven women, 80 percent were lecturers and assistant professors and 20 percent were professors. None of the central administrators and division chairpersons (equivalent to the deans) was a woman, and usually only I and one or two other department heads were women. The women faculty members were not organized around common issues, communicated very

infrequently with each other, and were not represented on most committees and decision-making circles. The few women on campus were invisible. Central administration made no effort to increase women leaders.
Male and female middle management faculty members were not interested
in mentoring me, and the campus was a fairly lonely place for women.

One thrust women did make in the early 1980s was the beginning of an
annual women's conference on our campus. Since there were few women
on campus, I went off campus and formed a committee of volunteer LDS
women. Together we began what was to become an annual conference for
LDS women in the islands of Hawaii. LDS women statewide wholeheartedly
supported the conference, and a number of women from the other islands
spent several days in the dorms and classrooms learning, sharing, and supporting each other in our roles as Christians, wives, mothers, and women.
While these conferences fulfilled the needs of many LDS community
women, perhaps two ways they helped women faculty members were,
first, by allowing us an opportunity to present a paper and build our re-
sumes for continuing faculty status and promotion and, second, by focusing on women on a campus led predominantly by men.

The campus scene in 2007 was somewhat different, with women making up 21 percent of the 126 full-time faculty members: 21 percent of the
faculty were professors, of which 3 percent were women; 33 percent were
associate professors, of which 4 percent were women; 34 percent were assistant professors, of which 9 percent were women; 4 percent were instructors, of which 3 percent were women; and 6 percent were lecturers, of
which 4 percent were women. One male had no academic rank.

In 2007 ethnic minority women, specifically Asian or Pacific Island
women, made up 9 percent of all faculty members. Furthermore, women
comprised 14 percent of central administration, 0 percent of deans, and 27
percent of department heads.

In 2006 women administrative staff and faculty organized and established the Academic Women's Network. The mission of AWN is to address
the concerns of women administrative staff and faculty as well as gender-
specific issues across campus and beyond through networking and mentoring. AWN participants are committed to promoting the accomplishments of our colleagues in their research, creative work, teaching, service,
and administration. Central administration supports AWN and under-
wrote training and conference attendance for four women faculty members in the past year.

Despite the increase of female faculty members and the efforts of AWN, there are many lingering barriers for women faculty members. We still need to communicate more frequently, regularly, and meaningfully with each other. A lunch bunch is scheduled to start meeting monthly, and an exercise group looks to be in the making per my suggestion; nevertheless, we women still need to meet and mingle with the men.

Another enduring barrier is low representation on a number of committees and in decision-making circles. Customarily at least one woman sits on the Continuing Faculty Status (similar to tenure)/Promotion Review Committee and the Faculty Advisory Council. This year there is no woman representative on the latter. We need women representatives at least on all significant committees. Getting women on significant committees could be a task for AWN.

Some men are open to women's concerns, and some women are taking on direct and indirect advocacy roles. We need to teach boys to respect and seek the input of girls, and we need to teach girls to make recommendations in the classroom and at home. The most understanding and supportive dean I have had was a gentleman who was married to a social work academician. We need to cultivate more minds to see the needs and power of not only men but also women.

Thirty years ago my strategy for overcoming challenges consisted of basic survival by being a "nice, quiet, Japanese girl." After a few years of ignoring the obnoxious attacks of a colleague degrading me for being a "woman social work teacher with an Ed.D.," I finally grew up and stood up. I practiced in the mirror numerous times and finally told him as strongly and loudly as I could that I did not appreciate his belittling remarks and that I never wanted to hear them again. He laughed—I maintained my immovable position—and he stopped violating me. Since then, he has treated me with respect, and he publicly seeks my ideas.

Today I speak my mind. Today I hear my voice even though it may be a solo recommendation. What has happened in the last thirty years? I do not think it was mentorship since I had no formal or informal mentor. I do not think it was collegiality because there were few colleagues who stood with me. I did little networking in my early years, but I did make concerted efforts to increase my relationships as time passed. I did not enroll in formal education and training in leadership and administration, but I did spend three weeks as a group facilitator helping female college students become leaders. Part of the program consisted of listening to a number of top-level women leaders in our nation's capital, and that helped broaden my perspective of women in leadership positions.

My institution has the same strategies, policies, and supports for the advancement of not only my career and the careers of other women but also the careers of men. The university makes available to all faculty members competitive funds for research purposes, conference expenses, and publication costs. In the past I have received professional development funds to conduct research projects in Samoa, Tonga, Fiji, and Hawaii; present research findings at national and international conferences; attend select conferences and workshops; take students to Cambodia for three weeks to learn about poverty and the Cambodian social welfare, economic, educational, and health systems and do service learning; and publish two books and a number of chapters and journal articles. These professional development funds, of course, have enabled me to be actively engaged in creative endeavor, with the ultimate result of being promoted whenever I have applied.

We as a university would probably do well to make leadership programs available to our faculty members. A good proportion of our faculty members seem to be under forty, and a leadership program could be beneficial to them directly and the university and student body indirectly. I recently proposed this idea to my fellow department chairpersons at the College of Arts and Sciences meeting and intend to follow up when I meet with the dean of the college.

Professional social work organizations could well support women faculty members by offering leadership workshops at conferences or online. "How to Progress in a Male Dominant University" workshop could help conference attendees from small colleges that have few women mentors.

Today I am a full professor and have been for about the last two decades. In reflecting how I learned to be a leader and administrator, part of it came from teaching social work concepts such as advocacy, social justice, networking, self-assessment, organizing, and lobbying and then modeling what I taught in the classroom and office and at home, in church, and in my community. Applying what I was teaching and accomplishing my goals testified to me of their validity and solidified these behaviors and beliefs in my life wisdom. In addition, living for the last thirty years and encountering a number of empowering as well as difficult situations have helped open my eyes to who I am, what I fight passionately for, and where I intend to leave my legacy.

Life Experiences

Throughout my professional career, I have made a resolute effort to serve. I feel that I have been served by many who came before me and am responsible to reciprocate for those yet to come. The realization that there is a plethora of leadership positions in professional organizations, community associations and organizations, and church positions and the insufficient number of eager servants made a major impact on my drive to serve and lead. At times I appreciated what the leaders had done to further the cause, and at other times I sat back disappointed in the half-hearted effort of my leader and strategized how I would have done it "better." I knew I had to run for office, be appointed, or simply volunteer.

I was not much of a leader in high school or college. As far as I am concerned, I was probably one of the common citizens Paul Rogat Loeb described in *Soul of a Citizen*—an everyday person who felt strongly about an issue. My early experiences at leadership occurred at church. Then I began teaching social work and became involved in the National Association of Social Workers Hawaii Chapter as chairperson of numerous committees and offices, eventually becoming president in 1988–1990 when Hawaii gained licensure. My last two major positions on the national level with NASW were as the Asian-Pacific Islander American Caucus chairperson from 2000 to 2004 and prior to that as a member of the national Board of Directors from 1997 to 2000. On the local level, I have been the chairperson or member of the Committee on Inquiry since 1991. My leadership with the Council on Social Work Education has not been as extensive, but I did sit on the Commission on Educational Planning from 1987 to 1989.

I have also been active in the national Asian Pacific Island Social Work Educators Association since 1985 as the secretary, treasurer, and/or CSWE symposium chair or cochair. We meet annually at the CSWE annual program meeting.

As my four children were growing up in the 1980s, I felt an especially strong commitment to my community as well and kept active as a Girl Scout leader, soccer team mom, Boy Scout counselor, Parent Teacher Organization president, and American Businesswoman Association officer.

Today I am a charter board member for the International Consortium for Social Development Asia-Pacific Region, national treasurer for the Asian Pacific Islander Social Work Educators Association, and member of the NASW Hawaii chapter Committee on Inquiry and of my community association.

Being actively engaged in the above organizations gave me ample opportunity to observe and learn from the leadership styles of both men and women, some of which I have incorporated in my own leadership and lifestyle. Working with others on common issues has also allowed me to learn how others think, analyze issues, use resources and technologies, collaborate, chair meetings, and resolve challenges. I have also been able to stay abreast of the changing profession and community, and this has helped me remain accurate when representing both the social work education perspective and the community perspective to the public. A major advantage of being in a leadership position is that I have had access to some knowledge that is not commonly known to the priority group I serve— BSW students—and I have been able to thus empower them with information about social work education, funds for graduate school, opportunities for learning in the community, etc. My students, family, church members, community, profession, and I have been the beneficiaries of my leadership experiences.

In addition to suggestions given earlier, the last note I would submit to students, faculty, and others in terms of developing as a well-rounded and effective leader and administrator is to gather information relevant to your situation, develop a realistic plan of action that leads to leadership and administration roles you would be comfortable having, and then living your plan. Enjoy what you do, laugh and celebrate along the way, and always look forward.

Keeping the Movement Alive

My small university of 2,400 students has students from seventy countries and is the most diverse university per capita in the United States. I believe I play several key roles while fulfilling my responsibilities to promote the movement to advance women of color in leadership and administration. As an advocate who sat on the university Admissions Committee, Faculty Advisory Council, and Continuing Faculty Status/Promotion

Review Committee, I have had opportunities to speak for equality and fairness for both women and men. As a faculty advisor and teacher, I have many opportunities to talk with female ethnic students and encourage them to continue their education beyond the bachelor's degree, consider seriously leadership positions in addition to direct services, and keep doors of opportunity open to politics and leadership in both professional and community organizations. As a model, I feel responsible to behave in a professional yet friendly way and to speak positively about my leadership positions in the department, university, and profession with students and others.

Currently, as the social work program chairperson, I am able to do the following to perpetuate the cycling of women of color into leadership and administration positions: (1) hire, work directly with, and mentor ethnic female social work student workers doing social work administrative assignments to prepare them for leadership positions; (2) encourage ethnic female students in my classes to graduate and continue on for their MSW and doctoral degrees, with practice experience in between; (3) plant the idea in ethnic women students to one day apply for faculty positions on this or another campus; (4) advise, teach, and mentor the Social Work Student Association officers, of whom about half are ethnic women, how to be effective leaders; (5) require that one workshop in the department-sponsored annual social work conference be devoted to leadership training for social work majors in general, with breakout sessions separated by gender; and (6) conduct research or creative endeavors with ethnic women students and inspire them to leadership positions.

As a mother, church member, and community resident, I do the following to help women of color move into leadership and administration positions: (1) teach my own children, extended family members, and community contacts to respect and support women as leaders; (2) teach, advise, and model for my daughter and female relatives leadership styles; (3) promote the leadership paradigm that includes both masculine and feminine styles and attributes; (4) include in the leadership paradigm room for retaining one's unique culture, identities, and values while developing new and vital skills for effective leadership; (5) encourage women and men to transform any values and attitudes that perpetuate traditional gender stereotypes to those values and attitudes that support equality, fairness, and social justice for women; (6) advocate and lobby formally and informally for the political agenda that promotes the feminine welfare on the local, national, and international levels; and (7) encourage women to learn how to use technology to further their goals and/or to get a degree.

Finally, there is a place for spirituality in teaching leadership skills and qualities. In my case, parents and adult leaders are encouraged to prepare both young men and women to be the fathers, mothers, and church leaders of tomorrow. LDS church programs require "shadow leadership" from adults as they help the youth teach lessons during family home evening, lead a family discussion, plan a family activity, or carry out church activities with their peers in Sunday school classes and youth/young adult activities. Youth and young adults are encouraged to follow Christ's example, develop character traits of a leader, and fulfill the tasks of a leader ("Teaching Leadership" 2007).

In conclusion, there are a number of strategies for pursuing one's aspiration to a leadership position, some of which were mentioned in this chapter. We who have been leaders are responsible for facilitating the development and entry of new female, ethnic leaders into the profession, community, and world. We current leaders are perhaps in the most opportune position for advancing feminine leadership through our own advocacy as we teach and mentor the leaders of tomorrow in our endeavors toward social justice for both clients and professionals.

References

Aburdene, P., and J. Naisbitt, J. (1992). *Megatrends for Women*. New York: Villard Books.

Carter, L. E. (2007). "Global Ethical Leadership and Higher Education: "Being the Change You Wish to See. In *For the Common Good: The Ethics of Leadership in the 21st Century*, ed. J. C. Knapp. Westport, Conn.: Praeger.

Center for Asia-Pacific Women in Politics (1999). "Panel III Political Empowerment of Women: Issues in Women's Political Empowerment in the Asia-Pacific Region." Symposium conducted at the Economic and Social Commission for Asia and the Pacific High-Level Intergovernmental Meeting to Review Regional Implementation of the Beijing Platform for Action, Bangkok, Thailand.

Chhokar, J. S., F. C. Brodbeck, and R. J. House (2007). *Culture and Leadership Across the World: The Globe Book of In-depth Studies of 25 Societies*. Mahaw, N.J.: Erlbaum.

Gandhi, M. (1913). *Indian Opinion*. Durban, South Africa: International Printing Press.

Harris, D. (1984). "Spiritual Power." *Ensign* 26–28 (November).

Hess, E. D., and K. S. Cameron, eds. (2006). *Leading with Values: Positivity, Virtue, and High Performance*. New York: Cambridge University Press.

Joiner, B., and S. Josephs (2007). *Leadership Agility: Five Levels of Mastery for Anticipating and Initiating Change*. San Francisco: Jossey-Bass.

Kahn, S. (1991). *Organizing: A Guide for Grassroots Leaders*. Silver Springs, Md.: NASW Press.

Kimball, S. W. (1979). "Jesus: The Perfect Leader." *Ensign* 6–9 (August).

Lesson 29: Developing Leadership. (2007). *The Latter-day Saint Woman: Basic Manual for Women, Part B*, 247. Salt Lake City: Church of Jesus Christ of Latter-Day Saints.

Loeb, P. R. (1999). *Soul of a Citizen: Living with Conviction in a Cynical Time*. New York: St. Martin's Griffin.

Pande, P. (2007). *The Six Sigma Leader: How Top Executives Will Prevail in the 21st Century*. New York: McGraw-Hill.

"Teaching Leadership Principles to Youth." (2007). *Guidebook for Parents and Leaders of Youth*, 27–28. Salt Lake City: Church of Jesus Christ of Latter-Day Saints.

10

Women, Leadership, and Power

If You Are Going to Wear the Pants, Do It in High Heels

MARIA E. PUIG

You get to know who can lead in a crisis, and, whether fortunately or unfortunately, I have had to deal with many crises in my lifetime. I am not sure if these experiences prepared me for the various leadership positions I have held throughout my professional career, but I cannot deny that these crises certainly helped to shape the woman I am and the leader I became. Not perfect, not always at my best, but certainly someone who was never afraid to take risks, stand up for what I believed, or "bite the bullet" and do whatever necessary to get the job done—correctly and well.

As best as I can remember, my first crisis came when my parents sent my older brother and me to the United States, as unaccompanied minors, after the Cuban missile crisis and the Bay of Pigs invasion. Finding ourselves in a foreign country, not knowing anyone, not knowing the language or where we were going to live and with whom, was certainly a crisis. However, much to my surprise—although at the time I had not realized it—my parents had raised us both extremely well. We knew to rely on each other and to be there for one another. We also knew that if we were going to survive this crisis, we had to be smart and strong.

A few years later I watched my mother and father come to this country, penniless and scared. They had willingly given up everything they had ever had, including the extended family they would never see again, so that my brother and I could live in this country. While both my parents returned to school to rebuild their professional careers, my father as a doctor and my mother as an attorney, I watched them work at whatever jobs they could find; my father delivering the *Miami Herald* and my mother working as a maid. That taught me perseverance, determination, and to have the courage to do anything and do it well in order to achieve a greater goal.

During my undergraduate studies at Florida State University, my father became quite ill, and this was another major crisis in my life. The two of us had always shared a very special bond; you might say he was not just my father, but my best friend and role model. Watching my father battle colon cancer and, a few years later, a major stroke that left him paralyzed and unable to speak, walk, or eat taught me valor and determination. For over a year my father endured this situation, having to be fed through a tube while being cared for by my mother and me. His positive attitude and continued love throughout this crisis taught me how a person's character and strength can still make your soul soar. Watching my father die a very slow death during the next year of my life taught me that I, too, was incredibly strong.

My next crisis occurred in my thirties, when, quite unexpectedly, I was diagnosed with cancer. To say that I walked out of my doctor's office in a daze is the ultimate understatement. It was more like I was on automatic pilot, a zombie, who somehow managed to drive home and then collapse. The most difficult part of this crisis was figuring out how I was going to tell my mother. We had lost my father two years earlier, and having to tell my mother I had cancer was the hardest thing I have ever done. Somehow, this crisis forced me to "pull up my big girl panties" and go forward. Fortunately, my cancer was caught early, at stage 1, and after major surgery I am happy to say that I have lived seventeen years cancer free and medically "cured."

However, the most challenging crisis I have ever faced was still to come. My mother was the most incredible woman I have ever known. She was intelligent, capable, strong as steel, with a great character and determination. My mother was our family's strength, protector, guide, and leader. Growing up with a woman who was both brilliant and strong but yet full of love and compassion was the best gift I have ever been given. And, all of a sudden, this beautiful and strong woman was dying. In 2003 I took a leave of absence from my position at Colorado State University to move back to

Miami to care for her. My mother had been diagnosed with terminal liver cancer, and doctors did not know how much longer she would live. Part of my dealing with the news was to deny that my mother was dying. Not my mother; not this pillar of strength who would do anything to protect and care for her family. I always thought my father had been my strength, but the reality was that it had always been my mother. To all of a sudden be faced with the certainty that she would no longer be there was my Achilles heel. I had never before felt, and probably will never again feel, quite so lost, weak, afraid, and totally alone. I watched my mother die on March 5, 2004. Somehow I survived another crisis. Which brings me to the present and to the first question: how did I pursue leadership and administration as I journeyed in my career?

Pursuing Leadership and Administration

My journey began quite normally, really. I started out my career as an entry-level case worker, working for the state of Florida, Department of Health and Rehabilitative Services, Department of Children, Youth, and Families. I was so happy to have been hired, considering I did not have a degree in social work and never before had done this type of work. Nevertheless, I talked my way into getting hired by convincing everyone that I could do the job. I wanted to work with kids, particularly kids who were in trouble and had pretty much been written off by their parents and society. I loved my kids, with all their warts and problems, and I loved the profession I was learning about. As often happens, your career begins to take shape, sometimes consciously and sometimes not. For me, this meant going back to graduate school to earn my MSW degree, and realizing that I wanted to pursue leadership and administrative positions within my agency.

Unlike many social workers who see themselves in direct practice positions throughout their careers, I never did. I wanted to be part of the group who not only had the responsibility for making decisions, but also had the ability and power to shape those choices. Administration became my second passion, and I quickly worked my way to the top. From my first entry-level case worker position, I was promoted to a case worker II position, then to unit supervisor, and then made a lateral move to work in the Department of Children, Youth, and Families (CYF) Program Office as a policy analyst. After working as a policy analyst for a year I returned to adminis-tration and management, as direct services supervisor responsible for child welfare operations—foster care, protective services, and adoptions—in the northern part of Dade County, Florida. My next upward move came soon thereafter, now moving into senior or upper management as the operations and management director for CYF in my district. I also went on to become the operations and management director for the Refugees and Entrant Program Office for District XI during the Mariel Cuban boatlift.

Soon afterwards I left the state to work for Dade County government as the division director for all juvenile services. I continued my work in Dade County for several more years until 1991, when I accepted a job at Florida International University's School of Social Work as the director of the Title IV-E MSW Program. It was during this time that I returned to school to pursue my Ph.D. degree in social work, which eventually led to my move to Colorado State University in 1996, when I was hired as an assistant pro-fessor. I earned tenure and was promoted to associate professor in 2001, and six years later I became the first leadership fellow in the School of Social Work. Currently I am the assistant director of the School of Social Work, which is a great position because it gives me the best of both worlds: I can continue teaching and working with students, while also fulfilling many challenging administrative responsibilities. Outside of my work at Colo-rado State University, I serve as a member of the CSWE Commission on Diversity and Social and Economic Justice, and I was the president of the Association of Latino Social Work Educators for four years.

If there was a blueprint for pursuing a leadership position, I would rec-ommend to the younger generation that they must first find their passion. Without passion, you will do your job, and that should never be acceptable or good enough. Passion will drive you to work harder and longer, and to take risks because you are doing what you believe in. Allow your passion to guide you, as it will take you to new levels that you may never have thought you could achieve. Although my first passion was always to work with and on behalf of kids, my passion for being an administrator was always a close second. I knew that in order to really help my kids, I had to be in a leadership position.

The third part of my "blueprint" plan involved having mentors. Often, many of my students ask what was the one factor that facilitated my pur-suit of leadership and administrative positions. Without hesitation I tell them it was having mentors who helped forge my career. Every new professional needs a mentor. Mentors helped to expose me to the inner workings of the organizations for which I worked. They taught me the written and unwritten rules that can often help or cripple a person's career. Mentors encouraged and protected me; they also opened doors and kept me in the background when it was not safe for me to be upfront. They guided, but they also provided me with countless opportunities where I could be challenged and learn. It was easy for me to develop the leadership "bug," as they slowly nurtured my talents and skills. Women, in particular, need to realize that no one has all the skills necessary to become a leader. Hard work and passion for what you are doing will get you recognized. Willingness to fail and learn will also get you accepted as a potential leader because we all—men and women—make mistakes. I certainly did. And they were some doozies! I am very open and honest with my students, so I let them know that I was fired a couple of times along the way.

Another component of my plan included being willing to take on extra assignments so that I would benefit from working with other administrators and leaders in the organization. These extra assignments not only taught me more about my job and the organization but also provided me and others in leadership positions with a way to see what else I was capable of doing. In a large and complex organization with thousands of employees, the more known you are as an entity, the more opportunities you will create for yourself. The message here is to not shy away from new possibilities, as these will open doors for you later on in your career. As I applied for and was promoted to progressively higher administrative positions, often the men and women who were doing the interviews and the hiring were people in the organization with whom I had previously "volunteered" to work. I know that there were times I got the promotion because they remembered me from situations where I had been a member of their team working on that extra assignment.

I would also remind young women that if they choose to pursue leadership and administrative positions, they need to be realists and recognize that there will be barriers. Even now, there will be social, organizational, and even peer-created barriers. Although women have made tremendous progress in the past twenty-five years, organizations can still be difficult places of employment, and men and women can still be hard on one another. You will be criticized; sometimes by other women, and sometimes by men. You may even run into women who will try to make it difficult for you. As frequently as women are supportive and part of the "sisterhood," equally often they are each other's worst enemies. For all the progress women have made, they can still get bitten by the jealousy bug, and then their competitive instincts take over. Not always, and certainly not with all women colleagues, but it can and does happen, so keep your eyes and ears wide open. Remember the saying, "keep your friends close but your enemies closer." It really does pay to follow that philosophy.

It would be dishonest if I did not acknowledge that the majority of my mentors were men. Twenty-plus years ago there were not many women in leadership positions, and those that were protected their place in the organization. Some stepped up to groom and mentor up-and-coming younger women. Others did not. For me, the alternative was to seek male mentors and avoid that whole woman-against-woman trap. However, I must caution the reader, particularly if you are a young woman, and remind you that what worked and felt right for me may not work or be right for you. The mentorship relationship is quite special and unique, and each of you will have to figure out what you need and want out of it. Even now, although there are many, many women in leadership positions, I still have an inclination and preference to be mentored by men. It fits my leadership and administrative style, as well as my temperament and personality. Readers need to know that I have been criticized severely for admitting that I seek and prefer male mentors. However, I hope that everyone remembers that this is about *my* journey and *my* truth.

Leading and Administering Successfully

Personal Factors

In describing the personal characteristics and factors that contributed to my success, I have to say that it was believing that I could do anything, while rejecting the notion that I could do or be less. Every now and then, someone will tell me that my confidence borders on fierceness. I certainly did not want it to be perceived that way, but I also would not apologize for it either. Growing up with both a strong mother and strong father, but particularly, a very capable and strong mother, the thought that I could not do something I really wanted rarely crossed my mind (except excelling in statistics—ugh!). I truly believed that you are limited only when you believe and accept that you are.

I grew up with parents who were so far ahead in their "parenting" that occasionally I would say to my friends I either had the craziest set of parents or the best. Nothing in between. My parents encouraged my brother and me to be critical thinkers, to voice our opinions, and to back up those opinions with facts. We were also confident to challenge what others said and what we heard or read. Both our parents took us to work, light years ahead of the time it became "in" to take your daughters or sons to work. They believed that exposing us to their work and careers would broaden our understanding of them as people. It also showed us that they had other roles, lives, and personal interests besides that of being our parents. My parents talked to us as adults and never belittled our ideas or goals. As a little girl I wanted to be a doctor and follow in my father's footsteps, so he took me into surgery and let me watch him operate. Similarly, I would accompany my mother to her office and to court.

With parents like mine, the focus, needless to say, was on education and hard work. They instilled in me a love of reading and learning and a willingness to try new things. My parents also allowed me to fail because failure teaches you to get up, to try again, and to dust off your disappointments. I have not always succeeded, but I have always gotten up to try again. I now try to instill similar values in my students: to be lifelong learners, to think for themselves, to question, and to always try and try again.

Going back to what I mentioned earlier about being a mentor and the need for mentors, I believe that it is really important for women in leadership positions to mentor other women. Part of being a responsible and effective mentor, though, requires encouragement and feedback that lets the person you are mentoring know when she or he could be doing something better. Even when the feedback you receive is negative, and I would be lying if I did not say it hurts, it can still help to make you a better leader and administrator.

As young women, as you explore and assume leadership and administrative positions, learn to develop your own style. For me, it meant being very comfortable with power and my ability to exercise that power, without losing my own feminine identity. At a time when women leaders dressed in manly suits and imitated men who were leaders, I was the complete opposite. I wore skirts and dresses and the highest heels I could find. I still do. I have never believed that in order to be taken seriously as a woman in a leadership position, I had to buy into the idea that power and womanliness are mutually exclusive. They are not! Also, do not let anyone make you feel that because you are a woman, and a powerful woman at that, you are ruthless or pushy. I speak very softly and, most of the time, gently, but no one mistakes the change of tone in my voice when I mean business or when I am upset.

Cultural Factors

Were there cultural factors that impeded or encouraged my desire to become a leader? My answer would be maybe. As a Hispanic woman brought up in a somewhat traditional Hispanic home, I have to say that my culture neither impeded nor encouraged my abilities or desire to occupy leadership positions. In some ways I am also a cultural anomaly. From the time I was a little girl, I said I was going to be a doctor, lawyer, businesswoman, or the "boss" of something. I do not ever recall saying that I wanted to have children or to even be married—although I am. Culturally, I know these ideas do not quite fit the norm.

I also do not think, based on my experiences, that my ethnicity, race, or gender affected my professional choices or pursuit of leadership and administrative positions. There were many jobs I got and others I did not. However, I do not remember sitting around and thinking or feeling that I got the job or did not get it because I was a Hispanic woman. I also have to temper what I am saying and underscore the fact that for many other Hispanic women, and women of color, their experiences may have been totally different. Certainly, many of them may have been denied opportunities based on these factors. The truth is that I do not look or act like an intelligent Hispanic woman (whatever that is). I look and act like a confident, intelligent woman. I am also the type of person that has never thought of herself as an ethnic minority or a victim. I firmly believe the minute you think that way, you are treated like a victim.

It goes without saying that I am proud of my Cuban heritage, my culture, and my *Hispanidad*. I do not flaunt or hide it; it is what it is, and I will continue to embrace it.

Systemic Factors

Organizations are social institutions that do for humankind what individuals cannot do on their own. Organizations, however, are run by men and women and therefore are fallible and problematic, chaotic, obtrusive, effective, ineffective, and difficult to change. We cannot live with them or without them. Women, working in these environments, can and do face systemic problems that are difficult to challenge or change. Every fabric of an organization fights change, and the only way it happens is when all the stars have aligned to make it happen. We can legislate change and have done so over the past forty years, but legislation does not change the way certain people think, feel, and even behave.

Women have to remember that organizations are complex and that policies and procedures, particularly the "unwritten ones," are cloaked in ways that most people do not notice what may be going on. Women, then, have to be smarter and able to look at the problem, figure out how to break it down to its most minute detail, and tackle each part in a systemic and logical approach. We have all heard about glass ceilings and glass walls and now even glass elevators. But the biggest systemic barrier women, particularly younger women, still face deals with the "mommy-track" issue.

I remember some of my women colleagues not applying for positions they were highly qualified and educated for because they wanted to have a baby. It was not that the organization would have denied them maternity leave or job security. It was because they knew that if they accepted the promotion, they would have to compromise how much time they could give to their roles as mothers. In some circles this problem still exists. In others, organizations are stepping up and providing in-house day care and flexible schedules, or even job sharing so that moms (and dads) can continue with their careers while fulfilling their roles as parents.

In my case, when I was in my late twenties and thirties, the organizations in which I worked knew I was not going to have children. It was not because I had stamped that message on my forehead. The organization knew because of the jobs and assignments I accepted. If truth be known, I also believe I was rewarded for the decision to not have children. There were certainly other women equally if not better prepared to assume some of the positions for which I was hired and to which I was promoted. However, I was willing to travel at a moment's notice; I could be gone on an assignment weeks at time or stay in the office working until eight or nine in the evening and on weekends without having to rush home to take care of the children. Was that fair? No, but it was the reality of the times, and it may still be in some organizational settings.

Organizations also expect that as you progress, you will continue your education. There are administrative positions that will always require having an advanced degree, in combination with hands-on experience. A strategy I used and encourage other women to use is to benefit from any tuition reimbursement program their organization provides. I earned my MSW degree while working full time, but the state of Florida paid for the majority of my tuition. It saved me from having to take out loans, and all I had to do was to continue working for the state a few more years. It was a win-win situation for both. I also took advantage of training, seminars, and other learning opportunities, as these provided learning possibilities and also chances to network with others in the organization.

Networking is an art; it is all about learning how to talk with people effectively, while "selling" yourself. The art part comes in by not looking like you are trying too hard to sell yourself. Women have become very effective at networking and creating networks of their own. Networking also facilitates mentoring and the forging of new friendships that can help young professional women grow and become more effective leaders. Networking can also lead to the development and implementation of leadership programs that can further women's skills, knowledge, and confidence in the workplace. I have participated in and been the beneficiary of several leadership fellowships, and through these programs increased my abilities and knowledge of the organizations in which I worked. Networking and leadership programs also encourage diversity in the organization, which continues to be more and more important. Diversity is necessary, not just because it is the right thing to do, but because it is the right thing for organizations to do. Having said that, I would like to add this caveat for any networking program women may undertake. I would recommend that you also include men in your networking attempts and programs. They are part of any organizational structure, and the sooner women learn to effectively work with and communicate with male colleagues, the better we will be at climbing the organizational ladder.

Part of networking also involves our participation in social work organizations, such as the National Association of Social Workers, the Council on Social Work Education, and the Association of Baccalaureate Social Work Program Directors. These professional organizations historically have given many women opportunities to develop their leadership and administrative skills, and we should all continue supporting their efforts in these areas.

Life Experiences

It goes without saying that we are all products of our life experiences. As you can tell by my previous discussions about my parents and family, they played the most significant role in my life. Although I may innately have had the talent and desire to become a leader and administrator, the confidence to pursue this goal was rooted in my upbringing and related life experiences. Personal confidence plays such an important role, not only in the way you see yourself, but in the way others see you. The two are inextricably connected. Confidence led me to pursue every dream I have ever had, and confidence also buoyed me when I failed. My advice to students and young women starting out is to do things that will help develop your confidence and then tackle other challenges that will test your boundaries and make you grow. Every small step along the way will help you to see how talented and skillful you are, and I believe that confidence begets success and even more confidence. It is kind of like the chicken or the egg argument. Were you successful because you were confident, or did confidence bring on your success? It is probably a combination of the two.

I also would advise young women to maintain a personal life that is truly yours and apart from your professional one. Sometimes you need that separation, that space, so that you allow family and friends to become just as important as your career to your overall well-being. I am guilty of letting my professional life take precedence over my personal one, and it cost me dearly. My first marriage ended in divorce because I put my career and my ambitions ahead of my husband and marriage. I also let my extended family down on many occasions because it was more important to be at work on the weekends than to be enjoying a family dinner with them. Looking back, and I have only a few regrets, I would give anything if I had spent more time with my mother and father and less time in the office. Because we all learn from our mistakes, and because I am older and hopefully a little wiser, my second marriage is more important to me than any career or job I could ever have. I am no longer pursuing the next ring on the ladder, the ultimate high-power job. Been there; done that. What I now value more than anything else is my time and freedom, and, most important, the balance between my personal and professional life. To all the young women pursuing the "dream," learn to keep that balance. That is the only way all of your successes will truly be sweet.

Keeping the Movement Alive

The best way that I can help to "keep the movement alive" is to be the best teacher and mentor that I can to my students. I love being a professor and getting to know all my students. The best part of having this career is the times when students come and talk about their goals and dreams, and you reminisce about your life when you were in the same position and state of mind. There is a certain naiveté students bring that I believe you should not shatter. Let them enjoy it while they can.

To all the young women who want to pursue leadership and administrative careers, I hope you will always remember that I am here to help you and to be by your side to support and look after you. You will be amazed at how comfortably you will fall into the role of woman leader. I was always blown away that I had that job and felt incredibly lucky to have had a wonderful administrative and leadership career.

My last piece of advice is that you begin with yourself and do the things you need to do to become the best person—not just woman—you can be. You will have a better and greater chance of changing the world if you do.

Note

Like most good efforts, this chapter comes from my heart and mind. It has taken me most of my adult life to understand and appreciate the love, nurturing, and sense of security and confidence my parents instilled in me. I dedicate this chapter to both of them, but particularly, to my mother. You were and will always be my source of strength, my role model, and the most loving and caring mother any young woman could ever have had.

To both my parents: Gracias, por todos los sacrificios que hicieron por nosotros, pero mas que nada, por el carinoy y el sentido de seguridad que siempre nos dieron.

11

American Indian Women and Administration

Once Upon a Time

JOYCE Z. WHITE

Once upon a time, storytelling "was the medium through which people learned their history, settled their arguments, and came to make sense of the phenomena of their World" (NCTE 1992). For American Indian people, stories are a way of teaching. Children may not hear admonitions, but they remember stories. My grandmother told me many. They stressed perseverance, hard work, and the gifts of our traditions. No one in my family had completed high school. Her dream was that I would get my diploma, work in an office, and be protected from the hard life that had been hers. Her stories made her dreams mine.

It was a long way from her kitchen to where I am now, looking out my window across the soft green of our campus, and where I am director of a school of social work. In looking back, what can I identify that will help other women who have limited access to opportunity, education, and mentoring move beyond the boundaries that hold them back?

Muller (1998:36) notes that "culture is an integral factor in understanding people and organizations . . . racial-ethnicity and historical processes influencing the position of people in organizations today needs to be addressed." Three-fourths of American Indian women in senior administrative and leadership positions are employed in government, education, or by a tribe. Few enter the private sector. American Indian women are disadvantaged in the pursuit of leadership roles because American Indians in general are disadvantaged in society. Poverty, family dysfunction, low expectations, negative attitudes, and stereotypes affect access to education, employment, career advancement, and wages. A 1991 study of 115 American Indian female managers in education found that the majority are seen first as Indian even in non-Indian situations (Warner 1991). In addition, these women often had to cope with patriarchal views held by American Indian men—a legacy of centuries of colonialism. Because men and women tend to have different paths to leadership roles, women may not be encouraged or prepared to seek leadership roles (Amodeo and Emslie 1985). Muller (1998) in a survey of American Indian women leaders found that most supervised employees were also members of minority groups of color, typically American Indian or Latino. Half the women managers were the first in their families to have gone to college and the first in their organizations to have a higher-level position.

American Indian social workers in a study by Weaver (2000) reported painful experiences of racism, isolation, intimidation, and demands to adapt to the dominant culture. In the academic world, they experienced discrimination from faculty and students alike. American Indians tended to be at the lowest faculty ranks and were less likely to receive tenure and promotion than any other minority group of color (Schiele and Francis 1996).

Tammy Trucks-Bordeaux writes from a Native American woman's perspective in *Academic Massacres*, which explores her experiences as an Indian student attending a midwestern state university. She writes, "had I known that the eight hundred mile journey from my home . . . meant plunging into a world void of the faces, culture and beliefs so dear to my own, I would never have left" (2003:416.). This sense of alienation and discrimination is a recurrent theme in the anecdotal accounts and literature by and about American Indian women professionals. Voss et al. (1999) summarize that what is seen as appropriate and confident behavior in the dominant culture is based on high evaluation of the individual.

American Indian nations differ in language, beliefs, and even family structure. However, there are similarities across groups. The traditional American Indian worldview is that the well-being and harmony of the group takes precedence over wishes of the individual. Family and kin are more important than the individual self (Voss 1999; White 1995). Women are often brought up to be unassuming. In the white world, you have to "show that you're good," in contrast to tradition, which stresses humility and modesty.

When traditional American Indians, in keeping with their cultural values, put community and family before self, school, or the organization, this can cause problems in the school or work environment. For example, religious commitments can cause tension between American Indian employees and their supervisors. An American Indian who has to leave the workplace for several days in order to travel a long distance and take part in a healing ceremony for a family member may be viewed as lacking motivation or commitment to her or his job. Traditional women, for example, may not tell their non-Indian manager about their tribal or family commitments or religious roles for which they use vacation or sick time. This might happen because religious and spiritual practices are not shared with outsiders who might misuse sacred teaching, songs, or materials.

In the traditional native world, academic and economic achievement may be viewed as less important than in the dominant society. A person may be held in high esteem because she or he possesses important characteristics, such as living in a traditional way, passing on the wisdom of the elders, or performing religious ceremonies. Time is also perceived differently. The Anglo view of time is linear and represented by "planning." Completing tasks on a timetable is important. Native concepts of time are more flexible and people-centered. Meeting needs of people is more important than completing tasks.

What is it, then, that allows some women to function in the dominant world in spite of the obstacles? Most of the women in Muller's study were encouraged by family members to get an education and move beyond the tribal world while still respecting and maintaining ties to their traditions. Career expectations were set early. They learned to move between two worlds, using "switching" techniques to negotiate different cultures and roles.

My Story

My story is similar to that of other women in Muller's study. I grew up in an extended family that discouraged me from putting myself forward. I lived with my grandparents and was the "old people's child." This child, usually first born, is expected to care for the elders. In earlier times, I would have carried wood, tended the fire, made sure there were meals, brought water, and given physical care and support as my grandparents aged. My mother was working as a ranch cook in another state, but a strong sense of family and flexibility of nurturing roles among the adults around me compensated for her absence. My resiliency is, I believe, the product of a context in which there was always someone who loved me. Family included not only parents and grandparents, but various "cousins" who might be related by blood or not.

We worked together in other people's fields. Sometimes we stood in commodity lines to get beans, rice, canned cheese, ham, and powdered milk. We fried our bread in big iron skillets. There was no indoor plumbing, often no electricity. From poverty we learned frugality, respect for the earth's gifts, and patience.

I graduated from high school at sixteen. I wanted to join the military but was too young. My parents wanted me to marry a twenty-five-year-old man from the city. He was a good person who had a steady job and wanted a wife, but I did not want to marry. A missionary priest arranged for me to attend a boarding school. His vision was for me to enter a religious order of women. Our schedule was the same as that of the novices—up at 5:30, Mass at 6:00, breakfast at 6:45, and so on. The transition was difficult, but it taught me structure and organization; it also developed regular habits that allowed me later to function within the Western time frame. I was placed in shorthand and typing classes, which gave me secretarial skills. I used a telephone for the first time, saw a dentist, and learned the basic rules of middle-class life, such as changing socks daily. I got eyeglasses. They opened a new world. I could see leaves of trees, blades of grass!

I wanted to go beyond high school, and I applied to a small college in the Midwest that had been established to educate children of freed slaves and Indian women. I was accepted and got on a Trailways bus with one suitcase—all I owned. To this day, I do not know how my tuition was paid.

By my senior year of college, I knew I wanted to study medieval and Renaissance literature. I applied for a Woodrow Wilson Fellowship that would support me through graduate school. At that time, only 11 percent of these fellowships were allocated to women. I cut my long hair as an offering and to bring the courage I needed for the interview ahead. I met with a group of what seemed very old men. I received the fellowship and applied to schools listed in a graduate program guide I found in the college library. Yale and the University of North Carolina at Chapel Hill both accepted me. Carolina wrote a personal letter, so I went there.

the reframed mission of the university and the school. But organizational life has its own imperatives. The MSW coordinator retired, and I was asked to take her place. I agreed to do so on the condition that I serve only until a new coordinator was named. I took an educational sabbatical, during which I completed my course work, passed my qualifying examination, and developed a dissertation proposal. I then returned to campus and began to enjoy my faculty role, unencumbered by administrative responsibilities. I started to think that the "pure" faculty role was its own reward. But those halcyon days were numbered. I was simultaneously offered a position in the provost's office and as associate dean. Once again, I consulted with colleagues, weighing whether to accept one of the offers or to remain a faculty member without administrative responsibilities. In the end, I chose to become associate dean, thinking that this kept me doing what I enjoyed most: academic leadership. I served as associate dean for almost ten years and as interim dean when the dean retired. As interim dean, I amassed a team, once again searching for the "right people" (Collins 2001) of great intelligence and energy and strong commitment to the organization, and together we began to transform the school, reframing the vision, establishing goals to reach it, and involving the faculty at each point of planning and implementation. After a national search, the provost and president asked me to be dean. Supported by the vast majority of faculty members, I accepted the position. Only with 20/20 hindsight am I now able to identify the pathway for becoming a dean and to address the "do's and don'ts" of pursuing that position.

Do's and Don'ts of Pursuing a Leadership Position: A Personal Blueprint

Pursuing an academic leadership or administrative position now is quite different from what it involved when I began my journey in the last third of the twentieth century. However, there are some directions that are relevant and summarize my own movement into leadership. I believe that faculty members interested in becoming program chairs, associate deans, or deans must consider the following:

- Earn a doctorate in social work or a related field.
- Develop a clear scholarly agenda and follow it with discipline.

There were few women students and no female faculty in the graduate English department. I definitely did not fit in. There were obvious social class and cultural differences. I had no money to eat out or shop with the other women. I did not feel an easy camaraderie with my professors as did many of the male students. A kindly older professor frequently said, "Darling, why should a pretty girl get a Ph.D.? You'll never find a man to marry you." There was a brilliant but less charming faculty member who taught Old English and chain smoked, throwing his cigarettes out the window. He delighted in ordering young women to conjugate "cunnan" (to know) with the inevitable wrong word that made me blush.

I got a job typing dissertations in the Department of Urban Planning, which introduced me to the study of communities. By the end of my first year, I was homesick and burdened with guilt that my stepfather was dying and I was not helping my mother and two younger brothers and sister. I surrendered my fellowship, which was through the Ph.D., and took a job teaching in a medical school in a southern city.

I taught college English for six years, married, and had a child. The world was changing rapidly in the 1960s, and my ideas with it. The college of medicine where I taught merged with a professional institute to form a large state university. I wanted to return for the Ph.D. degree, which was now the terminal degree, so I could continue teaching. My husband objected. He believed women should be at home.

Nonetheless, I applied to the only state university offering a Ph.D. degree in English. It was the first year they were required to accept women. They told me, "We have to take women, but not married women. It's a waste of resources." My husband's world views and mine were vastly different and we separated. The judge denied me and my daughter support. I was a feminist and had a master's degree so I had no right to support for myself or my child. His action was retaliation against all women who dared to go outside the confines of home and motherhood.

American society was changing rapidly. I wanted to understand what was happening and why. I wanted to be part of creating a better world for the poor, for people with brown skin, for old people and children. I could see many similarities to the Middle Ages—disparities in wealth and social class; crime; restrictions on rights of women; child abuse and neglect; lack of access to education, health care, employment, or even basic sanitation. It was not a large step from world past to world present. A colleague suggested social work. I agreed to meet Dr, Susan Vignola and some other social workers. It was a far broader field than I had realized, one that opened numerous opportunities. I began classes toward an MSW degree at VCU that fall.

Dr. Edward Carpenter, chair of the administration sequence, became my mentor. I enjoyed his classes and long discussions with him. I admired his work with communities and began to realize that it would take profound social change to bring about social justice for people of color, the poor, and those at risk. Dr. Carpenter was also Native American, and he helped me to understand that being from a different background was not only okay, but a rich source of strengths and perspectives for work with communities and organizations. He encouraged me to submit papers to several national conferences, and they were accepted. I was a research assistant for Dr. David Saunders, whose mother Beatrice was managing editor for *Social Work*. I was a stringer for *Practice Digest*, worked part-time for NASW Press, and had a second-year placement in the governor's office. There I did A-95 planning and review of block grants. My thesis on interdisciplinary health care teams was with Dr. Jean Harris, an African American physician and director of health and human services for the state. Another of my instructors was Dr. Grace Harris, who was denied admission to the university where she now taught. She got her degree elsewhere but became a member of the faculty at the university, eventually becoming dean of the School of Social Work, and ultimately a vice president. All of these people were warm and generous members of groups who had experienced oppression. They had succeeded and believed I could.

Several of my professors encouraged me to continue for my Ph.D. degree. I received a full scholarship from the National Institute of Alcoholism and Alcohol Research. While in the doctoral program, I worked in continuing education, eventually moving from the role of assistant to interim director. Doctoral students of color seemed to have an unusually difficult time completing the program. Some staff and faculty overtly stated their belief that people of color were less capable than whites. There was pressure to conform to the ways of the dominant culture. This is consistent with Hilary Weaver's (2000) survey of American Indian faculty and students. Some of her respondents believed that university faculty and field instructors had deliberately tried to change their communication and ways of interaction.

Participants in Weaver's survey said they were given the impression that the Anglo way was the only correct professional way to do things. They saw this as a negation of self and believed they had no choice but to adapt or fail. Adaptation came at great personal cost to many. Indigenous students in her survey experienced depression, diminished confidence in their ability to complete training, withdrawal, and a higher dropout rate. They were discouraged by not being included in Anglo events or given recognition in sororities, fraternities, and honor societies. Forming coalitions with other minorities was not always possible because of differences of language, beliefs, and the reality that other people of color had often internalized white majority perceptions of Indian people. Values and behaviors of students from other minority groups were sometimes culturally alien or shocking to traditional First Nations students.

Professors of color were helpful to me—like Dr. John Matsushima and Dr. Pranab Chatterjee, who became my dissertation director. Dr. Chatterjee brought the perspective of the colonized to his lectures. His classes helped me to recognize that I had bought into a perspective that defined people by their limitations and defined poverty as individual rather than system failure.

While working on my dissertation, I was asked to be director of a new halfway house for alcoholic women. The job required multiple skills— working with a board, setting up programs, raising money, writing grants, ensuring that accreditation standards and legal requirements were met, such as compliance with the zoning and electrical codes, as well as working directly with the women and the community. My next job was as social work director for a large teaching hospital. I learned how to collaborate with other units of a complex organization. I built a seventeen-person department, which included a clinical psychologist, oncology services, and services to divert chronic emergency room malutilizers. This saved the hospital considerable money. I found I was good at motivating staff and helping them move upward, enjoyed working collaboratively with other disciplines, and could take a leadership role.

I had not learned much about finance, budgeting, or program evaluation in my doctoral studies, and I welcomed the chance to add to my skills. I had always feared firing people, but I found that I could do that, too. I always tried to counsel the person toward something more suited to their talents and interests.

I also developed a strong belief in compassion. This does not mean accepting substandard performance, but it does mean being aware of where a worker is at the moment. Sometimes a slip in performance is related to something going on in the person's life. It may be transient. Sometimes the person is not capable of doing his or her job and no one has addressed that. Some people do not fit into a particular organizational culture and should be encouraged to leave. I think that sometimes in social service agencies we tend to let poor performance go too long without addressing it. Too often I find that I prefer coming up with a "reason" the person is performing poorly; meanwhile, the organization and other staff are suffering since they have to do the work that is neglected or done badly. It is easier to let people remain than to let them go. It is easier not to tell people reasons they are being let go. However, it seems more unkind than explaining how their talents and the needs of the organization do not match.

I remarried. My partner and I each came to the marriage with a child whose other parent was elsewhere. We began to feel as if we were running a travel agency getting the children back and forth between households. We moved to be nearer both children, and I took a position as a clinical director for a family alcohol-drug treatment agency, worked part-time in a family agency, and eventually had my own private practice. I juggled demands of my research, family, dissertation, and trying to build my career. I was envious of men who had wives. They did not have the child and household responsibilities I had.

I became active in state professional organizations. Social workers in the state were seeking state licensure at the time. I gave technical assistance to organizations serving the elderly as there was no state organization for the aging. My networking through volunteer service led to my being recruited for a full-time faculty position at a Historic Black College and University. While there, I taught in both the BSW and the MSW programs and coordinated a grant for services to minority elderly, which contributed to establishing the state agency on aging.

At that time, there were fewer than ten American Indian members of the Council on Social Work Education. There had been more when I was a master's student, but the drop in federal funding meant there were fewer training programs to prepare social workers to work with Indian people. I was nominated for the council's House of Delegates. There was a proposal to take American Indians off the list of represented groups because of their small numbers, but with the support of Latino and African American colleagues this did not happen. I was nominated and elected to the board of CSWE, and I sent a mailing to all the social work programs in the country. We had our first meeting in 1989. Dr. Mike Frumkin and Dr. Rochelle Gershowitz arranged space for us on the Saturday preceding each annual program meeting so we could meet. I acted as president of the group for a time; Dr. Hilary Weaver is now in that position, and the American Indian/Alaska Native Social Work Educators meet annually at the program meeting, maintain a list-serve, and have a full-day symposium on Native American issues.

I next took a job at a small, rural, faith-based university. While the mission and setting were evangelical and conservative, there was strong support for social work. My experiences there led to my realization that social workers really do share common values, and that socialization into the profession is a profound and life-altering experience. When the director left to care for his elderly mother in another state, responsibility for seeing the baccalaureate program through initial accreditation was mine. The Association of Baccalaureate Social Work Program Directors group provided a network of generous, talented people who freely shared curriculum materials, syllabi, and advice. My program received initial accreditation.

I was offered a salary increase to develop another new baccalaureate program nearer my home—I would not have to commute the 140-mile round-trip every day. I served as program director, then chair of the departments of social work, sociology, and criminal justice, and finally division head. I learned about university structures, the research and statistics needed to compete for resources, federal regulations, student aid, larger-scale scheduling, and universities as systems.

My youngest daughter's admission to one of the few public high schools in the United States that offered a major in harp led to my adventure in a university for the deaf. I sailed our boat to Baltimore's Inner Harbor and moored it, becoming a legal resident so my youngster was eligible to attend the school. I joined the faculty at Gallaudet University, the only liberal arts university for the Deaf. I had no experience with the Deaf or with American Sign Language (ASL), so I asked to attend the summer language institute before I began teaching in the fall. My family was the cheering section as I encountered life in an unfamiliar language and culture. I was hesitant about being over fifty and in a dorm with so many young people, but I soon had a posse of friends who helped me with my signing, talked to me about their romances and careers, and invited me to join them at the many deaf clubs around town. By spring semester I was lecturing in ASL.

I soon realized I would not reach the high level of ASL proficiency required for tenure. I was also beginning to fall behind in my professional knowledge. In addition, Dr. Janet Pray, chair of the department, was moving to institutional planning. Thus I accepted a position with a new MSW program seeking accreditation. The director had left at the end of the first semester. As with many new programs, there were tensions between BSW and MSW faculty, and each day was a challenge of negotiating differences among faculty and between faculty and administration.

However, this job allowed me to be part of a graduate school within a larger state system. I learned about recruitment, marketing, and admissions. The graduate dean was organized and competent and had great talent in creating a team. She taught me how to negotiate a large state system and compete for resources. This was also my first experience with collective bargaining. My social work training was helpful to being a competent administrator. Working with people is a great part of administration, and the ability to listen is important. People often want to be heard more than they want an immediate solution.

I am now director of a school of social work. We offer an interdisciplinary doctorate with a track in social work, a large MSW program at four locations, a BSW program, and interdisciplinary and certificate programs. For me, the route to where I am was serendipitous. Each new job has been an adventure. I accepted opportunities that came along, but I had no clear course of action. If I had known sooner what was necessary to succeed, I believe I could have done more and undoubtedly made a greater contribution to our profession.

I took on administrative roles early in my career as an educator. However, I would advise having tenure before taking on an administrative position. The career life of a chair or dean or even program director is limited. It is a job that can make it difficult if not impossible to continue research and publication. It is also a job that requires one to make decisions people do not like, with expected consequences.

I believe that administration is a service occupation. It is the support system for delivery of services and research and instruction. The root word is minister, and I believe that my role as a leader and administrator is to support the practice or teaching of my colleagues. I am there to keep resources flowing, to make sure there is money, equipment, and adequate support staff, and that people have what they need to do their best. I must keep the whole in mind, as well as how my agency, program, or department fits within and supports the whole. It is about being a good steward.

Succeeding: Leading and Administering Effectively

Every woman will emphasize different traits and practices that have contributed to her success. I can only list mine. They include networking, having a passion for what you do, finding and being a good mentor, being organized, having integrity and being credible, accepting responsibility, presenting self as a competent professional, evidence-based decision making, understanding the context of your work, civility to all and particularly to the lease-paid staff with the humblest and dirtiest jobs, being curious to learn, and laughing a lot.

- Networking. Networking is vital to leadership and administration. My involvement in professional organizations and the community has been valuable. Networking gave me a chance to observe women such as Dr. Wilma Peebles Wilkins, Professor Ernestine Brittingham-Brown, Dr. Carmen Ortiz Hendricks, and many others. Successful women of color believe in what they are doing. They know that what they are doing is important. They are enthusiastic. They are not cynical. They do not need to gossip, although they have keen ears to hear what is going on around them. All have personal warmth and interest in others, can collaborate across disciplines, and get things done. All of them do what they say they will do. They are organized and goal directed. They do not pretend to know what they do not know. Above all, they are generous in sharing their knowledge and encouraging newcomers.
- Passion. This word is overworked, but a belief in what you are doing matters. If you do not believe in what you are doing, how can you project your enthusiasm and support for your program? How do you find strength and motivation to persevere? Successful women in leadership positions find ways to "keep the faith" and not to be overwhelmed by all that has to be done. They draw from many sources—prayer, religious belief, or participating in worship services and the life of their church, temple, synagogue or mosque. They draw strength and hope from spiritual practices, meditation, sports, exercise, volunteer service, music, the arts, dance or other creative expression, gardening, and doing things with their family. All have many dimensions to their lives.
- Mentoring. Leaders need mentoring, and more than one mentor. They also need to be mentors—not only to pass along wisdom, but also because

one learns from teaching others. I attribute my ability to succeed to many mentors—my grandmother, who valued education; two elementary school teachers, who wrote me encouraging letters until their deaths. Some were my professors. Some were colleagues through a professional organization, such as Dr. Dean Pierce and Dr. Mike Frumkin, who supported American Indian men and women having a voice in the Council on Social Work Education.

• Organization. To be successful as a leader and administrator, you need reasonable planning and organizational skills, an ability to work as a member of a team, and an ability to meet goals and deadlines. You need to cultivate patience, persistence, stamina, and focus. My Catholic education emphasized order and the dignity of all work. I believe that all work has worth, so no task is beneath me.

• Credibility and integrity. Credibility is a sine qua non. The organization depends on the leaders' clarity. If you are not reliable and misrepresent facts, you lose the trust of others. This is true in small matters as well as large. Oddly, getting older, gaining weight, and wearing glasses seem to have added to my credibility!

I would rather understate what I hope to achieve than overstate it. When I enter a new setting or begin a new program, I prefer to wait, observe, make few initial changes, and consult with faculty, staff, and clients as appropriate about what needs doing.

• Curiosity. I want to live forever and experience the future. My interests are broad; I read voraciously in many fields—social science, history, health care, social work. I also read the *New York Times* daily. Curiosity is, to me, eagerness to know, to understand, to learn.

• Responsibility. As an oldest child, I have a strong sense of responsibility. I feel responsible for the people whose livelihoods are affected by my decisions. I try hard to be nonjudgmental, to see strengths, and to encourage people. I believe in collective wisdom. I also try to acknowledge my mistakes and not to blame others. Responsibility also includes being present, being on call, giving extra time when necessary, and designating someone in charge when you do take time off.

• Presentation of self. Having the nicest house or car has never mattered much to me. One is told to dress upward in the corporate world, however, because appearance makes a statement about the institution for which you work and projects competence and savvy. The days of having to dress like a man are fortunately gone. Simplicity keeps attention focused on the work. A colleague keeps a small bag packed with travel necessities and reserves a set of interchangeable knits—a neutral jacket, skirt, and/or slacks and top, a top in a contrasting color, and a pair of simple mid-heel shoes. Three pieces, three outfits, and no worry about wrinkles.

I see younger women not taken seriously because they dress in attire more appropriate for an evening out or in jeans and an informal top and thong sandals. Good advice to me was, "Don't wear anything to work, ever, that you would wear to a bar, the beach, or bed unless your work is in one of those places!"

- Evidence-based decision making. It is easy to fall into a crisis management mode in a busy and ever-changing environment. This is a bit like oversteering a boat, with resultant instability. Having a mission, goals, plan, and ways to assess outcomes is like steering to a compass point, taking into account unexpected events along the way. It keeps the vessel on course.

My experience is that people in authority—and especially those who manage budgets—like numbers, a logically presented case, and to know pros and cons. When I make a case, I find it helpful to have at hand enrollments, credit hours generated, faculty-student ratios, evidence of productivity by whatever measures the university uses, as well as how the proposed plan will further institutional mission and goals. Good data allows you to operate from a position of strength and confidence.

- Civility. Respect for others, courtesy, and civility are good "manners." If you do not know the rules, *Miss Manners Rescues Civilization* is contemporary and humorous. While we think of manners as knowing which fork to use, it is much more about civility and treating others as you would like to be treated. Every person in the organization should be treated with respect—faculty, students, support staff, maintenance, and housekeeping staff.

- Understanding of the context. It is important to become part of the life of your institution. This can be through service on committees or attending institutional activities such as art exhibits or basketball games. You can gain helpful tips by getting to know other people at your level within and outside your institution who can tell you how they deal with similar situations and help you understand the particular culture and norms of your workplace.

- Laughing, being joyful, taking care of yourself, and celebrating your traditions. At the risk of sounding like a replay of "Things Learned in

Kindergarten," I have found that a sense of humor in the face of life's unpredictableness and absurdity keeps me in balance. My life, family, and career have given me much joy. A wise elder told me to make a time each day, preferably a regular time, to take a few minutes and be thankful for the good things the day has brought and the good aspects of people with whom I have interacted.

Taking care of myself has been the most difficult task for me. I enjoy my work, my hours are long, and I used to fall asleep and wake thinking about problems, many of which were beyond my ability to resolve. Caffeine, erratic mealtimes, and insufficient exercise tells on one. Each of us can find our own reprieve from the cares of work—prayer, meditation, exercise, time away, playing with children, making music, stroking a pet, re-centering, knitting—whatever helps us to be more serene. For me, it is being outdoors. If our lives are out of balance, it is possible that our decisions are out of balance.

Part of taking care of ourselves is ensuring that we receive adequate compensation for our work. This is something at which I have not done well. I think other women share this reluctance to assert our worth. Possibly, we are so happy even to be considered that we sell ourselves short and give up negotiation below where we should. Imagine my consternation when I learned I was making $20,000 a year less than the man who had done my same job eight years before! It can be difficult to get figures from a private university, but most states publish salaries, including those of university faculty and administrators. The *Chronicle of Higher Education* publishes average salaries for each rank and university each year, and a comparison of schools can be useful in asking for an appropriate salary. This is where a mentor can also be invaluable.

Finally, we must celebrate our traditions, keep them alive, and pass them on. From the teachings of our elders, from the wisdom of the past—which sometimes must be retaught and relearned—we have much to offer that can change the world and help bring about peace and justice for all beings.

The Next Generation: Keeping the Movement Alive

Women have traditionally had leadership roles in indigenous cultures. Pressure to assimilate, prohibitions on speaking one's language or holding religious ceremonies, cultural destruction, and government policies have diminished the leadership role of women in many nations. How can we support women to take leadership roles and restore the balance between male spirit and female spirit?

For one, we can support our indigenous colleagues across North America and throughout the world. There are many movements that allow us to do this. In our profession, we can support organizations that bring us together and create opportunities for us to share our learning. One of the joys of having been involved in the American Indian/ Alaska Native Social Work Educators group has been seeing a new generation, a generation that is growing in numbers and whose preparation allows them to assume leadership roles in our profession.

The number of indigenous people in social work education and particularly in leadership positions remains small. There is much that can be done to recruit, retain, and promote those entering the profession. We must find ways to draw from traditions and values that can make a significant contribution to social work, not only with indigenous peoples, but with all peoples. It is important to support colleagues in social work education—recruiting students, finding resources so they can go to school, encouraging them, helping them to balance all the parts of their lives, making opportunities available for doctoral students, supporting students to complete dissertations, to find jobs, to do research. We need to do more to mentor new faculty as they work toward tenure and promotion, to support them as they begin to publish, to give honest feedback that helps them to identify their strengths and overcome their weaknesses.

Note

In honor of my grandmother, Leila, whose dreams made mine possible, and with the hope my daughters will share those dreams.

References

Ambler, M. (1992). "Women Leaders in Indian Education." *Tribal College Journal of American Indian Higher Education* 3 (4): 10–15.

Amodeo, L. B., and J. R. Emslie (1985). "Minority Women in Administration: An Ethnographic Study." Paper presented at the Annual Conference of the

National Association of Women Deans Administrators and Counselors, Milwaukee.

Gair, S., D. Miles, and H. Tginsibm (2005). "Reconciling Indigenous and Nonindigenous Knowledges in Social Work Education: Action and Legitimacy." *Journal of Social Work Education* 42 (2): 179–90.

Johnson, V. (1997). "Weavers of Change: Portraits of Native American Women Educational Leaders." Doctoral dissertation, Michigan State University, Dissertation Abstracts International, 59(01), 36A (University Microfilms no. AAT98–22466).

MacNeill, B., K. Horn, and J. Pereze (1995). "The Training and Supervisory Needs of Racial and Ethnic Minority Students." *Journal of Multicultural Counseling and Development* 23 (4): 246–59.

Muller, H. J. (1998). "American Indian Women Managers: Living in Two Worlds." *Journal of Management Inquiry* 7 (4): 28.

NCTE Guidelines, Teaching Storytelling (1992). Available at http://www.ncte.org/about/over/positions/category/curr/107637.htm (accessed February 20, 1992).

Russell, R., and R. L. Wright (1991). "The Socialization of Minority Women in Educational Administration Positions." Paper presented at the Annual Meeting of the Canadian Society for the Study of Education, Kingston.

Schiele, J., and A. Francis (1996). "The Status of Former CSWE Ethnic Minority Doctoral Fellows in Social Work Academia." *Journal of Social Work Education* 32 (1): 31–45.

Souers, T. J. (1992). "Circles of Power: Life Histories of Native American Indian Women Elders in Education." Doctoral dissertation, University of Oregon. Dissertation Abstracts International, 53(10), 3462A (University Microfilms no. AAT93–05237).

Taylor, M. J., and K. M. Stuss (2007). "Native American Women Who Lead Human Service Organizations." *Journal of Ethnic and Cultural Diversity in Social Work* 15: 123.

Trucks-Bordeaux, T. (2003). "Academic Massacres: The Story of Two American Indian Women and Their Struggle to Survive Academia." *American Indian Quarterly* 27 (1–2): 416–19.

Turner, C. (2002). "Women of Color in Academe: Living with Multiple Marginality." *Journal of Higher Education* 7 (1): 74–93.

Voss, R., V. Douville, A. Little Soldier, and G. Twiss (1999). "Tribal and Shamanic Based Social Work Practice: A Lakota Perspective." *Social Work* 44 (3): 228–41.

Warner, L. S. (1991). "Red Women, White Policy: American Indian Women and Indian Education." Paper presented to Women and Society Conference, Poughkeepsie, N.Y.

Weaver, H. N. (1998). "Indigenous People in a Multicultural Society: Unique Issues for Human Services." *Social Work* 43 (3): 203–12.

—— (2000). "Culture and Professional Education: The Experiences of Native American Social Workers." *Journal of Social Work Education* 36 (3): 415–48.

White, J. (2001). *Social Work with the First Nations: A Comprehensive Bibliography with Annotations*. Alexandria: Council on Social Work Education.

—— (2002). "Supervision of American Indian Social and Human Services Workers." In *Workplace Diversity: Issues and Perspectives*, ed. A. Daly. Second ed. Silver Springs, Md.: NASW Press.

White, V. S. (1995). "A Perspective on Native Cultural Values," ed. Michael Yellow Bird. *Proceedings.* First Nations Social Work Conference, Kansas University and Haskell Indian Nations University, Topeka, Ks.

12

A Leadership Motif for Women of Color in Leadership and Administration

SHELLEY ANN RICE-WYCKOFF

Pursuing Leadership and Administration

Contrary to the typical road where one actively seeks leadership and administrative positions, I have never actively sought such positions. While it was a secret dream of mine for years, becoming a leader and administrator in the field of social work was quite unplanned. Becoming a practitioner was my goal, but as I began to engage in activities, including teaching and social service consultation to nonprofit organizations and government institutions, it became apparent that people in leadership roles and administrators could have a profoundly positive impact on individuals who otherwise might not receive assistance. My primary motivation was helping people in need. If an administrative position became available, I would consider taking on that challenge if it enabled me to enable others.

That is exactly what happened. The person in charge of the undergraduate social work program at Alabama A&M University had applied for an educational leave to pursue a doctoral degree. The program needed a temporary replacement for that person, so I assumed what I thought was a temporary position as director. As interim director I started to view things from a somewhat different perspective, and I saw many needs. As my understanding of these needs crystallized, I began implementing solutions, such as initiating a master's program in social work (there was only one in the state of Alabama), developing very close relationships with the local social service organizations to establish student field placements, participating in state and national professional organization activities, and laying the groundwork for national program recognition.

All actions focused on opening doors and providing opportunities for developing new, competent social workers for a region in great need of them. In addition, I was involved in writing grants to secure tools, equipment, and resources for students. I also focused on involving students and faculty in local and state politics and being an active participant on campus committees and boards, such as the Promotion and Tenure, Academic Standards and Curriculum, Graduate Council, University Grievance, Commencement, and Founder's Day committees.

Leading and Administering Successfully: Personal Qualities

One of the characteristics that has contributed to my success in administration has been my engaging personality. By nature and inclination, I am a warm, encouraging, and empathic person. All types of people feel that they can come to me and discuss issues personal and/or political. They do not feel belittled or tense, confident that they will get a listening ear, with no personal motive or agenda on my part.

Indeed, my leadership style is genuine, and my goal is to do the right thing for my colleagues, the students, the institution, and the profession. In fact, my leadership style directly relates to and is absolutely relevant to social work values, ethics, and practices. It is my firm belief that social work administrators and leaders should be knowledgeable about the subject matter, be willing to learn, possess a sincere motivation, accept diversity, and above all maintain a very high standard of personal conduct.

Furthermore, I firmly believe organizational decision making must be shared as much as possible. There are several reasons why this is important. First, it represents the ethical principle of respect and self-determination, for which all persons have some responsibility, as well as the ability to assist in making decisions that directly affect what they do and how they do it. Second, I view shared decision making as a training tool. Based on the principle that one person does not have all the answers, it encourages collaboration and team effort. These elements are key to having a productive and effective organization. Third, the shared decision-making process develops leaders. One needs to know how to be an effective follower in order to be an effective leader. Regardless of one's leadership position in an organization, that person is a follower in some capacity. Everyone has to answer to someone.

On a personal level, my leadership style has been impacted by both my immediate and my extended families. In my large family, the reality of birth order dictated leadership roles. As one of the older siblings, I was expected to cook dinner several days during the week because my mother worked outside our home. Clothes had to be washed and other chores had to be done. The responsibility of sharing household chores with my siblings was definitely a training ground for leadership. The younger siblings were constantly looking for examples, good or bad, to emulate. Again, my parents gave me recognition because I was responsible and mature in carrying out their delegated assignments. As I grew older, my parents continued to rely on me for leadership in family matters.

Cultural Factors: Linked to My Leadership Skills

I grew up in a low-income family in the urban South. Seeking a better way of living, my father and mother moved from Prairie Point in rural Mississippi to Birmingham, Alabama. My father was a hard-working, industrious man. Armed with a fifth-grade education, he worked in the coal mine and steel mill at night and remodeled and built houses during the day. Our large family included eight children; everyone had tasks to perform. My father insisted that we always stay busy.

In elementary school, recognition, praise, and leadership opportunities were given to students who were excellent spellers, who turned in neat assignments, participated in class discussions and engaged readily without being prodded, dressed neatly, and were respectful to adults and peers. I worked hard to be one of these students selected to serve as an example of good character, interpersonal skills, and academic excellence. I was often the first to be included in spelling teams and reading circles. I enjoyed being the best speller, having the highest grades on assignments, participating in school programs, and seeing my name printed on posters in the hallway for exceptional work. For me and others like me, this recognition from teachers and peers was a primary motivation for working hard. It increased our competitiveness and desire to shine, to excel, and to be recognized for achievement. To achieve felt good!

This approach continued throughout high school as I became involved in even more activities. I was kind to my peers and accepting of people from different backgrounds, a plus in interpersonal relationships. Students used attributes such as friendly, genuine, down-to-earth, helpful, fair, and willing to help individuals who were struggling to describe me. This recognition motivated me to seek leadership opportunities. On summer breaks, when I was not working, I participated in enrichment programs for knowledge acquisition and skill development, which allowed me to meet new people. Through these programs, I was exposed to role models, good and bad, to individuals who were goal oriented and organized, and who kept their eyes on the prize. Being in the midst of achievers motivated me to stay focused. I continued developing my work ethics when at age sixteen I began working during the summer in factories in Long Island, New York, and Cincinnati, Ohio.

As a college student at Tuskegee Institute, a prestigious private Historically Black University in the South, I was privileged to be reminded of great leaders who had created the school. Their courage, knowledge, and desire to succeed against the odds served as a beacon of light demonstrating that obstacles were meant to be removed and/or pushed aside. I was in a disciplined and hard-working environment, and through networking I obtained financial support by working in the cafeteria and library. I worked hard, going to work very early and staying late. My values have thus been developed and characterized by discipline, hard work, and never giving up in achieving a goal.

As a Black woman, I needed to be "overly" prepared, and I was willing to go the extra mile to accomplish the goals I set. I constantly looked for opportunities that enhanced my goals, and I participated in activities that increased my knowledge of people and things, but most of all I remembered what it meant to be given an opportunity to attend college. Subsequently, it became my privilege to afford the same opportunity to others I would meet along the way.

Another experience that prepared me for leadership was raising two daughters. As young children, my daughters viewed me as an important role model in their lives. They saw me constantly striving to develop myself personally and professionally as a professor at the local university. While teaching full time at Alabama A&M University, I enrolled in a doctoral program at Vanderbilt University in Nashville, Tennessee. This required extensive time traveling and being away from home and studying while at home. The multiple roles of wife, mother, educator, and student were time-consuming as well as challenging. My daughters were in awe and very supportive, and amazed at my ability to handle these multiple roles and to do them so well. I completed my doctorate, including my dissertation, in three years, and at my graduation ceremony I put my diploma in the hands of my daughters.

During my tenure as a doctoral student, as I studied and completed assignments, my daughters also completed their assignments and readings. They earned top grades and valued education. They were encouraged to do their best and always gave 100 percent effort to their tasks. Because of their involvement in many extracurricular activities, they learned to carry out multiple tasks and to work hard to secure their own success. They were skilled at looking at or thinking about the consequences of self-destructive behaviors and thereby selected a better path. They valued delayed gratification in order to achieve their aspirations. They credit my leadership traits and role modeling for their ability to achieve their goals of becoming physicians. They also credit my leadership influence for their perseverance and courage, work ethics, and ethical principles, and they have kept their eyes on the prize.

Likewise, my church has had a major influence on my leadership style. First Missionary Baptist Church has a wealth of ministries that welcome member involvement as leaders and followers. Active involvement in church ministries has been an integral part of my life since childhood. Through participating in plays and programs and representing the church as a delegate at conferences, I honed my comfort level as a leader. As an adult in the church, I planned and implemented seminars during Family Month, served as cochair for the Annual Women's Day Program, and served on the Usher Board and the Board of Directors of the Church's Child Development Center and Academy.

I also planned and delivered presentations at workshops for teachers employed by the church's academy and child development center. The leadership roles in the church were excellent training ground for developing my leadership skills and confidence. As a result of years of service in the governance of church activities, I have confidence in my ability to get things done. I complete tasks without procrastination. I work with members of committees, sharing the workload necessary for achieving our goal. I have had to make decisions and perform analytical groundwork in order to arrive at certain decisions. Reporting the work of the committees required developing good oral and written communication skills.

Leadership roles in the church required teamwork, not turf building. All persons involved are commended for completing their tasks in a quality manner. Individually, each member's input was valued and accepted; each was treated with respect and dignity. Church service was an excellent training camp for future leadership roles that require good problem-solving techniques, decision-making skills, respectful use of confrontation skills, communication skills, respectful interactions, honesty, trust, fairness, maintenance of confidential information, and appreciation of diversity. All of the knowledge and skills gained from my life experiences have helped me meet the challenges of academic leadership.

Life Experiences

As a student in graduate school, I was assigned a field placement at a Veterans Hospital in Gary, Indiana. I worked with Vietnam veterans returning from the war. This was one of the saddest experiences I ever had. Many soldiers sat all day and night in a catatonic state, immobilized from the medicine. Medications were necessary to keep them from having horrible dreams and flashbacks, and in many cases it kept them from harming themselves or others. Many of the social workers had much empathy and patience with each patient. They were giving of themselves to help these very young people who had encountered traumatic events that had changed their lives forever. This experience provided me with an early example of the power of small groups. Social workers met in small groups, discussed issues, and sought the best ways to help the patients. There was an air of collegiality, teamwork, and common purpose. The clients were a priority. They were not used for personal power and prestige.

As irony would have it, I married an army officer as soon as I received my master's degree in social work. After our marriage, we immediately went to live in a very small town in Kansas, a town that had very few social service agencies. There were no vacancies for a person with a master's degree in social work. As I continued to look for a job that I believed I was destined to do, I took jobs at Wal-Mart and a clothing store to help my husband make ends meet. The experience of working in the public sector as a salesperson and cashier reaffirmed some basic characteristics about myself as well as affording me an opportunity to meet and interact with many people from all walks of life. However, I yearned in my heart and soul to be able to provide services to individuals and families as a professional social worker. I knew I had to be patient, but while I was waiting, I would do the best job that I could to carry out my responsibilities and tasks that had been assigned to me. I had a responsibility to my employer and was grateful for employment, even though my expertise was totally unrelated to the work I was doing. It was important that I treat each customer with respect and dignity. This experience taught me patience and humility and confirmed that I could be a dedicated and productive follower even though I had higher aspirations.

Finally, there was a vacancy at the local social service agency as a social worker in the child welfare division, and I was selected for the job. My life dream was beginning to unfold. I loved my coworkers, my job responsibilities, and the work environment. While there, I received my state license to practice. A monumental moment! The collegial office atmosphere was conducive to excellence. It was about social workers helping social workers to help families. I came away from this experience with a greater appreciation for the concept of competence and professional relationships. I wanted to always be prepared and able to offer individuals options that could help their situations. That required being abreast of the latest practice intervention techniques. Personally, I wanted to constantly learn and develop more and more. I felt obligated to provide my best. This experience also afforded my first challenge in understanding organizational culture. Being the only African American in an all-white agency that had a significant African American clientele meant that I was expected to be the office resource on African American issues. Somehow, I was expected to know all about African American traditions, rituals, behaviors, and mannerisms. Sometimes I felt pressure and unrealistic expectations, and at other times I felt good about being there to offer my assistance or offer what I knew to help.

When my husband left the army, we moved to Huntsville, Alabama. In Huntsville, my first job was that of field director for the Girl Scouts of North Alabama. It involved developing troops and training troop leaders in various communities in the Huntsville area. The job also required spending much time with children in their troop activities. This experience brought to the forefront the importance of being a role model, creating opportunities to build character in others. This experience also highlighted the disparity of community resources. As a spokesperson for the Girl Scouts organization, the need for verbal communication skills in dealing with the public became an important aspect of job success. Adults became motivated to become leaders based on my ability to talk enthusiastically about the benefits of developing young girls into productive citizens and building character. Although rewarding, this assignment was not my idea of a social work practitioner's role; planning interventions with individuals and families. My heart, as a social worker, was providing direct services to individuals and families. I continued to look for social work positions.

Not long after, I accepted a job at Alabama A&M University as the director of field instruction for an undergraduate social work program. I loved the university environment and the prospect of helping students reach their potential. I grew in awareness of community resources for family support systems. I was in constant contact with agencies locally and statewide that could provide good social work experiences for social work students.

As the director of field instruction, I still had the desire to work as a practitioner, so I worked part-time with Family Services as a therapist. These experiences were rewarding and made me aware of professional liabilities, the difficulties in satisfying more than one organization even though they have similar goals, the impact and power of decisions on organizations and people, and the need to be able to effectively plan and implement training programs. These somewhat different positions also taught me the importance of ethical behavior, self-assessment, the development of thorough intervention planning, the danger of shooting from the hip, and the use of supervision as a valuable resource for developing options for various issues. Another valuable lesson I learned is that holding down two jobs that require your very best (particularly if you are a perfectionist as I am) will result in burnout. That was hard to learn but satisfying work.

As a result of having a nine-month contract at the university, I was free to obtain other employment during the summer. I spent the summer serving as a consultant. My consulting job with the Internal Revenue Service (IRS) headquarters in Washington, D.C., had a significant impact on my leadership development. This agency was concerned with their employees' well-being. I was asked to develop an Employee Assistance Program. The IRS was a very structured macro organization and unique in that diversity was not only from a race perspective but also from an organizational culture perspective. The job required extensive travel throughout the United

States to examine the Employee Assistance Program for many large organizations, such as Chicago Transit, major airlines, and large food companies. This experience provided me with an opportunity to put everything I had learned to date in action and apply it at a highly visible and senior management level. It gave me the assurance and awareness that I could operate in any realm with confidence through my abilities to perform in an effective manner by just being me. I spent several months with leaders of large organizations, senior managers, mid-level managers, and employees. I was able to witness leadership in a different environment, first-hand, at its best and worst.

Systemic Factors Affecting Leadership/Administration in a University

One of the greatest challenges as a leader in an academic setting has been getting and maintaining qualified faculty. There is high demand for a genuine, caring, knowledgeable faculty, who are willing to devote time and energy to developing an academic program as well as themselves. There is a need for faculty who sincerely desire to develop students as critical thinkers, lifelong learners, and professional helpers. Even when one is able to identify potential employees, there is the problem of sorting out fact from fiction when it comes to qualifications. Often, one really does not know the extent of the prospective employee's skill, knowledge, and personal attributes until that person is hired, and then it is too late. What one thought would be an asset may turn out to be a liability. Leadership, at this point, requires that the administrator figure out how to deal effectively with the situation and still maintain a productive program.

Another challenge for leaders has been to instill and maintain a high level of dedication for a successful program in all faculty. It would be unrealistic to believe that all motivation is the same, but there should be consistency in the primary program goals. It is a challenge at times to keep focused as a number of issues and situations are constantly occurring on the individual and group levels.

Nevertheless, Topping (2002) suggests that understanding one's followers or employees—their capabilities, aspirations, personalities, and interactions—has a bearing on how they need to be led. Significant research on generational mindsets as it relates to workers discusses four categories: (1) matures, ages 55–69, (2) baby boomers, ages 37–55, (3) generation Xers, ages 21–36, and (4) generation Yers, born after 1980. Matures tend to buy into the status quo and often seem to possess a traditional sense of dedication to their company and job. Baby boomers are generally skeptical about authority, have desire for personal freedom, and push for a casual work environment and for working at home. Generation Xers seem to have less loyalty to their employing organization and greater interest in luxury and the finer things in life, with a premium on individuality and entrepreneurship. Generation Yers, the younger generation in the workforce, seem optimistic and have much faith in technology. They depend on multimedia and seek much stimulation (Topping 2002). An effective leader must be somewhat familiar with the motivational factors of all these generations in order to effectively utilize their capabilities and recognize their special needs and aspirations, and to remain cognizant of how to foster effective teamwork across generations.

Additionally, the application and evaluation of Maslow's hierarchy of needs for employees become a part of an effective leader's tools. One has to keep these need levels in mind with each employee, recognizing how they affect the work situation and environment (Neck and Manz 2007). When one considers all of the factors that affect the workplace and its people (e.g., the theory of individual needs and the idiosyncrasies of each generation that now exist in the workplace) with organizational pressures to produce quality goods and services at a competitive price, an effective leader becomes paramount to organizational success. Balancing the company's requirements while allowing individual employees to self-actualize with a mixture of at least three generations of people can be a daunting task, requiring special and skilled individuals as leaders and administrators.

The use of mentors is another method that is well documented as a means to develop effective leaders. Throughout my career, a significant number of persons in leadership roles have provided me with invaluable assistance. I consider them to be my network of peers and colleagues, with undeniable expertise and experience in the practice and education arenas. Indeed, they have been my informal mentors from afar. According to Topping (2002), the point of mentoring is to provide advice and guidance on career and long-term development issues. In terms of the concept of mentorship, study participants indicated that the attributes of a good mentor include being a good listener, having the person's best interest at heart, garnering much wisdom from personal experiences, being trustworthy, being candid, understanding the politics in the organization, and enjoying watching others succeed. Great leaders have an inherent desire to help others succeed.

Networking has also played a significant role in facilitating my successful leadership and administration. Networking across the profession has provided access to persons across the country with expertise and experience in all facets of social work education and practice, as well as good common sense and life experience. I have been able to examine effective methods, procedures, and activities and have culled selective elements for application in my program. Being in a position to compare programs has likewise afforded me an opportunity to determine if my program is unique in its day-to-day operational difficulties, which in turn provide conditional verification. It has become a confidence booster to know that a number of the same issues are present in most programs, and that we are all in it together.

Keeping the Movement Alive

My role and responsibility in keeping alive the movement of promoting women of color in leadership and administration is to dispel once and for all the stereotypical notion that great leaders are male, masculine, tough, competent, unemotional, and detached. Women of color should not even consider these stereotypes but become even more determined carrying out our historical legacy of uncompromising leadership. Women of color must emulate the legacy with thoughts of women like Johnetta Cole, Oprah Winfrey, Shirley Chisholm, Condoleeza Rice, Sojourner Truth, Mary Bethume, Harriet Tubman, Rosa Parks, Madame C. J. Walker, and others who were brave, tough, determined, persistent, and competent. Women of color have always been leaders!

As a member of national community organizations (Delta Sigma Theta and 100 Black Women), I realize that women's organizations have been instrumental in keeping the movement alive. Many of our activities afford members the opportunity to develop leadership skills, serve the community, as well as promote leadership aspirations. Goals in working in community organizations include promotion of high educational, moral, and spiritual efficiency. Such activities provide morality, teamwork, work ethics, commitment to helping vulnerable and oppressed populations, and social justice. Service and leadership are advanced; many of the activities are geared toward cultivation of young ladies to become productive citizens and potential leaders.

It is my special responsibility and privilege to create opportunities for women of color to become leaders. Promoting educational excellence and lifelong learning are essential. I strive to encourage young women to carefully plan their educational background and to recognize the need for "people skills" for communication and developing relationships. I also encourage them to build traits of fairness, consistency, competence, knowledge acquisition, decision making, problem solving, listening skills, flexibility, candidness, honesty, patience, role modeling, respect, courtesy, mentorship, and networking.

Creating opportunities for women of color include identifying different or nontraditional on-the-job experiences that could be utilized to develop knowledge and skills. Such examples could be planning a community job fair that requires partnering with community agencies; developing a unique project that increases visibility of the unit or organization; designating mentors for new employees; or developing an orientation handbook for new employees. Delegating various tasks allows prospective leaders to do the job independently and to develop confidence.

Women in leadership positions must refrain from being unfair, uninformed, incompetent, rude, mean-spirited, unethical, demanding, dishonest, inflexible, overly opinionated, and inconsistent. They also should be encouraged to grow and to develop to their full potential. Opportunities for learning and growth must be embraced. They should strive to become caring role models who are committed to teamwork, confidentiality, motivation, initiative, common sense, perseverance, and ethical problem solving. When tasks are delegated, it is important to allow the person to follow through instead of watching their every move. A supportive environment is essential to developing confidence, understanding accountability, and independent follow through.

Conscious role-modeling behavior that exemplifies confident leadership, mature self-presentation, self-sufficiency, and perseverance is imperative. It is likewise imperative that a leader have the foundational knowledge to achieve the desired goal. A leader must make sure that educational preparations are consistent with one's desired area of leadership. Lifelong learning is essential. Seeing other women learn and grow by seeing and doing becomes a time of celebration and excitement about growth and success. This is not a time to feel that the one you helped is now outshining you. A great leader should be proud to have contributed to the growth of another woman of color. To be happy about the growth of another is the real test of the character of "a leader." My responsibility is to be generous and congratulatory when accomplishments are made by those whom I have helped.

Modeling the ethical principle of treating all people with dignity and worth is another important responsibility in keeping the movement alive. I strive to help those who are watching realize that they too must work diligently to help followers feel significant, that they truly matter, and that they are valued. This builds positive relationships.

An additional responsibility is to help women understand their unique work environment and the importance of staying current in their field of knowledge and practice because in our technological age, information becomes obsolete quickly. To be competent in the business environment, it is important that we practice continual learning, such as improving our technical skills. Our knowledge base must be current, diverse, and broad. When new and different skills are needed, it is important that we are aware of the need and the venue to acquire the skills.

Needless to say, if we have the privilege of grooming leaders, we need engaging and creative interpersonal skills and networking expertise. Thereby we can build collaborative partnerships, resulting in a pool of available persons with essential decision-making capabilities. Being aware of this expanded knowledge base and expertise makes it easier to access needed information.

My responsibility includes embracing a strong value system and principles essential for effective leaders. In essence, I must "walk the talk" through my daily actions. I value people and treat them with utmost respect. Listening to others and attempting to understand their perspective, their challenges, and their ways of doing demonstrates respect and value. Valuing diversity and making fairness a fixed norm in my daily work has helped build a cadre of caring relationships.

Teaching is an important and essential role in my field of expertise. First and foremost, I impart to adults knowledge and skills needed for their ensuing positions. Knowing the agenda and having a plan for the teaching/learning process help to establish the road map for the development of workers in the social work field. Daily and routine activities can be restructured to optimize learning attributes for potential leaders.

Being a professor and administrator at Alabama A & M University for over thirty years has afforded me the opportunity to keep the movement alive since the student enrollment in the Department of Social Work is 90 percent female and approximately 95 percent Black. I consciously try to serve as an inspiration on many levels and to motivate future generations of professional social workers for years to come. I am involved in community activities, and I encourage students to become involved in activities that will help them to stretch and grow, both personally and professionally. They are reminded that whether tutoring children, reading to older people in nursing homes, leading a meeting, serving on committees, or volunteering at a hospital, all such interaction develops competencies necessary for future leadership.

Modeling effective leadership is worth its weight in gold since people follow examples. The work environment must focus on development through doing. As a leader, my role is to enable development by providing essential support, experiences, education, and resources. I must also encourage involvement in community activities, such as advisory boards, boards of directors, and quality control committees. When serving on community boards, I challenge them to serve in leadership capacities. I also encourage media utilization and interviews for developing oral and written communication skills.

Blueprint for Leaders

Over the course of my thirty-three-year career as a professional social worker, I have worked for and with every type of management and leadership style: strict and rigid; flexible and fluid; individually strong and weak; mean and kind; knowledgeable and not so knowledgeable; men and women; young and old. In each case my internal evaluation was making a mental note and indirectly attuning me to those qualities I wanted to possess. As a result, as a leader I now know when to lead and when to follow; when to be rigid and when to allow flexibility. Experience has also taught me the value of having vision and the confidence to make a way out of no way; it has provided me self-assurance and strength with humility.

Prepared and motivated, I see every day as an opportunity to help someone through the day-to-day routine of life, for it is the common nondesign events that shape individual lives in either a positive or negative fashion. I am thankful for having had the opportunity to experience the many vicissitudes inherent in my profession. Without them, it would be very easy to become a one-dimensional leader.

For those aspiring to leadership positions, it is important to conduct a self-assessment of one's leadership traits and the principles on which these traits are built (Frigon and Jackson 1996). Self-assessment requires the challenge of knowing one's self and also careful planning to achieve one's full potential. A leader must be aware of personal values in order to withstand and resolve challenges and possible conflicts and thereafter make critical and ethical decisions. Therefore, you must also know what you really want to achieve and have a clear understanding of the principles, traits, and leadership skills to achieve desired ends.

One must make educational preparations and build a knowledge base consistent with the desired leadership goals. Lack of competence in knowledge and leadership skill will result in disarray and dissatisfaction negating team work. If you are not knowledgeable in the area that you are leading, followers will quickly detect this lack of competence. Thus, one must be knowledgeable and committed to lifelong learning. Read, read, and read some more. Attend state-of-the-art seminars; read current journals that focus on development in your area. Provide opportunities for your followers to continue to develop. Take advantage of training that improves oral and written communication skills. Then, network to develop a professional support system as well as your comfort in engaging with diverse people. If one is accustomed to getting things done independently, this habit might have to be revisited since leaders must advocate and practice teamwork and shared vision if the goal is to come to fruition. Leaders will suffer burnout and alienation if work is done in a vacuum without the involvement of all players.

An effective leader and administrator must become as well rounded as possible. Begin by talking to leaders and administrators in the area. If at all possible, secure a mentor. This will prove an invaluable asset to individual development and possibly minimize mistakes along the way. With or without a mentor, I believe that ongoing leadership and administrative management training is essential. One needs to be skilled in time management, multitasking, and assertiveness. An effective leader must be able to handle a number of activities at one time. Knowing when to take on more and when to say no is also very important. There is a point when one can take on so many activities and tasks that the quality of work suffers, as well as the person's physical well-being. Since an administrator today must be able to speak effectively and clearly in public, a public-speaking course that includes all communication skills, such as listening, observation, attendance, body language, summarization, and appropriateness by expression type, is highly recommended.

Another essential area is the ability to mediate and/or deal with difficult people and difficult situations. This involves one's ability to understand all types of people and to logically develop workable agreeable solutions. Having sensitivity to the feelings of others as well as knowing how to satisfy the psychological needs of persons involved is a critical leadership trait. Attention should be given to all aspects of the environment, including body language, meaning behind words, seating arrangement, and the location of the discussions. Any difficult situation or person requires the leader to carefully and thoroughly research all aspects of the particular issue at hand. It is absolutely essential for leaders in difficult situations to stay calm, remained focused, and consider all facts to facilitate good judgment.

In addition, persons seeking leadership or administrative positions must be aware of the budget process. Regardless of what the administrative position, financial resources will play a major management role. It is absolutely imperative that one becomes quite familiar with the budget process and system as it relates to the company, agency, institution, or university, for it will provide you with knowledge and strategies for acquiring and utilizing resources in a particular area.

As a female in a leadership and/or administrative role, sometimes one has to battle male stereotyping that suggests you are timid, emotional, and motherly. Some males may have a tendency to support one who exhibits some of these traits versus one who conducts herself assertively. Establishing oneself as a confident leader or administrator who happens to be female is necessary. Be who you are and conduct yourself in a manner so that gender is a nonissue.

Final Thoughts

Frigon and Jackson (1996) defines leadership as "the art and science of getting others to perform and achieve a vision." However, my life experiences put leadership in a different frame of reference. In a mystical sort of way, leadership is an idea, a state of mind, a concept, something unexplainably found in some people who have no special training in the area at all, whereas others may have spent a lifetime trying to perfect this quality. This idea of leadership is totally integrated into my being, whether I am in my kitchen or in the office of a university president. It is something that I live. Leadership is very much like Christianity. The extent of my Christianity is not based on what I say but on how I unconsciously live Christian principles, and thus it is ever evolving.

Living leadership involves tenacity, genuineness, confidence, compassion, discipline, perseverance, humility, and approachability. It also involves commitment, appropriate focus, inclusion, integrity, and ethical behavior. A healthy dose of these elements is needed to be able to look beyond the "here and now," beyond the energy and mundane activity. One must envision the future and apply that vision to the present, thus creating insight, hope, consistency, discipline, and structure.

Persons who have a combination of vision and life experiences inspire, raise thoughts, and spark imagination, consistent with individual values. Optimism is a hallmark of an effective leader with truth and reality, where decisiveness and accountability go hand in hand. Effective leaders understand that taking action may sometimes result in errors and failure. These shortfalls are not totally negative for they may become needed stepping stones for the next success. Great leaders acknowledge responsibility and accountability for shortfalls and move on. This process may prevent the individual tendency to unduly focus on the negative and overlook or forget past positives. When expeditiously implemented (taking responsibility), it also gives those persons looking for something to criticize little fuel for their fire.

Second guessing and criticizing decisions come with the territory of any leader. These reactions seem to increase exponentially when one tries to take an organization to a higher level of accomplishments (Strock 1998). Good leaders understand this phenomenon and have included it as part of the success plan. A good leader has a combination of three levels of skill sets—that of a leader, a manager, and a worker. The primary elements of leadership include vision, strategy, and the ability to communicate. The primary element of management includes proficiency in manipulation of resources to maximize quality and output of products and services, while a worker's primary concern is focused on the details of getting the job done.

Generally, the ideal management strategy involves empowerment of staff and/or some form of decentralization of authority. Staff selection is important in every organization, but it becomes extremely important when it comes to delegation of authority and staff empowerment. Success or failure will be a direct result of how much the leadership vision is shared and supported by the staff, particularly if the vision requires continuous individual training and self-improvement. Good leaders understand the importance of having the appropriate support staff as well as a vision. A leader with vision is ineffective if the staff does not share the vision; the most appropriate action then is to replace the staff with those who support the vision. However, this sometimes is the most difficult action to accomplish and in most cases impractical. Then it becomes the leader's job to enlighten, educate, and encourage staff to embrace the new direction and/or vision.

Empowerment of staff can be one of the most important actions taken by a leader; however, empowering staff to accomplish their job with minimal supervision and no established priorities opens the door for others to set priorities for you (Strock 1998). When that occurs, personal agendas most often result in the organization responding to nonproductive activities and actions unrelated to the growth and/or improvement of organizational effectiveness. The effective leader remains alert to these possibilities and strives to prevent such nonproductive activities. This leads me to say a cautionary word about meetings. Typically, time management courses will indicate that meetings and presentations are undoubtedly the greatest single time consumer of a leader. Learn to minimize meeting time and maximize the event. For example, turn meetings into a management communication tool with implications that affect more than the subject matter at hand. This could eliminate the need for some future meetings (Strock 1998).

Good leaders have a unique perception of "time." Time is needed to develop and implement a proposal; time is spent at the office or on the job; and then there is timing. All are important, but timing has special significance for good leaders. Timing can determine the difference between success and failure, good results and bad, a go or no-go decision. Knowing when to take your hands off an important proposal, knowing when it is time for that new colleague to step up, knowing what the forces of change are bringing, and knowing when the work is done are significant elements of time and timing that good leaders seem to inherently possess. They know when it is time to move on.

Note

I am grateful for this opportunity to share my experience in leadership and offer encouragement and advice to others in the field of social work. I thank my husband for encouraging me, advising me, and supporting my efforts.

References

Frigon, N. L., and H. K. Jackson (1996). *The Leader: Developing the Skills and Personal Qualities You Need to Lead Effectively.* New York: AMACOM.

Neck, C. P., and C. C. Manz (2007). *Mastering Self-Leadership: Empowering Yourself for Excellence.* Upper Saddle River, N.J.: Pearson Prentice Hall.

Strock, J. M. (1998). *Reagan on Leadership: Executive Lessons from the Great Communicator.* Roseville, Calif.: Prima Publishing.

Topping, P. A. (2002). *Managerial Leadership.* New York: McGraw-Hill.

Conclusion

Continuously keeping current and future generations of women of color on the rise in academia is a responsibility that belongs to systems of all sizes and levels—from the micro to macro—and warrants supports and resources from the top to the bottom of the academy. The voices of women of color in this book are living testaments of the truths that a journey alone to the top is overwhelmingly difficult if not impossible, and that longevity as a leader and administrator may be compromised if the necessary supports and resources are not accessible.

Researchers, such as Riessman, discuss the use of narratives for various purposes, including political work and understanding the human experience on the micro, mezzo, and macro levels. For the women of color in this book, the narrative was a vehicle used to recall, process, engage, and lead an audience, particularly future generations of women of color, through their journeys as leaders and administrators in social work education and in the academy (Bamberg 1997; Riessman 2008). In turn, these narratives will validate the experiences of other women of color, mobilize their resolve to lead and administer effectively, and foster a sense of connection among them and for future generations of women of color rising in the academy. In essence, the significance of these narratives is in demonstrating the flow of power in the academy and how these women of color have successfully navigated their way through a system that is predominantly white male and historically oppressive to people of color, thus, rising to the top.

As validated in the book on strengths and survival of women of color as social work educators (Vakalahi, Starks, and Ortiz Hendricks 2007), the realities of those women of color in the academy who are in leadership and administrative positions continue to be one of great struggles and challenges on both professional and personal levels. The implications of race/ ethnicity and gender continue to be issues that these women grapple with on a daily basis. We hope that through this work we have honored and paid homage to pioneering leaders and administrators who have successfully led and administered in a system that has historically been oppressive and discriminatory. We hope that we have advocated for inclusion and partnership with all women and men in academia in ensuring the timely rise of women of color to leadership and administration roles. We hope that we have recognized and promoted respect for leadership styles and issues that are relevant to leadership development of women as well as provided lessons learned for future generations of leaders and administrators.

As offered in the introductory chapter, it is hoped that the voices of these women of color leaders and administrators would inspire positive changes and more timely responses from individuals and institutions. It is a call to decision makers in academia who recruit and retain administrators to join in this critical work to ensure that the women of color in this book are not representative of exceptions to the rule, but rather the rule. The lessons learned about successful negotiation of university, college, and departmental environments and beginning occupation of positions of power in academia testify that these women have been instrumental in promoting social change and social justice to the ethos of the academy. These accounts would inspire conversations and debates and raise consciousness on the university, college, and departmental levels to organize and advocate for collective equality and justice.

Lessons Learned on Leadership Development

Overall, the similarities in author response to structured questions from the editors represent a group career narrative and a collective story about a career trajectory, which in turn symbolize a group identity. Although this book contains only selected accounts, the themes show a collective representation of women in academia. As a whole, these women attest to the unique role of the profession of social work in providing a career trajectory for all women, and especially women of color, and a pathway to success and leadership opportunities. Furthermore, the women emphasized that leadership and administration is a journey that requires not only personal commitment and resilience (nature) but also the support from systems in one's environment (nurture). Likewise, the women affirm the importance of personal leadership development with a greater emphasis on mentoring and preparing the next generation of women of color in this journey. The following are specific themes drawn from these narratives pertaining to the pursuit of leadership and administration, leading and administering successfully, and keeping the movement alive.

The women in this project entered leadership and administration through diverse ways, some accidentally and others planned. In pursuing leadership and administration in the academy, these women of color talked about the crucial role of self-assessment/evaluation and identification of one's passion for leadership and administration, as well as one's leadership philosophy and style and understanding of the cultural context of institutions. Self-knowledge is a critical first step. Furthermore, they discussed the importance of timing, being in the right place at the right time, as well as taking the time to consider options very carefully. Likewise, these women discussed the need to develop and master management and administrative skills and competencies appropriate to the emerging task—for example, the critical nature of listening very carefully to others, taking the time to weigh every option and consequence, documenting experiences, and staying on task, as well as the need for lifelong learning, training on resource acquisition and usage, public relations and community engagement, skills in negotiation and strategizing to overcome barriers, consensus building, team building, flexibility, image management, and building bridges across diverse cultural and political lines.

To lead and administer successfully, always begin with a vision, mission, goals, and objectives (blueprint); keep the big picture in sight; and never be afraid to define one's leadership paradigm from one's cultural stance. Understand the integral role of balance between personal and professional lives, inclusion and appreciation of others' contributions, service, authenticity, multiculturalism and multidisciplinary, in effective leadership and administration. Cultivate strengths, particularly feminine-based strengths, and individuals' intuitive and creative strengths. For instance, cultivate resiliency and self-confidence, humility, courage, hard work, effective communication, and trust in the process. Because of the public nature of leadership and administration, the sense of insecurity, isolation, and lack of acceptance is inevitable. However, one must maintain effectiveness as a leader and administrator through relying on mentorship, collegial supports, networking (formal/informal), institutional commitment and support (i.e., equity and affirmative action policies and programs), and professional organizations (women's and social work organizations). Most important, never underestimate the power of family and cultural community supports, spiritual connections, and lessons learned from one's life experiences. And take more time to laugh at yourself and with others.

Keeping the Movement Alive

Keeping the movement alive requires extensive mentorship, particularly for the completion of doctoral studies, role modeling, and honesty about the challenging road of administration. Several contributors noted the importance of male mentorship in their quest for effective leadership development, and the authors concur that it is important for all women to accept and take full advantage of male support, as women of color develop power within organizational structures; they should also advocate for other women of color to occupy positions of power and then provide necessary support, opportunities for national and international visibility and networking, and teach the importance of staying true to one's cultural roots yet being savvy living in the dominant culture.

The academy has come a long way in terms of developing leaders who are women of color. However, progress has been extremely slow and often inconsistent, and there is still more work needed to be done in terms of increased recruitment and retention of women of color in leadership positions. The responsibility lies not only in the academy but also in individuals with the passion for leadership and administration, organizations that are capable of providing financial support and communities who must actively advocate and act upon opportunities for leadership. The "special" and "piecemeal" type programs alone have not worked. Thus, leadership development programs supported by proper funding must be established and maintained through collaborations between institutions of higher education and the communities in which they exist. Continued mobilization of communities to support their leaders and administrators in the academy can be effective in increasing the numbers of women of color in such positions in the academy. Reform of policies that advocate increased opportunities and representation of historically oppressed populations such as women must continue to be at the center of the discussions of decision makers.

In addition, support for mentorship, networking, and collegiality are specified as methods for leadership development in the voices in this book. In particular, the continuation of conference programs such as the National Association of Deans and Directors and Council on Social Work Education leadership sessions led by women members of NADD are strongly recommended. These leadership sessions provided personal description of women's paths to leadership as well as issues, concerns, and interest in becoming women administrators. NADD has long offered a mentorship program in which new and seasoned administrators are paired according to types of institutions. A significant aspect of this mentorship program, which aligns with the purpose of this work in terms of inclusion and collectivity, is the pairing of women with not only other women but also men. Informal venues for support of women interested in becoming administrators is a natural beginning for networking and a bridge to joining formalized programs. However, central administration funding for attendance at training for women in higher education administration, such as those at Bryn Mawr and at the American Council on Education Office of Women in Higher Education, is also important.

In reiterating the significant task of keeping the movement of women of color in academic leadership and administration alive, a strong and intentional partnership with mainstream women, men, central administration, and the larger community is imperative. It is our hope that through this work and commitment to social change and social justice, women of color in leadership and administration positions in the academy truly become the rule and continue to rise.

References

Bamberg, M.G.W. (1997). "Oral Versions of Personal Experience: Three Decades of Narrative Analysis." Special issue. *Journal of Narrative and Life History* 7 (1–4).

Peebles-Wilkins, W. (2001). "A Conversation with Women in Social Work Leadership: Insights and Advice." National Association of Deans and Directors of Schools of Social Work sponsored discussion at the Council on Social Work Education, Annual Program Meeting, Dallas.

Riessman, C. K. (2008). *Narrative Methods for the Human Sciences.* Thousand Oaks, Calif.: Sage.

Vakalahi, H.F.O., S. H. Starks, and C. Ortiz Hendricks (2007). *Women of Color as Social Work Educators: Strengths and Survival.* Alexandria, Va.: CSWE Press.

About the Contributors

Darlyne Bailey, Dean of the College of Education and Human Development and Assistant to the President, University of Minnesota

Carol Minor Boyd, Chair of the Department of Social Work, University of Mississippi

Priscilla A. Day, Director of the Center for Regional and Tribal Child Welfare Studies, Department of Social Work, University of Minnesota-Duluth

Sharlene B.C.L. Furuto, Associate Dean of the College of Human Development, BYU-Hawaii

Darlene Grant, Associate Dean of Graduate Studies, University of Texas-Austin

Maria E. Puig, Assistant Director, Colorado State University

Salome Raheim, Dean of the School of Social Work, University of Connecticut

Index